Pathways to the Future

"The future is not some place
we are going to, but one
we are creating.

The paths to it are not
found but made.

The making of those
pathways changes
both the maker and
the destination."

**Australian Commission
for the Future**

with best wishes to the reader

John Ipling

Published by the Sustainable London Trust, 7 Chamberlain Street, London NW1 8XB

The author thanks family and friends for their invaluable help:

Contributions
Chapter 1: Jake Ferguson; Daisy Froud; Paul de Zylva of Friends of the Earth.
Chapter 2: Emma Burlow; Mark Campanale; Jane Carlsen of the London Planning
Advisory Committee; James Farrell of the London Ecology Unit; Trevor Halvorsen;
Mayer Hillman; Robin Murray; Tara Garnett, Lucy Gillie and James Petts of Sustain.
Chapter 3: Alex Evans; Nick Hutchinson and Lesley Harding of Forum for the Future;
Perry Walker of the New Economics Foundation.
Chapter 4: Lindsey Colbourne of Projects in Partnership, Ian Haywood, Keith Patton.
Chapter 5: Victor Anderson; Sean Beane of the London Voluntary Service Council;
Dan Bloomfield of the London Ecology Unit.
Chapter 6: Roy Madron; Barry Fineberg.
Chapter 8: Martin Diamond; Chris Stratford.
Part 3: Daisy Froud; Jade Saunders; Liesel van Ast; Julie Brown of Growing Communities.

Editing and comments
Teresa Anderson, James Brander, Peter Challen, Max Dixon, Richard Douthwaite,
Louise and Patrick Grattan, Jane, Juliet and Zélie Jopling, Sarah McAlistair, Jacki Reason.

Donations
London Thames Gateway Forum and Daniel Dobson Mouawad.

The poem by Benjamin Zephaniah is reproduced with the kind permission of the poet and the Museum of London.

Photography by Jamie Macdonald

except:
p 14 West meets East, 16 ft x 12 ft photo-mural shown on six sites in London Docklands (artist: Loraine Leeson of *the art of change*, in collaboration with pupils and teachers from Central Foundation School for Girls, Bow); *pp 24 (top), 119* by David Stewart, reproduced with kind permission of Thames Gateway London Partnership; *p 60/61* by Will Curtis, *pp 64, 65* by Mark Scott, reproduced with kind permission of Heart of Thames Gateway Community Consortium; *p 69* Dragons' Gate, stainless steel sculpture in West India Dock Road, Limehouse (artist: Peter Dunn of *the art of change*, in collaboration with Anne Thorne Architects, 1996); *p 123* The Wymering Tree: 14 meter 'tree of life' in stainless steel (artist: Peter Dunn of *the art of change*, in collaboration with Anne Thorne Architects, 1999).

Designed, typeset and produced by ÆQUALIS, tel 020 8314 1613.
Layout by Shirley Trimmer and Andreas Goldner
Cover design by Shirley Trimmer
Additional artwork by Victoria Jones

Printed and bound in Great Britain by Blackmore Limited, Shaftesbury, Dorset
Printed on Chromomat Matt Art described by Performance Papers Ltd as made from chlorine free wood pulp originating from managed sustainable plantations, with minimum water usage and solid waste residue taken by local farmers for fertiliser.

Trade distribution by Central Books, tel 020 8986 4854.

Contents

Part 1 Exploring the pathways

Part 1 gives London a health check in terms of social justice and environmental sustainability. The diagnosis suggests that London is suffering from chronic growth-economy-itis. The prescription is a course of new economics and democratic participation.

Part 2 New Democracy for London

Part 2 describes the new Mayor and Assembly and suggests that there is an opportunity for London to develop forms of participatory government leading to justice and sustainability.

Part 3 People creating paths

Part 3 illustrates the creativity and diversity of Londoners and the organisations striving for justice and sustainability.

"thinking..."

If you have picked up this book there is a fair chance that you are a concerned Londoner. You are aware that London has lots of problems, and that these are a local version of wider problems. You have no doubt read other books about them. You are probably as well or better informed than me about some of the issues.

You are concerned. You see the need for change. You are perhaps also confused and rather pessimistic. In some areas it may seem to be obvious what should be done but this is not happening. In others urgent action has been, and is being, taken but the problems persist. Then there are those problems for which no one has any answers. You may well be wondering what chance there is of London's new mayor coming up with solutions.

For my own part, I have long seen that governments and local authorities were failing. I felt that the most helpful thing I could do was to support the numerous non-governmental organisations doing wonderful work for justice and conservation. I loved their philosophy, dedication, energy and spirit and enormously admired the skill with which they confronted powerful bodies. I was and remain 100% with them. But I saw that for all our efforts, in spite of the many great victories achieved often with massive public support, the overall situation kept on getting worse. I am not of a pessimistic inclination, but there seemed to be no good reason to be other than pessimistic.

I now believe that we have to start thinking differently. That is why I have written this book. Writing it has helped me, and I hope that reading it will help you, to think more positively and creatively about the future, in particular the future of London.

The change in the emphasis of our thinking that I believe is needed is that, instead of thinking about how to solve all those difficult problems, we have to think more about the **systems** that produced the problems in the first place, and about how those systems could be reformed so that the problems no longer arise. This I believe is where pathways to a better future begin. I do not pretend to have all or any of the answers. But I am sure that, provided we ask the right questions, the questions about the underlying systems, we can find the answers; and that, when we have found them, we do have the power to bring about the changes that we see need to be made.

Do not expect to find the solutions to London's problems in these pages. Rather, my hope is that the book may help you to think **in systems terms**. It is for you, for all of us concerned Londoners, to create the new ways that will make a better future for London.

To do this Londoners will need to act politically because to change systems requires government action. Like me, you may not think of yourself as a political animal: you may find the whole political scene off-putting. But, if we are to change the world, we need to start studying democracy, issues about the purpose of government, the nature of leadership and the decision-making processes, in systems terms. What sort of systems would enable us, you, me, the Mayor, the Assembly members, and millions of other Londoners, to turn our concerns into positive, effective, successful, satisfying action ?

This book is an attempt to answer that question. It says that suitable participatory processes have been developed. The only problem at the moment is that they run counter to the principles and practices, indeed to the whole culture, of the institutions of government.

The restoration of directly elected government to London offers an opportunity to break the logjam and move forward from the old, failed, problem-solving approach to the new systems approach which alone has the potential to un-lock our capacity to create a future of our choice, based on justice and sustainability. But this will not happen unless we make it happen.

I invite you to join me on the path sign-posted

"*...differently*"   John Topping

Exploring the pathways

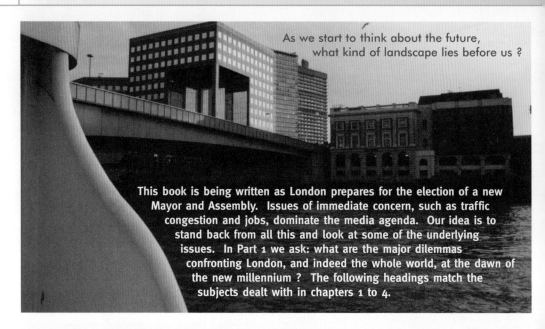

As we start to think about the future, what kind of landscape lies before us ?

This book is being written as London prepares for the election of a new Mayor and Assembly. Issues of immediate concern, such as traffic congestion and jobs, dominate the media agenda. Our idea is to stand back from all this and look at some of the underlying issues. In Part 1 we ask: what are the major dilemmas confronting London, and indeed the whole world, at the dawn of the new millennium ? The following headings match the subjects dealt with in chapters 1 to 4.

Social and economic justice

Whilst many Londoners enjoy increasing wealth, far too many are struggling: there is a marked contrast between the circumstances of rich and poor in London, highlighted by young people sleeping rough on pavements in the wealthy West End. The same is true in the global arena where the gap between the rich and the poor has doubled in the last 30 years. Our sense of justice demands that we take steps to reverse these trends. Otherwise the prospects for far too many children born today and for future-borns are appalling. We would like to build a local and global society that is acceptable to our humanity and sense of fair play, a society that does justice to the best, rather than the worst, of ourselves as human beings. There seems to be no reason why we could not do this. Yet we are not doing so. We are driven to ask: why is it that decades of dramatic technological advance and expanding 'economic growth' have been accompanied by a persistent growth of social injustice, at home and abroad ?

The environment

London's impact on the environment continues to increase as more and more of our food and other goods are flown in from afar. Over the last 30 years, 30% of the Earth's natural resources have been destroyed, much of it to meet the demands of cities like ours. London has to accept its fair share of responsibility. London is currently contributing to global warming and climate change. Our current path is plainly unsustainable. This is surely not due to any lack of knowledge or understanding or technological capacity to operate sustainably. Nor can London plead poverty. As Londoners, we need to be aware

Throughout this book 'London' refers to the area of Greater London, ie the 32 London boroughs and the City of London, which is the area for which the new Greater London Authority will now be the strategic authority. But, where the context allows, the word should be read as referring more generally and loosely to the aggregate of the economic activities of companies based in London and people living or working here.[1] 'Londoners' is used in a similar way, to include, for example, commuters.

of our unsustainable ways, to identify the forces driving us along these ways. Then perhaps we could work out what we need to do about it.

The economy

It is not hard to see the connection between consumer demand and damage to the environment. What is not so obvious, but many people now believe to be the case, is that the present economic system, which compels governments and corporations to strive for 'economic growth', **actually produces negative net benefits for society**: our economic system is the fundamental cause of the growing gap between rich and poor and the destruction of the environment. The reasons for this view are explained in chapter 3. If it is right, attempts by governments to alleviate the conditions of the less well off and limit the environmental damage caused by 'economic growth' address the symptoms, not the cause. The only cure is to change the system.

By 'economic systems' I refer to money systems and the rules governing markets, trade and corporations etc, ie the systems by which we manage the economic activities of production, distribution and consumption etc. The good news is that economic systems are man-made: they can be changed. The ideal would be a set of economic systems that would enable the whole of humanity to live healthy lives, would help to promote just and harmonious societies and would do so without diminishing the capacity of Nature to sustain life. Fortunately, 'new economics' has begun to offer us alternative economic systems that are specifically designed to achieve these desirable ends. Support for these ideas is spreading. London's long term future as a financial centre depends on adopting and promoting these ideas, not just at the margins of the economy but in lieu of the 'growth economy'. London, this great world city, could lead the way in exploring these new ideas and bringing about the changes needed.

But how much say do we have ?

Suppose it's right that the present economic system is flawed due to its inherent need for growth, and that there are people-friendly and eco-friendly systems waiting in the wings to be used, the next question is: what chance is there of our being able to get these ideas adopted ? Such ideas run counter to the accepted wisdom which favours 'economic growth' and the ever larger corporations that this system creates. In the last chapter of Part 1 we look at some of the decision-making structures in London and assess their effectiveness. What emerges is that whilst the know-how for participatory decision-making is well developed, its use is, as yet, marginal, simply because our political leaders see it as such. They are wedded to the notion of 'economic growth' and they see 'new economics' as of marginal importance only. As we reach the end of Part 1, there seems little hope of achieving the fundamental changes needed. At this point it seems that we may have reached a dead end.

It is only when we get to Part 2 that we explore how the Mayor and Assembly can interpret the role of leadership in a new way; and how, if they do so, the potential for discovering new ways forward will be limited only by our imaginations.

The role of the Mayor and Assembly will be to lead – to lead us

in making the new pathways the making of which will change us and our destination

1. The importance of a many angled view of a city is well explained by Marvin and Guy in an article in Local Environment Vol 2 No 3 1997.

The London Breed

Benjamin Zephaniah 1996

I love this great polluted place
Where pop stars come to live their dreams
Here ravers come for drum and bass
And politicians plan their schemes,
The music of the world is here
This city can play any song
They came to here from everywhere
Tis they that made this city strong.

A world of food displayed on streets
Where all the world can come and dine
On meals that end with bitter sweets
And cultures melt and intertwine,
Two hundred languages give voice
To fifteen thousand changing years
And all religions can rejoice
With exiled souls and pioneers.

I love this overcrowded place
Where old buildings mark men and time
And new buildings all seem to race
Up to a cloudy dank sky line,
Too many cars mean dire air
Too many guns mean danger
Too many drugs mean be aware
Of strange gifts from a stranger.

It's so cool when the heat is on
And when it's cool it's so wicked
We just keep melting into one
Just like the tribes before us did,
I love this concrete jungle still
With all its sirens and its speed
The people here united will
create a kind of London breed.

People – health and social justice

> Whether we look outwards at world trends, or inwards at London, the gap between rich and poor is increasing. Economic inequality is linked with environmental and racial inequality. Yet in the people of London we do have the resources to build a just and sustainable society.

London and the global poverty crisis

London is a world city and has to be viewed from a global perspective. A good starting point is *Caring for the Future,* the Report of the Independent Commission appointed in 1992 to study world population issues[1]. The Commission's approach was to look at the topic from all angles, precisely the approach called for in this book. In her preface to the report, published in 1996, Maria de Lourdes Pintasilgo, the Commission President and former Prime Minister of Portugal, made comments which illustrate how innovative, but essential, the all-angles approach is: "This approach did not prove easy. I was going to rediscover how the mentality of specialisation remains widespread, and how it functions as a dyke against new thinking, new ways of acting. Interdisciplinary knowledge, an inter-sectoral grasp of problems, integrated policies for action: these asked for a quantum leap forward. The Commission was clear in this regard: we would not extricate ourselves from the population problem by remaining within its boundaries."

World population

The Report began with population statistics. Two stand out

◆ the growth rate of the world's population peaked as long ago as 1965

◆ whilst the future cannot be predicted, due to all kinds of factors, current projections suggest that human numbers may peak around 2050 at 9.8 billion (the UN Population Division medium projection). This would add about 3.8 billion people to the current world population. All but 1% of these are likely to be concentrated in today's 'developing' countries, mostly in Africa or Asia, and the vast majority in urban areas[2].

World poverty

The Report then looked at poverty. Between 1970 and 1994 the number in absolute poverty had increased from 944 million to 1.3 billion. "The numbers mean that all the misery in the world has not shrunk despite three decades of development effort. Quite the opposite: this misery has grown in certain respects." The number of people without basic health services, the number who must drink unclean water, the number of those without rudimentary sanitation, all exceed one billion. Since 1994, the number in absolute poverty has increased to 1.5 billion.

World inequality

Significantly, inequality is also on the increase, both between countries and within countries. In 1970 the 20% of the world's people who live in the richest countries had 32 times the income of the poorest 20%. By 1995 it was 82 times. This is the trend. You may think that it could not have been intended by those in power; or you may believe that this was their intention; the point I am making is that the trends we have been witnessing for the last 30 to 40 years are **the result of the way the system as a whole has worked**. In more than 70 countries, incomes are lower now than they were in 1980; in 43 countries they are lower than in 1970. Most developing countries still qualify as, in a financial journalist's heartless phrase, "roadkill on the global investment highway"; a large proportion of the world's nations are in economic decline; and more are growing only slowly or sporadically[3].

It is interesting to note that, according to the Human Poverty Index, which takes account of deprivation, survival, knowledge, decent standard of living and social exclusion, the country in the industrial world with the highest percentage of the population classified as poor is the USA with 17%[4]. Despite its egalitarian rhetoric, the USA has become increasingly inequitable in the last two decades – it is the most unequal of all industrial societies in concentration of wealth, in distribution of income, and in access to health care and other social amenities. A recent study by the Centre on Budget and Policy Priorities reported by George Hagar, of the Washington Post, found that since 1977, the after tax income of America's wealthiest 1% has shot up 115%, the income of the richest fifth has grown by 43%, whilst the poorest fifth is getting 9% less than in 1977 and the middle-class households have made gains of less than 8% over 22 years. The USA is not likely to be a good model for eliminating poverty or reversing the trend for the gap between the rich and the poor to get larger[5].

Of course, if you compare the extremes of wealth and poverty, the figures get silly: three families – Bill Gates, the Sultan of Brunei and the Walton family (owners of Wal-Mart) — are said to have a combined wealth of £135 billion, equal to that of 600 million people living in the world's poorest countries. Gates's wealth alone increases by $106 million a day: two days' pay exceeds the amount spent to date on fighting Aids in Africa[6].

'The battle of our time'

After spelling out some of the practical consequences of poverty in terms of the conditions of life of the people concerned, the Commissioners stated that "the battle against poverty is a demanding one – the battle of our time. Population growth can deepen poverty; it leads, combined with laws of inheritance, to a fragmentation of land-holdings and living below subsistence levels. Although it is usually seen as the cause of poverty, demographic growth is, in fact, but one of the reasons for the persistence of poverty. The resources clearly exist to end poverty and exclusion, within countries and internationally, and they need to be used to relieve the growing number of poor nations". And, we might add, people.

The Commission then turned to *The ecological challenge*: "Poverty is at the root of deforestation, land degradation, and the destruction of coastal habitats. Hundreds of millions of poor people are forced, all over the world, to over-use their habitats in order to survive. This problem is exacerbated by growing populations. The destruction of the natural resource base is doomed to continue so long as the conditions of poverty remain unaddressed".

Then to *The economic challenge*: "Population growth, extreme poverty and ecological degradation are each and together rooted in the economic systems with which the world has been operating for the last 50 years. Economic and social development has been the principal quest of all nations, individually and collectively, during the past five decades. Development became equated with economic growth, progressively the exclusive preoccupation of policy-makers everywhere. This resulted in a proliferation of development models, strategies meant to boost economic growth"[7].

For economic growth, substitute sustainable improvement in the quality of life

The Report's review of global trends concluded: "As we have seen, the pursuit of economic growth has become a dominant concern the world over. Development is equated with, or even held to be synonymous with, economic growth only: it is thus evacuated of all social implications. This focus has by now overshadowed all other considerations, such as equity, environmental sustainability, employment and social cohesion." The Commission therefore proposed "that the concept of sustainable improvement in the quality of life becomes the central focus for policy-making in all countries. This would be an ongoing, dynamic task, leaving no room for status quo politics or excuses for inaction".

The disgrace of health and poverty in London

We have looked outwards and we have seen increasing poverty and inequality around the world. What if we look around us here in London?

London has great wealth. But is also has

◆ a serious level of absolute poverty
◆ extreme differences between rich and poor
◆ unacceptable levels of disadvantage among young people and people from ethnic minority communities.

These things inevitably lead to all sorts of other problems.

The challenge for London, for every concerned Londoner, is to explore how we can create a more just, a more equal, a healthier, safer, thriving society, here in London, as well as abroad.

Poverty in London

Of the 7 million Londoners, the proportion living in poverty increased from 14% in 1983 to 24% in 1992[9].

Unemployment among non-white ethnic groups is twice as high as the national average and for some ethnic groups is over 33%. The unemployment rate in London is now 8.1% on average but up to 21.5% in Hackney.

There are an estimated 100,000 homeless people in the capital at any one time, including 350 people sleeping rough, 30,000 non-statutory homeless, such as those living in hostels, winter shelters and squats; and 76,000 in statutory homeless households. There are 940,000 adults on income support; 750,000 receive housing benefit.

Our response

The extent of world poverty calls for a response from all wealthy countries, including our own. Indeed our Government is responding: it has called for urgent action to halve the proportion of the world's population living in absolute poverty by 2015[8]. London will take part in that response. But my reason for citing these passages from the Report of the World Commission is that I want to suggest that for London merely to contribute to the UK's efforts orchestrated by Whitehall would be inadequate and misguided. Never mind the UK as a whole, just for the moment, London itself has immense power on the world stage, the powers of the City of London, the power of London's huge corporate sector, the power of Londoners as consumers, above all the powers of Londoners as people, a highly cosmopolitan population with resident communities from all parts of the globe, arguably the most cosmopolitan city in the world. A great city like London has powers that national governments do not have. It has responsibilities to match.

London's future lies in a global context. There has to be a global vision for London's future. Up to now, London has been at the forefront of the pursuit of global 'economic growth', the very system that has evidently failed the world's most needy. London now has the choice of either continuing to play that role, or of urgently exploring ways of contributing to a reversal of the global trends towards increasing poverty and greater inequality: I believe we have to develop ways of improving the quality of life for all the world's inhabitants, especially for the poorest.

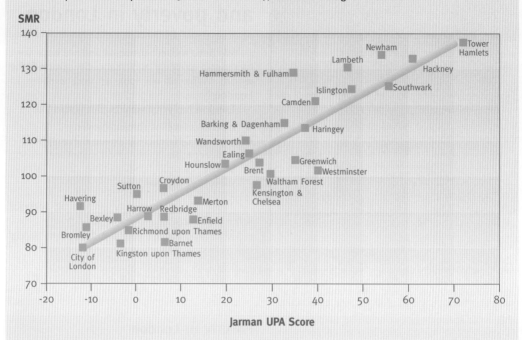

Standardised Mortality Ratios (under the age of 75; 1995)
compared with deprivation (Jarman UPA Score), London boroughs

This diagram compares health and social factors in London boroughs. The Standard Mortality Ratios (under the age of 75; 1995) shown in the vertical column reflect health. The Jarman scores on the horizontal plane reflect deprivation (England and Wales average value is zero). The areas with the greatest levels of social disadvantage have the worst health record.

Five London boroughs are among the top ten most deprived local authority districts in England. More striking perhaps is the fact that 40% of the population of London lives in electoral wards that are among the most deprived 10% of all wards in the country.

And yet 21% of households in Greater London enjoy a weekly income in excess of £650. Luxury flats are still being built, many for foreign investors.

How poverty affects health in London

There is a clear correlation between ill health and social factors.

The chances of dying under the age of 75 in areas of east and south London are almost twice as high as in the least deprived parts of the capital. In parts of Inner London rates of infant and childhood mortality are particularly high, well above national averages and over three times higher than in some Outer London boroughs.

Increasing inequality and its effect on health

"International economic developments do appear to be combining with the effects of technology to widen income disparities between rich and poor … . One suspects that this will continue. What this means is that economies are increasingly creating poverty and affluence co-existing close to each other."[10]

There is some evidence that the extent of inequality itself is associated with ill health[11]. London includes some of the poorest and some of the most affluent communities in the country, often living cheek by jowl. London boasts an equally wide range in terms of health indicators, from the very good to the very bad. In terms of income inequality, whilst average earnings in London are higher than those in the country as a whole, incomes in London are less equal than in the rest of the country. London has above average numbers of people on both high and low

Pathways to the future

incomes. And, whereas London on the whole is getting healthier than it was 50 years ago, this average improvement is deceptive: whilst some areas have seen big improvements, others have experienced drastic decline.

Poverty affects children

Throughout the capital there are communities with children who are suffering from the effects of disadvantage, deprivation and social exclusion. In 1991, 26% of children in Inner London and 15% of children in Outer London lived in overcrowded accommodation; 324,000 children were living in non-earning households. More than 2000 pupils were permanently excluded from schools in London in 1996/7.

Other statistics, not perhaps necessarily related to poverty, include:
◆ abortion rates the highest in the country
◆ hospital admissions for acute mental health twice the national average
◆ about 1000 births to girls in London under the age of 16 every year.

Poorer people are most adversely affected by traffic

It is the less well off areas of London that often suffer the worst traffic — heavy, fast traffic that divides communities, eg the M11 Link Road, the Old Kent Road, Westway[12]. It is also the people living in areas of lowest car ownership that suffer the worst traffic problems: Hackney, Tower Hamlets, North Kensington, parts of Harrow[13]. Injuries are a major cause of deaths in London with road traffic accidents contributing a significant proportion: in 1996, 2,600 children were injured on London's roads. There are studies showing that poorer children are more affected by accidents than richer.

Refugees

London has an estimated 220,000 refugees, many living in poverty. New asylum seekers are forced to live in temporary housing on restrictive food vouchers worth less than the level of income support. Asylum seekers experience widespread discrimination and harassment. A whole range of health inequalities follow.

Black and minority ethnic health

Pakistani and Bangladeshi households suffer by far the highest levels of deprivation, with 80% living below the poverty line.

Food poverty

Poorer families eat less well and make and have fewer food choices. The average family spends less that 9% on food; the poorest spend 40/50%. In low income areas, shops provide less choice of foods, prices are often inflated because customers cannot afford to go elsewhere, the food is often over-processed and low in nutritional value. These people are also less likely to be able to travel to extend their food choices.[14]

Fuel poverty

There is a gaping divide between those who fall into the category of the 'Fuel Poor' — those who have to choose between food, clothing etc and heating their home, and those 'Fuel Rich' — who can literally afford to be profligate with their

energy use. In London in 1996 over 4,600 people died because of 'Fuel Poverty'. Why so many deaths ? Poor housing stock and poor energy policy are key causes. Fuel poverty hits children and older people most severely and can be found in all boroughs.[15] The poor are less able to afford insulation.

A culture of racism

Racism is closely linked to economic inequality and is also a separate issue in its own right. It is an issue on which the Government is acting, but this is also a London issue because London is the UK's most ethnically diverse city.

Racism affects not only the police but also the professions including education and health; it affects many industries, even the arts. The relevance of the Macpherson report is not limited to the police. Huw Thomas has written: "He paints a picture of city life in which racism and racial disadvantage is deeply rooted – violence is its most dramatic manifestation, but there is a daily grind of institutional racism which shapes the lives of all those who engage with it (either as professionals or as users) ... . The lesson of Macpherson is that at present race structures urban life; that racial categories, like those of gender, suffuse institutional practices and social relations. ... Calls for socially mixed communities must be predicated on a belief that the mechanisms for distributing rewards in the city (jobs, especially, but also education and health services) are broadly fair, and demonstrably so; otherwise social mix will simply be a recipe for social conflict. But, as a recent review put it, 'the continuing evidence of social polarisation and of high levels of deprivation in our big cities suggests that there are wrongs to be righted'.

This is where the urban renaissance must begin – not solely with racial equality, but with social justice in general. This is not, indeed cannot be, a bolt on extra for specialised agencies. It must penetrate the activities of any agency involved in urban life. Otherwise, frustrations over trying to create enough durable, stable social mix will lead to an acceptance of social segregation as the only practicable option."[16]

A significant statistic is that 25% of Black African men are unemployed, compared with 7% white men, despite the fact that they are 30% more likely to have a higher educational qualification.

London Communities
of people born outside England

Country of Birth	Number
Irish	241,033
India	151,619
Jamaica	46,445
Kenya	56,993
Bangladesh	56,657
Cyprus	50,684
Pakistan	44,741
Nigeria	36,047
Italy	30,052
Uganda	28,244
Ghana	26,925
Sri Lanka	25,818
Australia	23,315
Turkey	20,426
South Africa	18,496
Hong Kong	18,398
New Zealand	18,379
Iran	16,856
Malaysia	16,163
Tanzania	15,452
Guyana	14,662
Mauritius	13,907
Barbados	13,466
Vietnam	11,858
Canada	11,626
Trinidad & Tobago	10,184

Source: Census 1991

Building on London's strengths

London has many strengths to help us to meet the challenges we face.

London's diverse population

London's cultural / racial / religious diversity is one its great attractions and strengths.

Nor is this diversity just a late 20th century phenomenon. London has always been culturally diverse. From the Roman invasion onwards its development as a major port brought various new communities in to settle, for example the Chinese in the Docklands. A significant number of London's communities have developed against the backdrop of Empire, slavery and the independence of Britain's former colonies.[17]

Pathways to the future

The qualities of Londoners

After the diversity of its population, I would have cited traditional 'British' qualities like integrity and a sense of fair play as fitting London to meet the challenges of the future. But as part of the ALG's *London Study* Ben Jupp and George Lawson of Demos did a study called *Values Added* which threw up some more interesting suggestions. They analysed Londoners' values to see how they might influence the development of London. They found that, compared with the British as a whole, Londoners are more open to learning from other cultures, more tolerant of traditionally frowned upon activities, like drug taking, more hedonistic — attracted by the buzz of the city – keen to balance different parts of their lives and also torn between the desire for a more community-centred, ethical lifestyle and their perceived need to put themselves first if they are to survive in the 'urban jungle'. The values of community solidarity and concern for the environment are held as strongly by young Londoners as by any other group, but they tend to emphasise more strongly personal experience, self-development, greater autonomy and openness and to be moving away from strong authority and traditional values of puritanism and security.

Whilst there were elements here on which to base a pessimistic vision of the future, Jupp and Lawson thought their analysis suggested that London could have a brighter future: "The new values of younger generations could act as a catalyst for innovative forms of social connection, perhaps centred around creative networks and new forms of learning. Greater tolerance and a willingness to take risks could bolster London's position as a centre for social, commercial and political innovation. Concern for the environment and enhancing social inclusion could be driving forces for a more sustainable city."[18]

This analysis suggests that Londoners are fully capable of meeting the demanding but exciting challenges referred to in this book. There seems to be no good reason why we should not become a less dependent and apathetic society, why we could not rebuild our local communities, become global citizens and live by our social and environmental values. And if we did so, life in London would surely be just as enjoyable, and also a lot more satisfying.

The problem as I see it is not that Londoners are incapable of change or that they are resolved against it. The problem seems to be deeper, and different: it is not a problem about human nature but about the systems that have grown up to dominate our lives, crucially our economic and political systems. In chapter 3 we discuss the suggestion that the root of the problem lies in our money system. In later chapters we explore the political processes whereby this could be changed.

The exploration of these radical pathways must be left to those chapters. Before leaving health and social justice however, I refer briefly to some of the features of the healthier and more just society that could emerge.

Education

Teachers will be seen to have a vital role in building London's future. What children learn about the world they are growing up in, and how they are encouraged to develop their potential, are going to be crucially important to the way London is able to meet the challenges of the 21st century.[19] As we shall see, London's new mayor does not have any specific powers or duties in relation to education (schools remain the responsibility of the borough councils and central government) but there is no reason why the Mayor should not take a lead in London becoming known for the excellence of the education young Londoners receive. The Mayor can be a champion for teachers and the education service and help make the links between education for citizenship (now part of the national curriculum), education for social justice, education for understanding our impact on the environment[20] and education for more local self-sufficiency.

Self sufficiency and volunteering

One current trend in the right direction is a shift away from 'high intensity' services, like hospitals, to 'low intensity services', for example, neighbours making sure that older people living nearby are visited frequently. In Camden it emerged recently that the number of people found in their homes weeks or months after their deaths averaged one a week. A pilot scheme to develop local 'self help' networks is being carried out by the North Camden Primary Care Group.

current funding programmes is that they can be accessed only by those already well versed in the intricacies of funding applications ... Local people in deprived areas will always be disadvantaged in relation to the sophisticated professionals if the issue of control of resources is not faced". She urges activists and workers to use existing programmes to build up a strong self-funded community sector. "The best sort of programme gives the community ownership and management control of all the resources it creates. This slowly builds up an alternative economic system at community level that makes local people better off by increasing their disposable income. It is particularly needed by those who cannot take up paid employment, because of age, disability or caring responsibilities."[21]

People need income

If local people are to play the key role in reducing social exclusion, they are going to need their own independent sources of income. So argues Alison West, director of the Community Development Foundation. "The problem with all

Not only do we need to identify the economic forces that are driving the trend towards a more divided and less caring society, but, to build healthy local communities, we also need to work out how to create funding systems to match the human resources going into things like care services. Both subjects are developed in chapter 3.

Environment and health

The Public Health Alliance is an independent voluntary association, which brings together a wide variety of individuals and organisations whose common aim is the defence and promotion of public health. In one of its reports, Sustainable Development and Health, 1995, Hugo Crombie expressed these conclusions:

"The best currently available environmental information shows that the current state of the environment is already damaging people's health and that environmental degradation is increasing and is likely to continue. Economic activity can result in environmental degradation but can also occur within environmental capacity limits. A move towards this sustainable state would be associated with improvements in human and planetary health.

The triad of health-economy-environment is closely interrelated and must be considered as one. There are a number of basic principles, which should underlie all health, environmental, and economic activities. These are:

◆ Patterns of living and consumption must occur within sustainable limits
◆ Economic activity is not an aim in itself but a method of benefiting people
◆ The precautionary principle must be followed
◆ It is important to empower communities in order to safeguard their health
◆ Health, and consequently environmental qualities, should be a basic human right. This implies a corresponding duty to avoid damaging the environment of others, including both those at a distance and those not yet born."

Detailed recommendations as to the economy follow. The report then lists matters of prime importance including

"Equity in health is paramount. This implies that the distribution of the major determinants of health, particularly wealth and income, must be equitable."

Taken together, the second of the basic principles and this last point have quite revolutionary implications. We will return to these later. I draw attention to them now to emphasise that the foundation on which they are based is not any kind of theory or doctrine: it is just health.

The Arts

Funding is also a big issue for the Arts. And in London the Arts make a major contribution to the money economy. Like agriculture, they are now termed an 'industry'. They play a major role in the appearance of our surroundings. They have great potential in terms of 'greening' the city and creating a new, more sustainable, urban culture. But these are not the issues I want to mention here. The more fundamental point is about the place of all the Arts in our lives, and in

the life of our city.[22] They represent a bulwark against the forces of the consumerist, 'growth economy' culture currently dominating our lives. They are surely a big part of the sustainable lifestyles of the future. In so much of the literature one sees London's attractions – its arts and heritage – represented as a means to an end: to make London richer, by drawing in tourists and visitors to spend money here. The reverse is really more important: the object of the exercise should be to promote life — fun, moving experiences, good relationships, entertainment, etc — all the things that London's civilisation, including its heritage and arts, offer us.

Whole books could be, probably have been, written on this subject. For me it is more personal: my children all learned musical instruments because this is a good form of training for life – it teaches you co-ordination, self-discipline, concentration, the ability to listen, to work with others, to be a performer, to be reliable. Those skills and qualities fit a person for many jobs. As it happens, my children have all become professional musicians. One of them told me recently something that illustrates the point I am making here: that all her friends are doing things with their lives that they believe in rather than doing jobs that would earn them the most money. This is wealth. Let us bear this in mind when we read in chapter 5 that one of the purposes of London's new government will be to promote 'wealth creation'.

Let us also bear in mind these kinds of educational needs when we consider the duty imposed on London's new government with regard to 'equality of opportunity for all people'. My children's musical education was subsidised from my income as a lawyer. We need an economic system that enables money to be provided for such purposes in ways that give equal opportunities to all.

People – health and social justice

Chapter 1
Notes and References

1. *Caring for the Future, Report of the Independent Commission on Population and the Quality of Life* Oxford. Passages quoted on pp 9, 10 are from pp 1, 18, 25, 29, 43 and 63.

2. *Which World?* by Allen Hammond, Earthscan 1998 p 73

3. *Which World?* p 75

4. *New Internationalist* March 1999, UNDP *Human Development Report* 1996 OUP. Hammond in *Which World?* at p 278 cites Edward Wolff of New York University, author of a recent study on equity trends, as concluding that America is "the most unequal industrial country in terms of income and wealth, and we're growing more unequal faster than the other industrial countries".

5. And see *Which World?* p 81.

6. *New Internationalist* March 1999, UNDP *Human Development Report* 1996 OUP.

7. See also Hammond's conclusion in *Which World?* at p 86 "In short, there is a growing recognition that environmental, social and economic concerns are closely linked and that economic development pursued in isolation might well fail as it has, so far, in most of the poor countries of the world".

8. "There can be no higher purpose than working to eradicate poverty and promote sustainable development in the world's poorest countries" Tony Blair April 1997. "Our goal, halving the proportion of the world's population living in absolute poverty by 2015, demands urgent action from the world's richest countries". Chancellor Gordon Brown.

9. All statistics and much else in this section are taken from *The Health of Londoners,* a report by The Health of Londoners Project, 1998 Kings Fund Publishers, a member of one of whose sub-groups, Jake Ferguson, has contributed to this book; or from the Election Briefing sheets produced by the King's Fund on various aspects of health in London. The *Health of Londoners Project* included reports on *Housing and Health, Refugee Health, Child Health* and *Transport in London and the implications for Health.*

10. *21st Century City that Works,* a report by Prof Douglas McWilliams, Centre for Economics and Business Research Ltd, part of the ALG's *London Study.*

11. See *Sustainable Development and Health* Hugo Crombie, Public Health Alliance, para 5.5 referring to work by RG Wilkinson. Increased wealth does not necessarily mean better quality of life. Whilst there are now 47,000 millionaires in Britain compared with only 6,000 at the beginning of the decade, surveys show that people are working much longer hours. Rising 'prosperity' (for some) is likely to be accompanied by continued social upheaval: more broken marriages, worsening drug dependency, workplace stress, loneliness and collapse in faith. The professional classes in particular will feel the strain of keeping up: *The Paradox of Prosperity* by the Henley Centre, noted in the Daily Telegraph on 16 September 1999.

12. Paul de Zylva, Friends of the Earth London Groups Coordinator citing the *Poor Show* report available from Lambeth Public Transport Group on 020 7737 6641.

13. Paul de Zylva citing study by FoE and the London School of Hygiene and Tropical Medicine.

14. Information for this paragraph supplied by Paul de Zylva.

15. Information for this paragraph also supplied by Paul de Zylva.

16. Huw Thomas in *Town and Country Planning* November 1999 Vol 68 No 11 citing B Robson: 'Vision and reality: urban social policy', in *British Planning: 50 years of Urban and Regional Policy,* B. Cullingworth, The Athlone Press London 1999.

17. Article by Steve Bruce, The Commonwealth Institute, in *A Mayor for London – Involving Student Citizens* Arts Inform and Institute for Citizenship December 1999.

18. Association of London Government *London Study,* Demos 1997.

19. The Institute of Education is leading a debate within the teaching profession about what kind of a curriculum is needed to meet the challenges of a "period of intense and rapid change".

20. See London Environmental Education Forum in Part 3.

21. *New Times* 8 October 1999.

22. *The Creative City* by Charles Landry and Franco Bianchini, Demos 1995, cites many interesting examples and is itself a good example of the whole-systems approach. The need for 'giving people a say' is also emphasised in this context. For an indication of the part that the Arts already play in London life, see for example the *Tower Hamlets Arts Directory 1999.* London Borough of Tower Hamlets, Arts and Events Office, listing an amazing array of art forms, arts centres and cultural organisations, and beautifully put together.

London's 'metabolism and ecology'

London's impact on the global environment is contributing to the rapid deterioration of the Earth's natural resources on which we depend for survival. This is unnecessary. The challenge for London is to become a sustainable part of a sustainable world.

● ●

The end of a millennium was a big milestone for western civilisation. But for life on Earth it was more like the minute hand on a clock passing one of the notches marking the seconds. The incredible explosion of life that is Nature has taken 3000 million years to develop.

In fact however this **is** a significant moment for Nature. What is significant about this particular moment on Nature's clock is that, for the first time in all those 3000 million years, Nature has produced a species that has become aware of just how Nature has developed throughout that period. Darwin began the process of discovery in the 19th century. Thousands of scientists have built on his work. Richard Dawkins has explained, in language we can all understand, the scientists' growing understanding of the processes that have been at work. David Attenborough and the BBC have brought the wonderful story, with all its beauties, its richness and amazing diversity, into the living rooms and bedside reading books of every family in the land. James Lovelock's Gaia theory seeks explanations for some of the interactions as yet dimly understood.

And yet, with the cruellest of ironies, this same, aware, and also intelligent, imaginative and innovative species also has the capacity to destroy other species, each one of them unique and impossible to recreate, to obliterate equally unique and irreplaceable habitats, and to dig out of the ground and release into the air 300 million year old fossils, the condensed remains of primeval forests, thereby speeding climate change to a pace to which current species have never before had to adapt. We have developed the capacity to do these things and, in spite of our awareness, we are doing them.

Full-scale global emergencies

1998 and 1999 saw the publication of two reports describing the state of the global environment at the end of the 20th century.

The Living Planet Index

In 1998 the WWF, together with the World Conservation Monitoring Centre and the New Economics Foundation, published the *Living Planet Index*, which measures changes in the health of the world's natural ecosystems since 1970, focusing on forest, freshwater and seas. It comes as no surprise that forest ecosystems have declined. It is less well known that during this period there has also been a very severe deterioration of freshwater and marine ecosystems. Putting these three together the *Living Planet Index* shows a decline of a horrifying 30% since 1970 "which can be interpreted as meaning that the earth has lost nearly one third of its natural wealth in that time".

The report also analyses global consumption patterns to calculate the burden placed on the natural environment by humanity through the

WWF Living Planet Index
A measure of the health of the world's natural ecosystems, 1970-1995

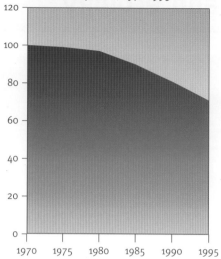

GEO 2000

In 1999 the UN Environment Program (UNEP) published GEO 2000, the Global Environment Outlook report. "Full-scale emergencies" now exist as a result of water shortages, land degradation, tropical forest destruction, species extinction, overfishing and urban air pollution in the world's megacities. The report pointed the finger at a wasteful consumer society in rich countries coupled with rapid population growth in poor ones.

Presenting the report, UNEP director Klaus Topfer said that the time to tackle major problems was fast running out and in some aspects, such as global warming and destruction of species, it was already too late. "It is absolutely crucial to give more thought to the future. Human activities have grown to the point where they affect the large scale physical systems of the planet and present-day actions will have consequences that reach far into the future. We can no longer be complacent and assume that the environment can look after itself".

These reports are not alone. Nor are conclusions such as those quoted confined to bodies specially concerned with the environment. Allen Hammond in his wide-lens survey of current global trends has written "Many of the trends considered here describe a world in which conditions are getting worse, not better. I wish it were not true, but that is what the data all too clearly show. Environmental conditions, for example, may be improving in the United States and in a few other wealthy countries, but globally they are deteriorating rapidly.. Moreover the analysis underlying this book suggests that if current trends continue, many of these conditions will get far worse"[1], threatening even the modest improvements made in the few wealthier countries.

production and consumption of resources such as grain, fish, wood and fresh water, and the emission of pollutants such as carbon dioxide (CO_2). "Globally, consumption pressure is growing rapidly – at about 5% per year – and is likely to exceed sustainable levels, at least for fish consumption, meat consumption and CO_2 emissions, if indeed they have not been exceeded already."

We Londoners make our own contributions to these processes, directly through our consumption of meat and fish and our carbon dioxide emissions, indirectly in many other ways. The only sane response is to reduce the pressures we exert, by eating less meat and fish, by emitting less carbon dioxide, and to take part in other ways, including the use of financial power, in achieving global reductions.

Consumption Pressure
A measure of the burden placed on the environment by people, 1995

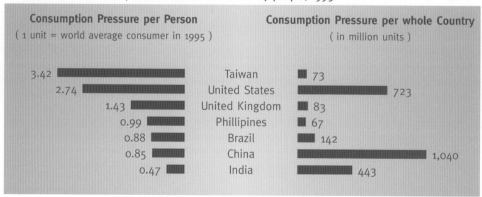

Consumption Pressure per Person (1 unit = world average consumer in 1995)		Consumption Pressure per whole Country (in million units)
3.42	Taiwan	73
2.74	United States	723
1.43	United Kingdom	83
0.99	Phillipines	67
0.88	Brazil	142
0.85	China	1,040
0.47	India	443

Pathways to the future

Climate change

Most of the emergencies highlighted by the Living Planet Index and GEO 2000 have been looming for decades. It is 30 years or more since many of us were concerned enough to start supporting the WWF, Greenpeace, RSPB, Oxfam and other organisations campaigning on these issues. However, even the best efforts of all these organisations have failed to reverse these tragic trends. In the meantime we have unwittingly brought upon ourselves a further nightmare prospect, which many now regard as the most serious of them all: climate change.

It's official

Global warming is no longer a theory: even official government documents acknowledge that it is a reality

◆ Since the 1970s, the world has warmed by about 0.15 degrees Celsius per decade.
◆ 1998 was the warmest year on record.
◆ In England, four of the five hottest years since the record started in 1660 occurred in the last decade; ten of the eleven warmest years in that record occurred after 1980.

These are startling statistics. Moreover the clear message from the scientific community is that this warming is due, at least in part, to the increasing concentrations of greenhouse gases in the atmosphere.[2]

The IPPC

The International Panel on Climate Change is the officially recognised group of international scientists who have consistently concluded that global warming will happen, that it will have major adverse consequences and that it has been and is being induced by emissions of various "greenhouse gases", namely carbon dioxide, methane, nitrous oxide, hydrofluorocarbons,

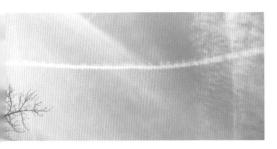

perfluorocarbons and sulphur hexafluoride. The largest impact comes from combustion of fossil fuels – coal, oil and natural gas which provide about 90% of the world's commercial energy used for electricity generation, transport and industry and in homes and offices.

For the UK also, the worst culprit is carbon dioxide, emissions of which account for 80% of our total contributions to global warming. On this issue, Londoners are directly implicated.

The chief meteorologists of Britain and the US

Two days before Xmas 1999 the heads of the Met. offices of Great Britain and the United States wrote a joint letter to newspapers warning of the seriousness of the situation, their end-of-century message: **global warming is now changing the world's climate rapidly, and humanity faces a 'critical' position because of it**.[3]

The seriousness of the situation was stressed by George Monbiot and Sir John Houghton, director of the IPCC, in a recent BBC Radio 4 programme. Monbiot distinguished two sets of effects of climate change: first were the readily predictable effects: dry climates would get dryer, wet ones wetter and there would be more floods, storms and other 'weather events'. These are effects we have already begun to experience: typhoons, hurricanes and floods have already done immense damage, resulting in millions of people being displaced and becoming 'environmental refugees'. The second category is the non-linear big bang effect like a change in the Gulf Stream which would have long lasting unpredictable consequences. Sir John Houghton insisted that the science was firm: the predictions had not changed for 15 years and had been confirmed by events to date. A half a metre rise in sea levels would result from the expansion of the water through warming.

The irony of the situation is that the countries in line to be hardest hit by global warming and climate change are comparatively innocent – sub-Saharan Africa, the Indian sub-continent, low-lying island states; whereas the industrialised countries, which have caused the atmosphere to warm, may be let off more lightly. However both speakers emphasised that the world is now a global village; they expressed impatience at the institutional inertia which is preventing governments and corporations from responding adequately, and at the intransigence of the USA and to a lesser extent of Europe. A world wide citizens movement was needed to put pressure on governments to take urgent action.

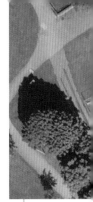

Serious already, catastrophic unless...

Two things are thus clear: that climate change is happening and that it is having, and will have, serious effects; secondly, that the effects will be catastrophic unless we do something about it. What, then are we doing about it ?

Rio, Kyoto and Buenos Aires

At the Rio Earth Summit in 1992 world leaders agreed the Framework Convention on Climate Change, which set a voluntary target of reducing greenhouse gases to 1990 levels by 2000. The UK is one of the few countries that met this target, but this was only achieved as a side effect of converting from coal to gas, which has less impact. "Since 1990 our total greenhouse gas emissions have reduced by about 7% whilst our economy has grown by over 13%", boasts the Government, without mentioning that this is how it happened.[4]

At Kyoto in 1997 the parties drew up a new Protocol under which developed country emissions of the six principal greenhouse gases would be reduced to 5.2% below 1990 levels by 2008-2012. The obligation to make these reductions would be legally binding when the Protocol has been ratified (expected in 2001). Three 'flexible mechanisms' were proposed to enable countries to achieve part of their legally binding commitments by action taken to reduce emissions abroad: joint implementation (JI), clean development mechanism (CDM) and international emissions trading, which enable countries that achieve greater reductions than needed to achieve their targets to sell the surplus to other countries (which in turn thereby buy the right to exceed their targets).

At Buenos Aires in 1999 a two year plan was agreed setting deadlines for progress on further negotiations, including a work programme for finalising the 'flexible mechanisms'.

The UK and the EU bubble

The Kyoto Protocol allows a group of countries to undertake joint commitments by forming a 'bubble'. The countries of the European Union have formed a bubble that is committed to an 8% reduction. They have agreed how the joint obligation will be shared amongst them: the UK's obligation is a 12.5% reduction.

Independently of these international agreements, the UK Government has set itself the objective of achieving a 20% reduction by 2010. To implement this and its prospective legal obligations the Government is developing numerous strategies on energy, business, transport, the domestic sector, agriculture and the public sector. The Government recognises that "we will only be successful if all sectors take action" and also that "the programme will bring other benefits too: warmer homes, a less polluting transport system and many job opportunities."[5]

Reducing our CO_2 emissions touches almost every aspect of our lives at home and at work, how we travel between the two and what other travelling we do. Taking part in implementing government policies means numerous actions by local government, public services, the private sector and individuals.

The Government's programme is by no means a business as usual agenda. There will be room for many initiatives.

The Government is to be congratulated on having played a useful part in the negotiations at Kyoto and Buenos Aires and for its support for a cooperative approach to implementing its programme. The international community and our own government are moving in the right direction. They need our support and full cooperation.

But is that enough ?

The UK Government's response to the challenge presented by climate change is ahead of that of many other governments, especially that of the US Government. But measuring performance by comparing governments gets us nowhere.

What really matters is what it happening out there in the atmosphere.

Pathways to the future

"The concentration of CO_2 in the atmosphere is climbing to a dangerous level. To stabilize the atmospheric concentration, the scientific community [this refers to the IPCC] believes that **global** *CO_2 emissions* **would have to be cut by about 60%**, *to a level that is within the capacity of the oceans and terrestrial ecosystems, especially forests, to remove CO_2 from the atmosphere. On average each person in the world currently burns enough fossil fuels to emit about 4 tonnes of CO_2 per year. Yet per person emissions in North America are around 20 tonnes per year, the European average is about 10 tonnes per year and the average in the developing countries is about 2.5 tonnes per year."*[6]

From this you can calculate how much an average European would need to reduce CO_2 emissions to bring their emissions down to the average level recommended by the scientists as necessary to stabilise the atmosphere. If the world average needs to be reduced to 40% of 4 tonnes = 1.6 tonnes, for the average European **that means a reduction from 10 to 1.6 tonnes**. Some readers may feel that they are currently responsible for a lot more than the European average. You will be able to draw your own conclusions!

The answer to the question "But is it enough?" must therefore be: well, it's a start, but only a start. The Government has, it is true, recognised that "further cuts in emissions will need to be made over time if dangerous levels of climate change are to be prevented"[7]. But a gradual transformation whereby we reduce our emissions probably to a tenth of their present level, is not on the Government's agenda. As a result of the Government's 'problem-solving approach' and its adherence to the gospel of 'economic growth', the real issues have not been addressed at all.

A 'systems approach' would require governments to invite the public (a) to join in defining the problem and (b) to join in working out how to solve it: two logically separate but vitally linked elements of a 'systems approach'. As it is, our government ministers, along with those of other industrial countries, are struggling to sell their programme to ordinary people by asking them completely inappropriate questions like "are you doing your bit?"[8]. Not surprisingly, the response is unenthusiastic. "Small steps like turning off unneeded lights or leaving the car at home once in a while really make a difference". If this is the level of change needed, people are unlikely to take it seriously. No wonder they do not take much notice.

Action on Climate Change

Highly important work is already being done in London. Amongst outstanding individuals are

◆ Mayer Hillman, of the Policy Studies Institute, who has researched the policy implications of climate change, especially those for our present lifestyles. His many contributions to the public discourse are, like Beethoven's symphonies, uncompromising. For example, every passenger, he says, on a return flight to Florida accounts for an average of 1.8 tonnes of CO_2. More than one year's ration! He has much to say on how we can modify those aspects of our lifestyles dependent on the use of fossil fuels, with important gains in terms of health and quality of life.

◆ Aubrey Meyer, founder and director of the Global Commons Institute, has pioneered the concept of 'contraction and convergence' – reducing the greenhouse gas emissions globally, whilst the per capita emissions from developed and developing countries converge. This simple concept is winning increasing acceptance. Should we not have a strategy for contraction and convergence between rich and poor in London ? Think how that could frame transport policy in a new light!

◆ David Fleming, an independent economist, is working on the mechanisms needed to enable the principle of contraction and convergence to be applied. He has demonstrated the advantages of domestic tradable quotas in which everyone has an equal entitlement of carbon units to cover their needs.

One London-based independent organisation which has been able to play an important part in the international scene is FIELD (Foundation for International Environment Law and Development). In acting for the Association of Small Island States throughout the climate change negotiations, at Rio, Kyoto and Buenos Aires, FIELD lawyers have been able to make significant contributions to the progress achieved in the negotiations.

Pathways to the future

The challenge for London

It should not be assumed that climate change will not affect London. The direct effects could be unpleasant and could cost us £ billions. "In south-east England, summer rainfall could be much lower. Droughts could be interrupted by intense thunderstorms. These would cause flooding, but would fail to benefit either water supplies or soil moisture. Coupled with stronger winds, such droughts could turn the south east into a landscape of drying rivers, desiccated soils, and forest fires in summer."[9] One of the Government's 34 indicators of the impact of climate change on the UK generally is the number of times the Thames Barrier has to be raised – and it has been raised more frequently in recent years. It will, like other barriers and sea walls, provide ever less protection from spring tides and storm surges as sea levels rise.[10]

The direct effect of climate change on London is not however the crucial consideration. The Earth as a global village. London is part of that village. The facts, the evidence and the scientific advice are there for anyone to judge for themselves. Yet London is not responding anything like seriously enough to the issues raised by the *Living Planet Index*, *GEO 2000* and the IPCC.

We therefore need to examine London's impact on the Planet in the light of the evidence we now have. Never mind, for the moment, the national programmes. As Londoners we need to ask: where is London in all this? Just as there is a challenge for each of us as an individual, so there is a challenge for each community, each organisation, each workplace, and for London as a whole. If we can start thinking differently within these various organisations and within London as a whole, that is going to help change attitudes throughout society.

At the moment, thinking by individuals is dominated by our personal circumstances and habits. At the other end of the scale government thinking is dominated by the belief that 'economic growth' is a good thing (more of that in chapter 3), its problem-solving approach (more of that in chapter 6) and the reluctance of elected governments to do anything that they fear will not command public support. It is possible that if London as a whole gets its thinking going on how, albeit over several decades, we are going to reduce our per capita CO_2 emissions to the global average recommended level, which, as we have seen, probably means a reduction to one tenth of our present levels, this will actually help individuals and organisations in London start to think through how this can be done.

Energy

Fossil fuels

It should be clear from our discussion of global warming that we need to learn how to live using less fossil fuel. Quite apart from that, there are two other reasons for not using fossil fuels as if there was a limitless supply:

◆ Fossil fuels are part of the world's natural capital and should only be used for capital purposes.[11]
◆ The supply is in fact limited. Oil discovery peaked 30 years ago. Oil is now being used up four times faster than new sources are being discovered. Shortages are predicted to develop within the next ten years.[12]

The average household is currently responsible, directly or indirectly, for about 24 tonnes of CO_2 emissions per year. About one quarter of that is attributable to domestic uses, mostly heating, another quarter is transport, mostly cars, the rest is use by commerce, industry and agriculture. There are three main routes to using less fossil fuel:

◆ Reducing activities that use energy
◆ Producing energy from renewables (non-fossil fuel sources of energy)
◆ Energy efficiency.

To achieve the eventual 90% reductions in our CO_2 emissions, we will certainly have to use all three routes. Note the unusual order in which I have placed them. Whilst energy efficiency offers the greatest savings, we need to pursue the other routes right from the outset.

Reducing activities that use energy

There are obvious possibilities in terms of travel. For example IT can reduce the need to travel to obtain goods, data and services. People, especially the better off, can arrange their lives so that they do not need to travel so much.

The most commonly heard call is for more use of public transport. On our route you will see a BEWARE sign here. Using public transport is

twice as energy efficient as doing the same journey by car, on average occupancies. But it still causes CO_2 emissions! Travelling 100 miles by public transport does more damage than travelling 40 miles by car.

Although many of the actions to reduce fossil fuel use involve initial capital costs, they will almost all reduce running costs.

De-materialising our economic activities

Closely related to the agenda of reducing the use of fossil fuels is that of eliminating all kinds of dissipative uses of materials. The only way any species can continue to live on Earth indefinitely is by not using up the capital resources it needs to live. At present we are both using up materials we should treat as capital not income, and we have "released into the atmosphere tens of thousands of new chemical and bio-chemical products, often with surprising results" (many of which, one might add, have probably yet to come home to roost).

Books like *Factor Four* and *Natural Capitalism*[13], present an exciting and sophisticated vision: "eliminating the concept of waste by redesigning production on biological models, with closed loops and no toxicity; reshaping commerce as a 'solutions economy' (shifting from goods to services, from stocks to flows, and from zero-sum transactions to relationships whose structure rewards efficiency gains and aligns providers' with customers' interests); and reinvesting in systematically restoring, sustaining and expanding natural capital."[14]

Eliminating waste altogether: eliminating the whole concept of waste! How is that for thinking differently! Amory Lovins, joint author of these books, sees it as a genuinely practicable possibility. His enthusiasm is infectious. The danger is that it lulls one into a sense that everything is going to be alright after all: technology and market forces, backed by suitable government action, will solve all our problems without our having to change our lifestyles. The Lovins route-map will be very useful. But there is another of those BEWARE signs here.

Renewables

This refers to harnessing the energy of the sun, wind and biomass to create electricity. (It does **not** include energy obtained by incinerating rubbish!)

Photovoltaics (PV) convert sunlight directly into electricity. It is considered to be the most suitable form of renewable technology for use in the urban environment. Greenpeace claims that two-thirds of the UK's current electricity production could be generated by photovoltaics on homes and offices[15]. Jeremy Leggett is London's leading photovoltaic campaigner turned entrepreneur: he is "completely convinced that the solar revolution is coming, and it is going to create a vast new business revolution".[16] Production is currently small-scale and expensive: economies of scale could cut the PV solar panels by a factor of four[17]. Both Shell and BP have started PV subsidiaries. The industry just needs a massive boost to realise its potential – just the kind of outcome that could be achieved from the kind of new governance for London described in these pages, with the Mayor as champion.

Solar water and space heating is another way of using the sun, this time directly.

Windpower is said to offer the possibility of providing 10% of the world's electricity by 2020.[18] The Triodos Bank's Windfund offers investors an opportunity to help fund renewable energy projects.

The Forest in the Square Mile

In *Creating a Sustainable London* we recorded a story told by Mark Campanale, who works in the City of London:

"A couple of years ago I attended a meeting typical of those which take place every day in the City of London. A group of Indonesian businessmen organised a lunch to raise $300 million to finance the clearing of a rainforest and the construction of a pulp and paper plant. What struck me was how their decision to replace this living, complex eco-system with industrial plantations had been reduced to a set of simple financial ratios. The City has evolved a financial system in which financial rationalism – the use of 'profit' as the basic measure of business validity – overcomes even basic common sense about protection of biodiversity. But not only would the future of that rainforest be determined by decisions made over lunch that day, the financial benefits of its destruction would go to institutional shareholders based in London, Tokyo or New York. Very little, if any, of the financial benefits would go to local people.

Therefore when thinking about the environmental impact of London, we have to think about the decisions of fund managers which impact on the other side of the world. In essence, the rainforest may be geographically located in the Far East, but financially it might as well be located in London's Square Mile".

The EU is looking for cities that aim to achieve 100% of their energy from renewable sources;[19] why not London ?

Energy efficiency

There is a wide open gate leading to this route, for householders, office managers, property owners, businesses and the public sector; and no lack of advice from numerous organisations. A combined heat and power scheme is described on page 131 of this book. Moreover this is a win-win-win agenda because, as well as reducing fossil fuel use, it provides jobs and results in a higher quality environment. The only things that have prevented more people from proceeding down this route already are our defective economic and political systems, subjects we will come back to in the next chapter and in Part 2.

Pathways to the future

Sustainable Cities

Cities obviously cannot be self-sufficient. They are, by definition, places where people gather to live and work, leaving the countryside for growing food and other crops and rural recreations. Cities are by nature highly dependent on external supplies. Taking up only 2 % of the world's land surface, they are homes to half the world's population and use over 75% of the world's resources. Their impact on the rest of the world is bound to be massive. There will always be give and take between cities and their hinterlands. London's hinterland extends to the whole globe.

Cities are defined by geographical areas and much of the give and take is in terms of the physical transport of goods. They are however also economic centres and cultural centres. Here the exchanges take the form of credits and debits, radio broadcasts and TV programmes, business trips and tourism and many other activities. London is said to be a 'world city': the context in which that phrase is most often used is where it is being stressed that London must seek 'economic growth' in order to maintain its competitive position vis-à-vis other cities in terms of financial services, tourism and air travel services. That is thinking in the out-moded and dangerous problem-solving mode[21]. For us, what makes London a world city are its cultural, financial and political relationships: these are part of what London is: they are part of its future, as well as its past.

Every city, and London especially, is a part of bigger systems, in terms of its economy, energy, climate, pollution and resource use. Which is why this book about pathways to the future for London has taken the shape it has: it does not make sense just to look at London. We have to raise our heads and survey the whole scene, all 360 degrees of it, all the way to the horizon and beyond into the future. We have to see how we can take part in creating world wide sustainable systems.

One of the effects of the kind of 'economic growth' we have witnessed in the last half century especially, is that cities such as London have become much more dependent on external supplies than they used to be. Herbert Girardet, who has written extensively about sustainable cities[22] and is a Sustainable London Trust trustee,

calls this *mobilisation*, not *civilisation*. Modern cities are defined, he says, by their demand for energy, depending on the routine use of fossil fuels for transport, electricity, service provision and manufacturing.

'Metabolism' means "the chemical processes that occur within a living organism to maintain life". 'Ecology' is "the branch of biology concerned with the relations of organisms to one another and to their physical surroundings".[23] I use these words metaphorically in the title to this chapter, to encourage us to think about the processes within the city and the city's relationships with the rest of the world.

Substituting circular for linear metabolisms

"Like other organisms", writes Girardet, *"cities have a definable metabolism. The metabolism of most 'modern' cities is essentially linear, with resources flowing through the urban system without much concern for their origin or for the destination of wastes: inputs and outputs are considered as largely unrelated. Raw materials are extracted, combined and processed into consumer goods that end up as rubbish which cannot be beneficially reabsorbed into living nature. Fossil fuels are extracted from rock strata, refined and burned; their fumes are discharged into the atmosphere.*

"In distant forests trees are felled for their timber or pulp, but all too often forests are not adequately replenished. Similar processes are applied to food: nutrients are harvested as food and not returned. Urban sewage systems have the function of collecting human wastes and separating them from people. Sewage is discharged into rivers and coastal waters downstream from population centres, and is not returned to farmland. Today, coastal waters are sullied with human sewage and toxic effluents as well as the run-off from mineral fertilisers supplied to the farmland which feeds cities. This open loop is not sustainable."

Girardet contrasts this with nature's circular metabolisms, where every output from an organism is also an input which renews and sustains the whole living environment.

"On a predominantly urban planet, cities will need to adopt circular metabolic systems to assure the long term viability of the rural environments on which they depend. Outputs will also need to be inputs into the productive system: for instance, with the routine recycling of paper, metals, plastic and glass, and the conversion of organic materials into compost, returning plant nutrients to keep farmland productive ... The critical point is that cities could massively reduce their through-put of resources, whilst maintaining a good standard of living and creating much-needed local jobs in the process." [24]

Many European cities have begun to address the challenges of urban sustainability much more urgently than London. Three hundred European cities have formed themselves into the European Climate Alliance working towards halving their energy consumption and CO_2 emissions by 2010. Now, that's more like it! How about London joining them, on the way to zero emissions by (say) 2025. That would be worth talking about, over the counter in the **local** shop!

London's 'metabolism and ecology'

How do the things we have been discussing in this chapter apply to London ? Here are some statistics to stimulate thinking.

London's metabolism compares unfavourably with other European cities, with about the highest per capita energy consumption:

"Seven million Londoners consume 45,000 tonnes of oil equivalent per day, a queue of road tankers from Chiswick to Piccadilly. With heat leaking through the roofs of houses, over half of it is wasted. Nearly 20% of it is used just for refuelling planes. London's own internal traffic uses up a further 23% of its fuel. Add to

The Metabolism of Greater London
Population 7,000,000

These figures quantify London's resource use. They are listed here to emphasise the huge potential for greater resource efficiency. London's waste output could be used as a significant resource for new recycling and efficiency industries.

Inputs	tonnes per year
Total fuel (oil equivalent)	20,000,000
Oxygen	40,000,000
Water	1,002,000,000
Food	2,400,000
Timber	1,200,000
Paper	2,200,000
Plastics	2,100,000
Glass	360,000
Cement	1,940,000
Bricks, blocks, sand, tarmac	6,000,000
Metals (total)	1,200,000

Wastes	
Industrial and demolition	11,400,000
Household, civic, commercial	3,900,000
Wet, digested sewage sludge	7,500,000
CO_2	60,000,000
SO_2	400,000
NOx	280,000

London's Ecological Footprint

London's Ecological Footprint, following the definition by Canadian economist William Rees, consists of the land area required to supply London with food, fibre and wood products, and the area of growing vegetation needed to absorb London's CO_2 output:

	acres
London's surface area	**390,000**
Farmland used:	
3 acres per person	21,000,000
Forest area required for wood products:	
0.27 acres per person	1,900,000
Land area required for carbon absorption (equal to acreage required for fuel production from biomass):	
3.7 acres per person	26,000,000
Total London ecological footprint (125 times London's surface area)	**48,900,000**
Britain's productive land	**52,000,000**
Britain's total surface area	**60,000,000**

that the tractor fuel and the fuel burned up in freighters and lorries that supply London … The flow of resources is linear, coming from somewhere, never mind where, and ending up as rubbish in a tip, or as sewage in the North Sea, or as atmospheric pollution. London recycles only 4% of its wastes, less than anywhere else in Europe. Vienna, for instance, recycles 43% … London's food supplies come from all over the world. Every Londoner has an acre of farmland available to him or her in Britain, and another acre abroad, on farms where animal feeds, wheat fruit and vegetables are grown … Fewer vegetables and fruit are grown in the vicinity of London than in most European cities and ever more is being flown in long distance in the cargo holds of jumbo jets, at great financial and environmental cost. For its own use London imports fruit and vegetables for over £400 million a year. Of this some 5,000 tonnes is flown in from places such as California and Kenya. This is done at a huge energy cost which is totally out of proportion to the nutritional value of the food imported. For instance, flying a mango into a London home from the tropics requires some 600 times more energy than the calorific content of the food itself. The same applies to fish… In fact, most of the food we eat today – bread, meat, rice, greenhouse vegetables – has a far greater fuel than nutritional content.

"London's electricity supply system relies on remote power stations and long-distance transmission lines, and is no more than 30-35% efficient. Yet the know-how exists to bring down London's energy use by 30-35% without affecting living standards, and with the potential of creating tens of thousands of jobs by using renewable energy such as wind and solar power, and more energy efficient systems such as combined heat and power stations."[25]

In short, London, the mother of mega-cities, is now an excellent metaphor for defining an unsustainable city. We are doing that which we ought not to be doing; worse, throughout the 10 or 20 years since the destructive effects of our global impact became more and more obvious, London has gone on blindly pursuing the same patterns of 'economic growth' which have been the driving force in making matters worse. And we are still.

As London embarks on the experiment of a directly elected mayor, what chance is there of a dramatic change of **direction** ? Could London become the world city that takes a lead in promoting the most enlightened developments in urban sustainability ?

Transport in London

This is not a book about how to sort out London's traffic problems. I will not even attempt to analyse the issues. I have already made some general points under the heading Energy. Here I merely add a few thoughts, in the hope of provoking some new thinking.

Reducing car use

Current proposals by the London Planning Advisory Committee (LPAC) envisage traffic reductions by 2005 of 40% within Central London, 30% within Inner London and 10%

within Outer London. These, it is suggested, will be achieved by a variety of mechanisms. These proposals are put forward for discussion with the boroughs as a basis on which the Mayor can take definite decisions when he or she takes office. The introduction to LPAC's consultation document making these proposals was written by its chair, Haringey Councillor Nicky Gavron. From this it appears that the motivations behind the suggested targets are

◆ health issues
◆ congestion costing business billions of pounds each year
◆ projected increases in cars in outer boroughs
◆ popularity with the 85% of people who travel into Central London in the rush hour by tube, bus or bike, and the nearly 40% of households who do not have a car
◆ less congestion making public transport (bus services) more reliable
◆ improving conditions for pedestrians and cyclists
◆ improving air quality
◆ reducing noise, and visual intrusion, fear, intimidation and community severance.

"It is not anti-car. But we have to learn to use cars more selectively, on those journeys for which they really are the most appropriate means."[26]

This looks like a thoroughly sensible set of proposals for solving the perceived problem. As a decision-making process, it bears all the

London's 'metabolism and ecology'

Negotiative Planning and the Reflexive City

Three models for city planning have been distinguished

Conventional Planning and the 'Fortress City'. In this model

- The problem is defined as one of 'taming trends', 're-assigning' and removing traffic and regenerating the economy
- The policy is relatively simple – there are Experts and there are the Policy Makers
- The image of the city is thus one which places a strong emphasis on protecting the integrity of its boundaries, keeping 'extraneous' traffic out and emphasising technologies of tracking, control and enforcement

The Progressive Planning and Audited City. Here

- The problem is one of 'environmental individualism' and lack of information – if only people knew the consequences of their actions they would surely change
- The Local Authority's role in this process is to form partnerships with different agencies, promote good practice and 'get the message across'
- The City is thus a highly audited one – flows, capacities and footprints are the key decision criteria – and decisions are made on the basis of this information

Negotiative Planning and the Reflexive City. This is the emerging model and is characterised by

- The problem is actually very serious, a recognition that there is a crisis
- Responsibility for finding a solution lies not solely with the local authority but relies on networks and partnerships involving a wide range of groups
- The vision of the city is a reflexive one, aware of its consequences and with users, employers and many other agencies involved in defining problems and developing solutions

*Urban Transport Plans: Emerging Logics of Transport Planning,*Robert Evans (University of Wales Cardiff), Simon Guy (University of Newcastle) and Simon Marvin (University of Salford)

hallmarks of the *Conventional Planning and 'Fortress City'* model described by Evans, Guy and Marvin (see above box), with some elements of the *Progressive Planning and Audited City* model. This has meant that

- basic issues such as global warming and justice, and the fact that we have more than one full-scale emergency on our hands, have been left out of account (except, implicitly, via the Government's Integrated Transport White Paper, but my point is that these are issues **for London**)

- many of those most affected by the proposals — car drivers and people most adversely affected by traffic — have not been involved in defining the problems and finding the solutions (though it may be envisaged that they will be 'consulted' in due course).

This problem-solving kind of government is all that is possible in the present political situation in London. It is the kind of highly professional activity that has taken the place of effective government in London for the last 12 years. It does not address the big issues, it does not create trust, it does not achieve cooperation. This theme is developed in chapter 6.

The election of a Mayor offers the opportunity for London to adopt the third of the Evans, Guy and Marvin models, the *Negotiative Planning and Reflexive City* model.

Alternatives to more underground lines

If the overriding considerations are

- massive reductions in CO_2 emissions and
- narrowing the gap between rich and poor,

these objectives are not achieved by building new underground lines (costing £320 million per Jubilee Line mile) for the better off to travel in ways that will entice them out of their cars, or for business visitors to travel from Heathrow to the City without being held up in traffic jams.

Some improvements that could well be made without too much expense would have immense benefits. An obvious example is improving facilities for zero energy travel, ie networks to encourage and facilitate cycling and walking: these would be

◆ good for neighbourhoods (traffic flows through residential areas cause community severance restricting access to facilities, driving out businesses and completely immobilising disabled people)
◆ good for health[27]
◆ good for reducing accidents, (currently running at 350 people killed and 6,500 serious road casualties per year in London)
◆ good for reducing the burden on health services, from treating heart disease in particular
◆ good for equality of opportunity
◆ good for the quality of life, good for the sense of well-being, good for equality of opportunity, especially good for children (they have been real victims of the car, their rights to a safe and convenient environment have been eroded steadily as adult mobility has risen leading to more danger and perceived need to restrict their freedoms to get around on their own, with adverse effects on their physical, social and emotional beings)
◆ above all good for the globe in terms of reducing car use and hence CO_2 emissions.

Spending public money on improving pedestrian and cycle facilities would also go well with the new agenda of policies to encourage more local living (ie lifestyles that do not require so much travelling) and more local community life.

Here I have to declare an interest: I am a cyclist and I love it. It gives me daily exercise and even in London it is a really pleasant way of getting around – very reliable, comparatively unstressful, even friendly: cyclists often smile and say hullo!

Fixing London's transport problems

Why is it that so little been done to reduce car use in London ? Why is it that the things that have been done are not always the best things that could have been done – the whole of the London Cycle Network would cost the same as 300 metres of the Jubilee Line Extension. Is it because of the opposition of car drivers ?

No, the reason has little to do with either transport or user lobbying power. The explanation lies in the areas of economics and politics.

◆ As to economics, the car is part of the 'growth economy'. Pedestrians and cyclists are not. Every additional car manufactured and every mile it is driven constitutes 'growth'. Walking is not 'growth', except to the extent that we have to have our shoes repaired more frequently; and cycling creates much less 'growth' than cars. As we shall see in chapter 3, our economic system demands 'growth'.
◆ As to politics, our communities simply do not have the structures or processes to address these issues effectively. The London boroughs are in some ways too small – transport is a cross-borough issue; and in some ways too big, in that they are not at one with their communities (we shall come back to this point in chapter 4) and they are subject to severe spending restrictions imposed by central government. Camden, for example has produced a Walking Plan: good; but little can be done to implement it due to lack of funding from central government: frustration. For the last 14 years we have had no London government which could have provided the necessary leadership. Finally, and most importantly, government at all levels is stuck in the 'problem solving' approach, which is ineffective. To crack transport issues needs the full participation of all the stakeholders, including the atmosphere and future generations! We return to this in chapter 6.

Air travel.

Any expansion of air travel or of any facilities for air travel , such as Terminal 5 at Heathrow, would be highly irresponsible due to the high fossil fuel demands of aircraft and the extra surface travelling generated by air travel. T5 presents a straightforward choice between the way forward marked 'economic growth' and that marked 'global future'. Taking the 'global future' route does not simply mean taking unilateral action. It means leading a movement for international action to reduce air travel.

Which path will London take ?

Food

Food is a major issue in the context of sustainable cities for several reasons

◆ food poverty in London
◆ 'food miles' – London importing much of its food from great distances, contributing quite unnecessarily to the CO_2 emissions, for which its population, as consumers, is indirectly responsible
◆ forests destroyed to grow food for export to wealthy cities like London
◆ communities in poor countries ceasing to be self-sufficient in food through their land being taken over for growing crops for export
◆ supermarkets reducing the viability of local shops, which can be reached on foot, thereby creating more car travel.

You can no doubt think of many more issues.

They are all tightly linked to our two big themes: the dominance of the 'growth economy' (some people are more interested in growing money than food!) and the modern city-dweller's total disregard for Nature. What better metaphor could there be for our estrangement from Nature than a child growing up to think of the supermarket shelf as the place where food is found ?

There are many ways out of this bad place. We highlight one of them: growing more food in London. Growing food in cities may strike you as being unrealistic but in fact many cities grow up to 30% of their own food and you may be surprised to know that there are still 30,000 allotment gardeners in London, not to mention all the private gardens, and that 14% of Londoners grow some fruit or vegetables. I happen to be one of these people and can assure you that it is one of my favourite things in life. I grow dozens of different kinds of vegetables and fruit: they of course grow themselves and the so-called grower is little more than a mid-wife and

carer: it always feels to me like a great privilege. I do a couple of hours on my allotment most weekends: it gets me out into the open air, gives me plenty of exercise and I enjoy a pint at the local pub on the way home. As you have probably guessed, I am an organic grower – no chemicals – with the result that I share some of the crops with other creatures. Still I always come home laden; and what I bring back is much appreciated. Home-grown veg certainly taste better, SLT volunteers will confirm.

In 1996 Tara Garnett wrote a report about growing food in cities and she followed it up last year with one on the feasibility of growing more food in London[28]. Her first report describes the wide-ranging benefits of growing food in cities. Her second report begins

"London could become a pioneer of urban agriculture for the UK, and even for Europe. The breadth and depth of expertise in the capital is impressive and, with a supportive policy framework, could significantly improve the quality of urban living."

She then sets out the environmental, economic, health, community development and educational advantages. So here is an opportunity for London to develop activities that meet the basic concerns in this book, in that they would

◆ save CO_2 emissions by reducing the amount of food imported into London
◆ address food poverty
◆ improve health, by providing exercise and fresh fruit and vegetables.

Growing growing

There is plenty of scope for growing more food in London as evidenced by the organisations and projects mentioned on pages 128 and 129 of this book. A key issue is access to land for community gardens and allotments for the most deprived members of our society, including many who have been used to growing their own food in their countries of origin. Here we are again, back to economics and politics. London currently grows more inequality than food.

What is lacking, Tara Garnett says, for Sustain, 'the alliance for better food and farming', is a supportive framework. Again, it's a question of London getting its act together.

Biodiversity

In the earlier part of this chapter we described how humans, although we have become aware of the wonders of the natural world, have at the same time developed the capacity to destroy it. What we have not yet developed is the capacity, as a species, as a nation, as a society and as a community, to stop doing these things. Developing that capacity, for London, is what this book is all about. London has a global responsibility. London also has a local responsibility. This section is about the particular part of Nature's diversity located within London, which must be our own special responsibility.

What is the extent of biodiversity in London ?

◆ 600 square miles of land, 40% green open space, half of that valuable wildlife habitat
◆ ancient woods at least four centuries old (and much older in many cases such as Oxleas, famed for its anti-road campaign, and Ruislip, next to my allotment), chalk grasslands, reservoirs, churchyards, wet meadows, railsides, canals, cemeteries, private gardens (nearly 20% of London is private gardens) and, obviously, the Thames, flowing through the heart of the city and perhaps London's most valuable and well known natural asset
◆ many rare species – 100 need special protection — and perhaps more importantly, an abundance of common ones, including a surprisingly rich flora, with 2,100 flowering plants and ferns growing wild.

Government agencies and non-governmental groups have been cooperating to conserve London's wildlife for years. The London Ecology Unit has played a leading part and a mass of expert survey work has been done by volunteer members of the London Natural History Society. The London Ecology Unit has developed a programme of site protection, with 1200 sites designated as being of either metropolitan, borough or local importance. The system has been successfully tested on numerous occasions at public enquiries: its purpose is to ensure that people in all parts of London have access to nature in their local neighbourhood and that provision of green space and nature is a major consideration in local planning issues.

Now nature conservation is being given a higher profile. A UK Biodiversity Action Plan, drawn up following the Rio Earth Summit in 1992, deals with the whole country, its object being "to conserve biological diversity within the UK and to contribute to the conservation of global diversity". To implement the UK plan requires concerted actions at the local level. In London, the response to this was the formation of the London Biodiversity Partnership in 1994 and partnerships at a more local level in many of London's boroughs.

So we will now have

- ◆ Borough Biodiversity Partnerships: every London borough should have its own local partnership and action plan. This is where local groups can cooperate with the public agencies and local people can contribute their own ideas. These borough partnerships are especially important as they will help to identify how specific action can be implemented on the ground, as an integral part of the wider process[29].
- ◆ The London-wide Biodiversity Partnership, a growing consortium of public, private and voluntary sector bodies which has been working towards a London Biodiversity Action Plan since 1994. The first volume of this consists of an audit which has just been published[30]. The second volume will specify the actions needed to conserve key habitats and species. For example, the Thames Estuary Partnership, which includes the Port of London Authority, property groups and water sports bodies as well as conservation organisations (see page 125), is taking on the Tidal Thames Habitat Action Plan.

One of the 'strategies' London's new Mayor is required to have is the 'London Biodiversity Action Plan'. In creating this the Mayor will no doubt build on the London Biodiversity Partnership's work. To have a statutory biodiversity plan for our capital city will a remarkable event. Moreover, since (as we shall see in chapter 5) all the Mayor's strategies are required to be consistent with each other, the strategies for economic development (the Strategy for the London Development Agency) and the Spatial Development Strategy, for example, are required **by law** to be consistent with the Biodiversity Action Plan. And of course, vice versa. Biodiversity is also listed as one of the things to be covered by the Mayor's four yearly 'State of the Environment Report'. It adds up to a remarkable statutory underpinning for the work that needs to be done on the ground.

It looks all very sensible and admirable. And it is not all just talk about generalities: for example, London Underground has completed an ecological survey of its railway linesides.

Will it be effective ?

To be effective, wide public participation will be needed. It is very good to read that the London Biodiversity Partnership is fully aware of this. This is a field where public participation has always been very strong: thousands of people are enthusiastic and active through the various societies and local groups. By contrast, government agencies have never been given the staff and the resources they need to do their jobs effectively; with the result that Nature has suffered massive losses in the last few decades, largely as a direct result of modern farming practices to supply our supermarkets.

All these audits and action plans will achieve nothing unless not thousands but millions of people get the message and act. That will not happen without political leadership, giving support, for example, to the London Biodiversity Partnership and its member bodies and to the work, for example, of the members of the London Environmental Education Network (see Part 3) in schools and ecology centres. This is a good example of where the Mayor, though not having a role in education services, can promote education about biodiversity, to attract the public participation needed to support the Biodiversity Action Partnerships.

Pathways to the future ? Leadership and education look to be the most promising. And please do not remove dead timber or dig out old tree stumps, if you can possibly help it, because that is where the larvae of the stag beetle live – large white grubs with stubby legs and a brown head; they take several years to mature. They are becoming scarce. It's their planet too.

Zero waste

Waste is a perfect case for illustrating the difference between the problem-solving and the systems thinking approaches.

The problem is that the landfill sites are nearly full. Solving it means finding another way of disposing of the vast amounts of waste produced by our modern consumer society. The North Sea is no longer an option. The land is full, the sea is out of bounds: it has to be the atmosphere. Incineration is the obvious answer. The scientists, funded by big business – there is profit in incineration contracts — have developed the technology to ensure that the fumes are healthy, at least so they say. The operation can be managed by a few large companies via a limited number of tightly-worded 25 year contracts: officials can keep control. These arrangements can even handle the waste stream getting bigger: come to think of it, this would suit the incineration companies very well. Science and big business have provided the problem-solver with the answer to the problem. They have also achieved 'growth'. It is business as usual, all very clinical and satisfactory. (A pity about all the toxins that did not go up the chimney and may therefore be in the ash: this can presumably be safely disposed of somewhere.)

The alternative, that of reducing the amount of waste produced by an economy that wants to 'grow', insisting that anything that can be re-used is re-used, altering industrial and commercial practices to ensure that goods are so produced and traded that they can be re-used, getting everyone including householders, businesses and public bodies, to recycle everything they can possibly recycle, and to compost all biodegradable waste, so as to end up with zero waste, all this looks horrendously difficult: how on earth, say the problem-solving officials to each other, could we manage all that, especially as market forces do not seem to be keen on it ?

Given the problem-solving approach and the 'growth economy', the officials and the big companies are bound to go for incineration. There is only one real difficulty: where to put the incinerator ? Since this is not a police state, every effort will have to be made to persuade local people to accept it: in the last resort they will have to be compensated in money.

Oh, but there is one other snag: that recycling target. In 1995 the Government set a target of 25% recycled household waste by the millennium. Unfortunately, in the next five years, we only achieved an increase of 2% to bring the figure up to 8%.

The systems approach, by contrast, starts with an analysis of the situation, just as we have done in this book. The outcome of that analysis is that we need to develop a zero waste economy. How can this be done ? Sadly, there is not space here to summarise Robin Murray's *Creating Wealth from Waste* [31]: it is all there, permeated throughout with systems thinking and very easily accessible. I quote from the preface by Tom Bentley

*"…the solution lies in understanding the role of the **productive system** – all those agents and institutions involved in producing a particular good, whether warmth, light, food or clean streets – as a whole. This way of thinking – which emphasises the intelligence and potential for innovation spread across a whole system, rather than the concentration of power and knowledge at the top – can be found in two spheres of society that, at first sight, seem like strange bedfellows. They are the leading edge of the knowledge economy, with its emphasis on networks, collaboration and creativity, and the emerging global movement of Greens, community enterprise and local economic development, which exemplifies innovative capacity, self-reliance and sustainability. Between them they are helping to shape a new path for capitalism…".*

London has a choice: to set off in **this** direction, or to set off in **that** direction.

This way is the way we are going at the moment, the way described by *GEO 2000* as "the wasteful consumer society in rich countries": it leads to still further destruction of the world's natural wealth – depleting it, perhaps, by another 30% in the next 30 years. It is making the rich richer at the expense of the poor, within London and all over the world.

That way leads to just and sustainable societies, societies that have learned to live in fraternity with each other and without depleting the natural capital of the Earth.

The choice is ours. Which pathway shall we choose ? It is not a choice to be put off for later. It is a question of direction. In which direction shall we go ?

Chapter 2
Notes and References

1. Article by Peter Johnston of the European Commission DGXIII – B *Sustainability in an information society* in *I & T Magazine* discussing the potential contribution of the 'information society' to sustainability in terms of environmental impact, materials use, energy use and transport.

2. *Climate Change Impacts in the UK The Agenda for Assessment and Action* DETR 1998; *Indicators of Climate Change in the UK* DETR 1999 and see http://www.nbu.ac.uk/iccuk/.

3. Joint letter by the chief meteorologists of Britain and the US printed in the Independent on 23 December 1999.

4. *Climate Change* DETR March 1999.

5. Ditto.

6. *Living Planet Report* WWF International, New Economics Foundation and World Conservation Monitoring Centre 1998 p20. The last sentence is slightly paraphrased as the text in the report refers to diagrams.

7. *UK Climate Change Programme* DETR 1998.

8. *Climate Change* DETR March 1999.

9. *Climate Change Impacts in the UK The Agenda for Assessment and Action* DETR 1998 pp 8,9.

10. *Indicators of Climate Change in the UK* DETR 1999

11. See chapter 3.

12. Dr C J Cambell, presentation to the House of Commons All-Party Committee 7 July 1999.

13. Paul Hawken, Amory B Lovins, L Hunter Lovins, *Natural Capitalism,* Earthscan 1999; Ernst von Weitzsaecker, Amory B Lovins, L Hunter Lovins *Factor Four,* Earthscan 1997.

14. *Harvard Business Review* pre-publication leaflet for *Natural Capitalism*: this book cites numerous examples of companies adopting these principles even within the existing economic framework. This whole agenda is strongly advocated by many non-governmental organisations including Greenpeace and Forum for the Future.

15. *Unlocking the Power of our Cities* Greenpeace.

16. See his web site at http://www.solarcentury.co.uk

17. KPMG report *Solar Energy: From Perennial Promise to Competitive Alternative* discussed in Green Futures November/December 1999. For Forum for the Future's Solar Millennium Project, contact Dr Ashok Sinha at Forum for the Future.

18. *Windforce 10,* European Wind Energy Association, Forum for Energy and Development and Greenpeace International.

19. *Positive News Summer* 1999.

20. Brent Cross, where IKEA's large London store is located, is however a prime example of a shopping centre sited for access primarily by car.

21. See chapter 6.

22. For example *The Gaia Atlas of Cities,* Gaia Books, Schumacher Briefings No 2 *Creating Sustainable Cities* 1999 Green Books.

23. *Concise Oxford Dictionary.*

24. Herbert Girardet *Journal of Contemporary Health* Autumn *1997.*

25. Herbert Girardet *Resurgence* No 167.

26. London Planning Advisory Committee (LPAC) 1999 consultation paper.

27. See *Transport in London and the implications for health* Neil Soderlund, Jake Ferguson and Mark McCarthy, The Health of Londoners Project.

28. *Growing Food in Cities* T Garnett 1999, National Food Alliance and Safe Alliance, 1996 and *City Harvest – the feasibility of growing more food in London*, T Garnett, Sustain.

29. See *Biodiversity Action Plans: getting involved at the Local Level* London Wildlife Trust.

30. *Our Green Capital (Introduction to the London Biodiversity Action Plan)* London Biodiversity Partnership, 2000.

31. *Creating wealth from waste* Robin Murray, Demos 1999.

Economics for the future

The force driving adverse social and environmental trends is apparently the current economic system's insatiable thirst for growth.
'New economics' offers alternatives that do not suffer from this defect.
Some of these are already in use.
It is possible to create economic systems that tend to promote social justice and environmental sustainability.

The word 'economics' comes from the Greek word meaning 'household management'. How should London's household be managed ?

Is this any of my business ?

The need for a discussion

Considering what an important subject it is, public discussion of economics is surprisingly limited. The impression is given that the economic system is something we just have to live with. Government spending, we are told, has to be severely constrained. Companies, on the other hand, have to grow if they are to survive. London's future, we are asked to assume, depends crucially on remaining a more attractive place for business than other cities with which it competes. London has to attract inward investment and tourists. London, we are frequently reminded, has continually to adapt itself to survive in an intensely competitive world economy. Anyone who questions these propositions is silenced with a dismissive "Get real!".

Yet a public discussion of economics is urgently needed because there is no doubt that human activity is directly responsible for the over-exploitation of the Earth's resources, climate change caused by global warming, the growing gap between rich and poor within countries and between countries and other unwanted effects described in the two previous chapters. Our global system of 'household management' is simply not delivering the outcomes we would like to see. In spite of the best efforts of the numerous campaigning organisations which enjoy massive public support, the destruction of the world's natural resources continues. Environmentalists call in despair for a fundamental shift in human consciousness, away from the blind materialism that characterises our behaviour as consumers, towards a more 'spiritual' awareness of our place in the natural order. Relief charities plead for a more compassionate society. But human irresponsibility and greed are only part of the problem. It is said that there is now overwhelming evidence that the economic system itself is flawed. Might it not be more practicable to reform it than to change human nature ?

Remember the point we made in the Introduction to Part 1 of this book: **economic systems are man-made: they can be changed.**

Demystifying economics

Fortunately a public discussion of economics has now been made possible by the work of authors such a Herman Daly, Hazel Henderson, Susan George, James Robertson, Walden Bello, Maude Barlow, David Korten, Paul Ekins and Richard Douthwaite and organisations such as the New Economics Foundation here in London. Let us call them all 'the New Economists' for

Economics about money

Mainstream economics is mainly concerned with the world of money. What is money ? It is the coins in our pocket, or the money in our bank account; it is a means of exchange; it is something we can put it aside to spend later; we can lend it to others or invest it in a commercial venture, thereby enabling the borrower or entrepreneur to develop; and it's used as a way of valuing certain things. It is indisputable that in the modern world money is extremely useful. Still, there are some questions to consider: where does money come from in the first place and what consequences follow from the way it is brought into existence ? These are extremely important questions which we look at in the next section of this chapter.

short. With their help we are now in a position to drag economics, screaming and kicking, into the same space in which we have been discussing people, metabolisms and ecology. And it is precisely by bringing it into this space that it becomes an accessible topic, a subject that relates to our ordinary lives.

Why should a book about London seek to demystify economics ? The answer is that the way in which London's 'household management' is conducted is a matter of extreme importance to all of us and to future generations. And as London is inextricably caught up in the global economy at numerous levels, not least as one of the world's leading financial and commercial centres, we need to understand the basic features of the whole economic system of which we are part and in which London is a star player.

Bringing economics into the discussion of London's future is in fact one of my main reasons for writing this book. So many of the reports, articles and books I have read about London's problems, and so many of the conferences I have attended, have taken the economy as something that we have no choice but to learn to live with. From the New Economists I have learned that this is not the case.

This presents a challenge: it is part of the challenge to learn to 'think differently'. Up to now you may have assumed that you would not be able to understand economics without special training, and that there would be no point in trying to because, even if you discovered that changes were needed, you would not be able to do anything about it. I hope to persuade you that both these assumptions are wrong[1].

Economics about people

By contrast, the New Economists see economics in terms of people's lives and the future of our societies. They are concerned with **all** the activities and resources that make for a good life, not just those products and services that are bought and sold. For them a meal cooked at home is just as much part of the economy as one bought at a restaurant. Fresh air, though not paid for in money, is as vital a resource as anything bought and sold. The value of money is subjective and depends very much on how well-off you are: ten pounds is worth far more in the hands of a poor man – who spends it on food for his family – than £100 in the hands of a rich man who spends it on buying an extra smart suit.

Real wealth or true wealth is something quite different from money because it includes all those things that money cannot buy. If you love music, the ability to get together with some friends and make music is part of your true wealth. Your health is part of your true wealth. Not that money is irrelevant to true wealth: in the modern world you need money to buy a musical instrument or to buy the food for a healthy meal. But money and wealth are still two very different things. We have to be constantly on the watch out for arguments that confuse them.

'Making money' is not the same as creating real wealth. 'Making money' can be nothing more than acquiring it from others. Watch out therefore for expressions like 'the wealth creators': they may not in fact be creating any wealth at all.

GDP and ISEW

It follows that money is a poor measure even of value, certainly not a good measure of real wealth. Similarly, GDP (Gross Domestic Product) is not a true measure of a country's prosperity. It is simply an index of the gross market value of a country's monetised transaction of goods and services, including negative elements like the costs of crime, accidents and armaments, excluding positive elements like the productive value of work done for self or love, and taking no account of damage to the environment not reflected in the prices of goods or services. To compensate for these anomalies the New Economists have constructed an 'Index of Sustainable Economic Welfare' (ISEW), which adjusts GDP by adding for beneficial but uncompensated work, and deducting items that represent a net loss of well-being.

For the UK the ISEW kept up with GDP until about 1974 when it peaked and since when it has fallen steadily: in other words, according to this index, the co-called growth since 1974 has actually been of negative value to society. People who have prospered since 1974 may find that difficult to accept. Not so those who have not prospered. No figures exist for London but an ISEW for London would take into account the conditions of life in parts of the city mentioned in chapter 1 and the impact on the environment of, for example, London's construction, production, trading and financial activities. London's GDP would no doubt show huge increases in the last 25 years with every luxury purchase in a Mayfair store and the billion pound costs of traffic congestion adding further to it, but who could say with any confidence that London's ISEW has not been steadily declining ?

'Economic growth'

Beware therefore of expressions like 'economic growth' being used to mean that it makes us better off. It's a fallacy that underlies many apparently responsible assertions. For example even Allen Hammond (whose informative book, *Which World?*, strengthened my resolve to write this book) writes "Since economic activity is now growing more than twice as fast as population, Earth's inhabitants in the year 2050 will be richer – or at least they would be if all people and all regions shared in that economic growth."[2] Even if the condition of equal sharing were satisfied, how true would this be if most of the extra activity had gone into armaments, wars and relief works following typhoons ? Economic growth means nothing in terms of prosperity without a close examination of the nature of the activities being paid for by the money flows which 'economic growth' measures.

The widening gap between rich and poor

As to the condition of equal sharing, this is negated by current trends: global disparities of wealth and income are rising rapidly, widening the gap between rich and poor regions. Between 1970 and 1990, for example, the gap between average per capita income in developing countries and that in industrial countries doubled from less that $9,000 per person to nearly $18,000 per person (measured in constant dollars). These gaps in income are likely to become even more pronounced in coming decades, increasingly dividing human societies into two: one of wealth, luxury, and power; the other of poverty, hardship, and often hopelessness. As mentioned in chapter 1 the gap between the income of the richest fifth of the world's population and that of the poorest fifth has nearly tripled in the last 30 years. By 2025, if current trends continue, the disparity between the top and the bottom fifths will be more than 100-fold; by 2050, depending on the projections used, nearly 200-fold[3]. As the example of the United States shows, the rising gaps between rich and poor are not restricted to developing countries[4]. The richest are everywhere getting richer at the expense of the poorest.

An inefficient system

An economic system that produces growth without regard to environmental and social consequences, as does our present system, is simply inefficient as a mechanism to encourage sustainable human activity. For example, it has failed to induce us all to be much more resource efficient. It is good at promoting 'productivity', meaning labour productivity, not resource productivity. Numerous exciting opportunities exist for profitable business achieving energy savings: market forces can be used to promote these; but the current system fails to do so[5].

The consumer society

It is the current economic system that is also responsible for the increasingly consumerist lifestyle which has come to dominate the urban condition. Due to the failure of the planning system administered by local government to stand up to the financial giants, much of this now takes place in supermarkets and shopping centres with huge car parks, away from the high streets, many of which have suffered a sad decline. More and more of our lives seems to be about getting money or spending it: is this the way we want it to be ?

London and the New Economics

London's economy and the culture of the City of London, the Square Mile, is at present tied to the 'economic growth' agenda. This is a suicide car bound for a precipice. If London wants a long term future, as a city to live and work in, and as a world financial centre, as a great world city in every sense, then the challenge for London, including the City, is to come to terms with the imperative of living in harmony with the natural world and earning its living in a way that contributes to social well-being. London is ideally placed to become a centre for the design and implementation of sustainable economic systems, both for the global marketplace and in its own backyard. The New Economics presents London with many opportunities. Some of them London can develop without government intervention. Others would require government legislation or international cooperation: there, London can lend its considerable influence:

London can become a driver for changing the global economy. Some of the possibilities that London could investigate, experiment with and, if sound, promote are mentioned in the following pages.

There is a pool of talent and creativity in London, much of which is currently wasted in largely useless activities, such as the derivatives market[6]. The New Economics offers an exciting agenda, requiring new thinking, whole-systems thinking, a dialogue between experts in many fields, to redesign the economic systems that are currently failing us. In systems terms, all the parts of the system need to be engaged in the task of reforming the system. London's opportunity is to be the place where all this goes on.

So long as business people feel that looking after themselves and their shareholders is all they can do, London will continue to be a negative force in the world. This book is about the tremendous potential London has for positive, constructive action. London, as an active participant in the global economy, can become an active player in the resolution of global dilemmas. Key global issues at the dawn of the third millennium include the role of money, the role of multinational corporations and the role of technology. London is one of the world's leading financial cities, in some fields it is **the** leading financial centre[7], certainly an important driver of the global engine for economic growth. It is also home to some new thinking about the distinction between economic growth and true wealth, suggesting that London needs to grow out of its obsession with money and redefine the bottom line in terms that recognise that distinction. Several initiatives for the constructive use of investment money are based here, as are numerous multinational corporations many of which have begun to question their most hallowed assumptions. Through its commercial networks London has access to the latest manufacturing and information technology.

The changes needed to redirect London's metabolism and ecology, as indicated in chapter 2, call for the development of new financial instruments and 'products'. These will not be designed in Westminster or Whitehall. The necessary skills are located further down the River. The challenge for London is to become a world leader in the wise use of finance, corporate regulation and technology to enable humanity to reverse out of its present course and take on a beneficial role in, quite literally, the future of human life on Earth. London could and should be at the forefront of a world movement offering hope for the future to the many, not just the few.

The case against 'economic growth'

The effect of 'economic growth'

We have seen that economic growth is not the same as improving welfare: when the figures for GDP are adjusted to indicate sustainable economic welfare (the ISEW), you find that the situation for the UK as a whole has been worsening over the last 25 years. This is now widely accepted. What is more surprising is Richard Douthwaite's finding in respect of the period 1955 to 1988 that almost all the extra resources the growth had created had been used to keep the system functioning in an increasingly inefficient way: "the new wealth had been squandered on producing forklift pallets and corrugated cardboard non-returnable bottles and ring-pull drink cans. It had built airports, supertankers and heavy goods lorries, motorways, flyovers and car parks with many floors. It had enabled the banking, insurance, stockbroking, tax collecting and accountancy sector to expand from 493,000 to 2,475,000 employees during the 33 years. It had financed the recruitment of over 3 million people 'the reserve army of the unemployed'. Very little was left for more positive achievements when all these had taken their share."[8]

'Growth' responsible for adverse trends

The idea that 'economic growth' has actually caused the destructive trends described in chapters 1 and 2 is more difficult to grasp and is one that many will find hard to accept. That however is Richard Douthwaite's case in his recently revised *The Growth Illusion*. Written to explain "why economic growth is the cause of our environmental problems and why its continuation, even if we take steps to limit pollution, cannot be part of the cure", his book describes the destructive effects growth has had in practice. The following are amongst the points Douthwaite makes (the headings are mine).

Growth is anti-social:

◆ In order to remain competitive and profitable, companies introduce labour saving technology, which puts people out of work[9].

◆ Growth causes the cost of social services (which have to be paid for out of taxes) to rise as a proportion of GNP. Could this be why governments are always struggling to find the money to pay for social services ? Is their problem actually the consequence the very same 'economic growth' that they insist will give them the extra money they need ?

◆ Growth tends to increase inequality.

◆ The growth imperative has been behind the push towards trade liberalisation.

Growth is inefficient:

◆ It leads to small companies being swallowed up or put out of business by larger ones, who thus win a bigger market share. For example, more superstores and fewer small shops. A National Retail Planning Forum report showed that a new superstore costs, on average, a net 276 local jobs, as independent grocers, village shops, newsagents and milk rounds close down; the number of shops in Britain had declined by 40% since 1940[10].

◆ larger firms are less efficient than smaller ones (where the large ones score is in their access to cheaper capital and their ability to build brand names and mount massive marketing campaigns; but only their owners benefit).

◆ growth increases choice only for a short period whilst new and old technologies exist side by side, otherwise only the better off are able to buy more and more sophisticated consumer goods and services.

Growth causes direct damage to people and the environment:

◆ Growth has led directly to damage to children and the environment – their interests are of course never taken into account by companies who introduce new technologies in response to competitive pressures.

◆ The technologies that fuel growth generally substitute fossil energy and capital equipment for human labour.

◆ The pursuit of economic growth led to the ozone crisis and to global warming.

This looks like a formidable case[11]. To borrow the language of the law, it is a prima facie case, which ought to go to trial. Many will still insist that growth is basically good, contending that it should not be abandoned, merely tamed to avoid bad effects. Douthwaite was surprised to discover

The limits to growth

Another fundamental point made about 'growth' is that it has limits. This was the proposition famously advanced in *Limits to Growth*, written in 1972 by a team led by Donella Meadows and Dennis Meadows, warning that there were limits to Earth's ability to withstand the impact of human activities. At the time the book was wrongly represented, by those who did not want to face up to its conclusions, as having predicted that the limits were set by the prospect of the resources of the Earth becoming exhausted. As Douthwaite points out, the prediction was about the **effects** of 'growth', not the resources for it. Douthwaite says that *Limits* was fundamentally correct. It has been born out by climate change due to the human induced global warming. We have already reached the limits to 'growth'. If so, this must be another reason for questioning it!

how many economists now think otherwise: early in 1998 he opened a week-long Internet seminar for almost 700 participants from over 50 countries expecting that it would take most of the seminar to reach some sort of agreement that, whatever growth might have achieved in the past, current growth is not benefiting ordinary people. Not at all. It took a bare 24 hours, so most of the rest of the seminar was spent discussing how the economic system could be altered to remove its need to grow.

If Douthwaite is right, a discussion about how the economic system could be altered to remove its need to grow must indeed be the next item on the agenda; and it is surely a discussion that ought to be taking place in London.

People working in the financial services sector make much of their living from growth. It is an imperative of the world in which they work[12]. It would be understandable if they were reluctant even to discuss the subject. People working outside the financial services industry are likely to take a different view. Not so long ago, listening to the BBC's Radio 4, I heard Kevin Hawkins of Safeways describe the competitive conditions in the retail trade as "a market which none of us would want to be in". The possibility that 'there is another way' would be an attractive proposition in the productive industries.

I wonder whether it's 'economic growth' that has pushed up house prices in London boroughs such as Camden where a family home is now unaffordable except by the very rich. "A shoe box now won't present much change from £100,000" commented the Camden New Journal on 11 November 1999 when reporting that Camden Councillor Jake Turnbull, 26 and recently married, earned too much money to be eligible for social housing (not that there is any of that to spare) but too little to buy even a one bedroom flat in the borough with the result that he will be forced to live elsewhere and have to resign as a councillor.

The case against interest

If 'economic growth' is bad and/or past its use-by date, attention has to turn to the forces that drive it. The capitalist system of lending money at interest or investing it for profit currently provides the City of London with much of its work. However a very serious case is now being made against the system. Given the scene set in the first two chapters of this book, it is time that London took notice of this, began to examine the arguments and, if they are valid, to explore how to develop other ways of servicing the global, national and local economies.

How it works at the moment

Capitalism as we know it enables people with spare money to increase their wealth by lending it at interest or investing it. It thus tends directly to increase the gap between the rich and the poor who do not have money to spare. For example Margrit Kennedy records that for Germany the richest 10% of the population receive twice as much interest as they pay, the next 10% peg even and the rest pay more than they receive[13].

The further charge now being made against the present capitalist system is that it provides the initial force that drives 'economic growth', simply because a company which borrows £100,000 from a bank at interest has to make another (say)

£150,000 over the next 20 years in order to be able to repay the loan with interest. To be able to do this, the company strives to grow. Similar considerations apply to money which is invested with a view to dividend[14].

The company in the above example may be able to win the extra £150,000 that it needs to meet its obligations to the bank by enlarging its business at the expense of other competing companies, some of which may be driven into bankruptcy. Or the whole economy would have to expand. Whichever way the extra £150,000 is produced, it is not too difficult to see the links between the need for borrowers to pay interest and the whole system's need for growth; and also why the system's need for growth may result in businesses being driven into bankruptcy even though they are well-run and are providing useful services without doing any harm to the environment. You probably know of some businesses that have suffered this fate.

It is argued that the payment of interest on borrowed money is thus at the root of the system's insatiable thirst for growth. If we want to eliminate the system's need for growth, interest rates will have to be gradually reduced, eventually to zero.

Zero interest, yes, zero interest!

Where a company which proposes to erect a building has to borrow money at interest to do so, it is unlikely to spend **extra** money (say, an extra £10,000) on long-lasting materials necessary to ensure that the building lasts more than 30 years. This is because the benefits provided by that extra £10,000 will only start to be enjoyed after 30 years, whereas throughout that 30 years the company would have had to pay a fortune in interest – compound interest — on the extra £10,000. In calculating whether of not to spend that extra £10,000 now, the company has to add that interest to the initial £10,000 as part of the cost of the long-lasting materials. To the company, those materials will seem extremely expensive.

Society thinks differently. Society as a whole does not have to pay interest – the bank and the building company are both part of society. Society wants buildings built to last, like the house I live in, built 150 years ago. Buildings

make use of natural resources, to which future generations of society have as much right as we have. We need an economic system that enables companies to build buildings like this house — built to last. A zero interest system would do this.[15]

Richard Douthwaite takes it further. "The principle of giving equal weight to the interests of future generations has a great deal wider import than the construction of longer-lasting, lower-maintenance buildings or truly productive power plants. It means, for example, that fossil fuels must not be used to satisfy our day-to-day needs directly, greenhouse effect or not. Oil and coal should be burned to develop renewable energy sources or to increase the world's stock of metals extracted from their ores. Such fuels must not even turn bulk metal into useful goods. That is the job of renewables, which must also be used to replace metal stocks as they are lost or corroded. The principle also means that land should be farmed only by methods that maintain soil fertility."[16]

A zero interest system would be like getting rid of a harmful addiction. The habit of using money to make money is like a drug, giving some members of society at least a daily high, but in reality dragging society down, at a physical level lowering its natural energy and at a psychological level reducing its self esteem and self confidence. It tells us that we have to be competitive to avoid the fate of failed economies, we have to keep embracing new technologies, we have to become more and more labour productive. It tells us that we can pride ourselves on having a modern successful economy. The truth is otherwise. We would all be a lot healthier and happier on zero interest[17].

That at least is the argument that is now being put forward. It deserves a hearing. It might even be right. It is already being discussed in London in forums like The Forum for Sustainable Currencies and the London School of Economics Green Economics Society. My aim here is simply to provoke a wider discussion. **Zero interest could be a pathway to the future for London. Why should not London lead the way in making the changes that will put money in its place, at the service of society, so that money is used for the benefit of society** ?

Bank-produced money

Most people, if they think about it at all, probably believe that money is created by the government or perhaps the central bank. Not so. In fact almost all money is created by the commercial banks lending it to their customers, whether on overdraft or loan account, but in any case, of course, at interest. Borrowers are going to have to engage in activities that will earn them enough money to repay the loan plus the interest. As we have already seen, this is what lies at the bottom of the economy's need to grow, a need that must be satisfied regardless of whether the growth is proving beneficial.

Money is thus created to facilitate the most profitable activities, but these are not necessarily the activities that would be of greatest benefit to society; they may well be harmful to the environment. Provided that the bank is satisfied that the borrower will be able to repay the loan with interest, it will be prepared to make the loan. Neither party to the transaction is likely to have had in mind any long term values or purposes. Neither Nature nor future generations are represented in the bank manager's office when the overdraft arrangement is made.

Furthermore, to be sufficiently profitable, the business activities that bank loans are made to facilitate will have to provide goods or services for people with money to pay for them. The system tends to promote the provision of services to the better off and to bar the provision of services for those without money, who may well be most in need.

So it is really no wonder that the system has the effects we have described. But what is the alternative ? Most people assume that we are stuck with the existing system: it seems to be firmly under the control of the financial bodies who make their living from it.

Not so. There are two complementary ways of creating credit. One is people-produced money; the other is government-produced money. Both are practicable.

People produced money

The most well-known long-established existing interest-free people-produced money is the Swiss WIR which was launched in 1934 to overcome the currency shortages of the time and now has 60,000 account holders. It is an independent currency system for small and medium-sized businesses, a tightly regulated system of mutual credit. LETS (Local Exchange Trading Systems) are another example[18]. Time Money, described by Perry Walker opposite is another. A similar one is Hureai Kippu (Caring Relationship Tickets) created in Japan by a group of 300 non-profit organisations for people providing health-care services[19].

What all these new money systems have in common is that their purpose is to facilitate some form of activity which the creators of the currency, be they government or non-governmental wish to promote. New currencies can be, are being, created to serve socially useful and environmentally friendly purposes. As they are interest free, they do not make the rich richer or the poor poorer.

A pathway for London might be to run down the interest-driven part of the economy and expand the zero-interest driven economy. This way might lead to people being able to use a range of currencies for different purposes, all tending to promote desirable activities, desirable for meeting people's needs, good for society and the planet.

If we got rid of the 'economic growth' generated by the need to pay interest or dividends on money lent or invested – the 'economic growth' that increases the gap between rich and poor and has an adverse impact on the environment – this would free up resources of people and materials for other uses valuable to societies. Such an economy would not **need** to grow, but **could do so** wherever this was beneficial.

These at any rate are the pathways that London can explore.

Pathways to the future

Time Money

What is it ?

A new kind of money which credits the time people spend helping each other. Participants earn credits for doing jobs – one hour of your time entitles you to one hour of someone else's time. Credits are deposited centrally in a time bank and withdrawn when the participants need help themselves.

Time is the unit of currency and everyone's time is worth the same. Help is exchanged through a 'banker' who links people up and keeps a record of transactions through the TimeKeeper software. By measuring the good we do for each other Time Money conjures up wealth: we can invest in each other and the places where we live and work.

Who is using it ?

People are growing Time Money locally through GP practices, neighbourhood centres, schools and housing schemes up and down the country:

- in **Gloucestershire**, Fair Shares is using time to re-build rural communities
- in **Peckham** local people have created an Hour Bank to provide care and support for each other without paying cash or asking for charity
- in **Watford** older people are re-designing council services through Time Swap
- in **Lewisham**, GPs and patients are prescribing Time Money to power patient support groups and self help schemes
- in **Newcastle** older people are using Time Money to value the contribution they can make to the health and well being of their local communities.

Why ?

Because we need to recapture wasted community assets

The market economy values what is scarce – but we want to live in places where there is an abundance of love and trust. The market economy excludes a growing number of us as unproductive and useless but we know that the help we give each other is as valuable as the things we can buy with 'real' money. Time Money offers us one way of resolving these contradictions.

Because we need to re-connect the social economy with the local economy

Time Money has no equivalent in the formal market but it can catalyse support for local economic enterprises like LETS, community businesses and high-street loyalty schemes by increasing the trust and confidence between people. Time Money can also mobilise surplus goods, like food or recycled computers, and use these to encourage participation.

Because we need more diverse and sustainable kinds of self-help

Where traditional volunteering encourages us to help 'those less fortunate than ourselves', Time Money transforms the nature of giving so that it becomes a reciprocal exchange between social equals.

What does Time Money do ?

It:

- replaces one-way social interactions or charity with **mutual aid**
- redefines participants as **co-producers** with something valuable to give rather than useless or needy people who are a burden on already over-stretched services
- makes **users** central to producing health, education or community services rather than passive recipients
- creates more responsive, participative and sustainable **community** services.

Perry Walker, New Economics Foundation

Economics for the future

Government-produced money

There are strong arguments for saying that it would be much better if money were spent into existence by governments instead of being lent into existence by banks[20]. As matters stand it would be difficult for the directors of London's commercial banks even to discuss such a suggestion. Moves in this direction will require leadership, vision and advanced decision-making processes. More of this in chapter 6.

Linking money to sustainability

At the end of 1998, 57% of the world's foreign exchange reserves were held in dollars, around three times the amount held in ecus, D-marks, French francs and sterling combined. This means that over the years, the US has received billions of dollars worth of imports and given nothing in return apart from paper notes and electronic credits. This is obviously wrong, yet another example of the richest taking advantage of all the others.

The effects of the currency problems of various countries in the last five years has been catastrophic for the environment and for poor people in the countries concerned. Unemployment rates in Indonesia, Thailand and Korea roughly tripled and between 50 and 100 million people fell below the poverty line as a result of the recent currency problems of those countries: massive human suffering caused by the economic system.

In *The Ecology of Money*, Richard Douthwaite has put forward an exciting proposal for currencies to be linked to the use of fossil energy, via the new international trading system for CO_2 emission rights. Bernard Lietaer, the former Belgian central banker and designer of the euro, in his foreword agrees with the importance of linking monetary issues to energy sustainability but suggests that a whole basket of commodities and services might produce a more stable international currency system.

For our purposes it is sufficient to take note that these sorts of ideas are being put forward. They are the sorts of ideas that need to be urgently explored to see if it is not beyond the wit of men and women to devise an international currency system that tends to foster sustainable economies.

The case for multi-level currencies

James Robertson and other New Economists argue for a multilevel currency system. Bernard Lietaer agrees: "We see mainstream politics getting behind complementary currencies as a consequence of the introduction of the euro. Complementary currencies will become more popular for local activities and regional politics and scarcity of currency will become a thing of the past."[21]

The electronic revolution offers opportunities to rethink our assumptions about money. The possibilities for e-cash (eco-ecash?) need to be explored through the sorts of participation processes described in chapter 4 and not left to be developed to meet the growth imperatives of big corporations.

The case for vibrant markets

The ideas outlined above are not anti-market. Quite the contrary. In *The Post-Corporate World* David Korten draws a sharp distinction between the 'mindful market' as described by Adam Smith more than 200 years ago – people self-organising to create their own livelihoods – and today's rapacious capitalist economy in which money and goods can be moved freely in search of maximum short-term profits without regard for the consequences for people, communities and Nature. David Korten is strongly pro-market, provided that the market is properly regulated, as envisaged and spelt out by Adam Smith. He is strongly against capitalism as we know it today. Capitalism is to the market what a cancer is to our bodies. We get cancer when a genetic defect causes a cell to forget that it is part of our body. The defective cell seeks its own unlimited growth, expropriating our bodies' life energies, without regard for the consequences either for itself or for us[22].

Capitalism Against the Market

	Capitalism	Healthy Markets
Dominant attractor	Money	Life
Defining purpose	Use money to make money for those who have money	Employ available resources to meet the basic needs of everyone
Firm size	Very large	Small and medium-size
Costs	Externalized to the public	Internalized by the user
Ownership	Impersonal, absentee	Personal, rooted
Financial capital	Global with no borders	Local/national with clear borders
Purpose of investment	Maximize private profit	Increase beneficial output
The role of profit	An end to be maximized	An incentive to invest productively
Coordinating mechanisms	Centrally planned by megacorporations	Self-organizing markets and networks
Cooperation	Among competitors to escape the discipline of competition	Among people and communities to advance the common good
Purpose of competition	Eliminate the unfit	Stimulate efficiency and innovation
Government role	Protect the interests of property	Advance the human interest
Trade	Free	Fair and balanced
Political orientation	Elitist, democracy of dollars	Populist, democracy of persons

Source: *Post-Corporate World*, p 41.

This position of being anti-capitalism as we know it and pro-markets is generally shared by the New Economists. Markets are seen as good servants and bad masters. The movement is anything but anti-enterprise. Many of the new ideas are designed to provide financial services for entrepreneurs not served by the mainstream financial sector. See, for example, the London Rebuilding Society proposal described below.

Nor are the ideas mentioned here socialist in the sense of requiring more state ownership or state control over the management of enterprises. They seek to give more power to people and to reduce the power of money and large corporations.

Following the work of theorists like Andre Gorz and Jeremy Rifkin, another aim of people-based economics should be to enable the advantages of labour-saving technology to be shared between workers, so they can all work shorter hours and have more free time, instead of some being made redundant and the rest having to work harder than ever.

I hope this discourse will help readers to think more logically about these questions. There is an awful lot of loose language about that is confusing. People talk or write about the bad effects of the 'market economy' or 'market forces' when what they probably mean to criticise is not markets but an economic system that depends on, and insists on, profit-led growth. Similarly, those who seek to defend or promote the existing system claim that the market economy creates jobs and wealth, without examining the overall effects of the existing money system. Loose language, whichever side is using it, only confuses the issue. It has to be challenged if we are to come to terms with reality.

Trading routes

London's role as a financial centre arose out of its function as a port. Its role as a commercial centre has survived the closure of the docks. London is still a major trading power.

◆ International trade has increased enormously in the postwar period. The volume of trade transacted in a single day in 1999 equals the volume of all commerce in the whole of 1949.

◆ Tariffs have been reduced from 40% to 4%.

◆ Trade is increasingly dominated by larger companies: transnational corporations account for 70% of world trade; the top 100 of these control 14% of the world's wealth.

◆ World trade is expected to increase by US$200 billion by 2005. By that date international trade is expected to account for 40% of national output in industrial countries and more than 50% in developing countries.

◆ International financial flows, only $20 billion per day fifteen years ago, are now more than $1 trillion per day; by 2015 they may reach $30 trillion per day[23].

The expansion of world trade has been accompanied by deregulation and privatisation, forced on governments by pressure from the multinationals' lobby groups, such as the European Roundtable of Industrialists (ERT)[24]. Even debt relief for the poorest countries is conditional on compliance with conditions laid down by the International Monetary Fund (IMF) (structural adjustment programmes) requiring the debtor country to reduce government expenditure, privatise state-run industries, devalue the currency and promote exports, all policies designed to give the private sector space for growth. Now it's increasingly widely recognised that these policies are hurting the very same (and **very** poor) people whom the debt relief should be helping.

The growth imperative strongly influenced Britain's entry into the European Economic Community (EEC). The expansion of global trade has been driven forward by the trade liberalisation rounds undertaken under the aegis of the General Agreement on Tariffs and Trade (GATT) and, latterly, the World Trade Organization (WTO). Although the WTO nominally exists to provide an impartial, rules-based 'level playing field' for trade, it is in practice dominated by the 'Quad' of industrialised nations: the US, Canada, Japan and the EU. And the governments of these countries are in turn dominated by the big companies; and, of course, by the 'growth economy' culture. "The United States and the European Union consider the multilateral trading system one of the world's principal bulwarks of peace, sustainable development, and economic growth; and a primary engine for rising living standards and broad-based prosperity in the future" declared the White House on December 17th 1999, following the breakdown of the trade negotiations at Seattle.

The British Government's policy is set out in its *Strategy for Sustainable Development A Better Quality of Life.* The following sentences "Trade and investment are crucial to poverty elimination. They bring resources that can help generate the growth needed to establish sustainable livelihoods" (para 9.1); and "Liberalising trade can help to ensure that resources are used efficiently, to generate the wealth necessary for environmental improve-ment, for development, for the spread of cleaner technology and for improved social conditions" (para 9.18) are good examples of the 'growth' mentality embedded in the thinking of government. True, the document conceded that trade can magnify unsustainable economic activity; but the second of the Government's principles, whilst affirming all governments' right to regulate for environmen-tal improvement, insists that "foreign imports and foreign investors are treated in the same way as comparable national products and companies". That gives the multinationals the legal right to force entry into any country, the only defence permitted to the country being to make regulations for environmental improve-ment. A country's desire to protect local indus-tries or ways of life or other local foundations of community wellbeing would not allow its government to impose a trade barrier.

Land value taxation or rating

London should explore forms of local taxation that promote equity and sustainability. One such idea, promoted by the Henry George Foundation, is land value taxation. This is a method of raising public revenue by means of an annual tax on the site value of land, that is a percentage of the value of the land ignoring buildings, crops and any other work. It is said to be more just, easier and cheaper – in the age of e-commerce, it will be much easier to collect than taxes on income and other transactions – and likely to reduce inner city blight and benefit the environment. It has been used in Denmark, Hong Kong, Australia, New Zealand and numerous cities in the USA, always, according to the Henry George Foundation, with beneficial results. Certainly worth looking at. And if found to be a good idea for London, the Mayor can lobby central government for permission to use it. As it is envisaged as taking the place of other taxes, not as an additional tax, there would be problems relating it to the national tax system.

Contact: Henry George Foundation, Suite 427, The London Fruit Exchange, Brushfield Street E1 6EL

In 1999 London charities joined campaigning organisations like World Development Movement and Friends of the Earth in support of a declaration addressed to the WTO at Seattle calling for a halt to further 'liberalisation' pending a thorough review of the effects of the expansion to date. The declaration was signed by nearly 1600 organisations from 90 countries. At a pre-conference Teach In at Seattle, Sara Larrain, a Chilean grassroots environmentalist asked exasperatedly "Why is it that people from the North think exports benefit us ? They are wrecking our environment and increasing inequality". The answer is that a lot of people from the North are well aware of what's happening and they too are exasperated by the failure of our governments to abandon their blind support for 'economic growth'.

The expansion of the 'global economy' has led to a general lowering of wages from which only the owners of transnational companies and of natural resources benefit. The existing WTO rules also pose threats to national environmental policies. In 1994 the WTO Dispute Resolution Panel ruled that US legislation requiring all shrimp sold in the US to be caught in nets fitted with a 'turtle excluder device' was protectionist and illegal. Likewise it is through the WTO that the US has been able to impose sanctions on European exports because of European reluctance to allow American hormone-treated beef to be sold in the EU; further sanctions are threatened because of the EU's insistence that the 'precautionary principle' should be applied to genetically modified crops.

There is no doubt that the expansion of world trade driven by the 'growth economy' has been damaging. Instead of the current presumption in favour of trade, a radical starting point would be to assume that trade is beneficial only if

◆ it only involves inessentials, so that it can take place out of choice rather than necessity
◆ it is between partners who are already using all their resources fully
◆ it is fair trade.

Fairtrade supports jobs in some of the poorest countries and communities[25]. Via the numerous charitable and commercial organisations promoting this trade[26], relationships of trust and mutuality grow up between workers and buyers. It is a form of commerce in which all Londoners can take part, in the knowledge that this kind of trade expansion and economic growth benefits people and the environment.

The pathways to the future seem to lie in these directions. This book, however, is not about particular policies. The object is rather to draw attention to the issues and to the potential for London, under the new leadership of a Mayor, to start using its massive influence constructively.

Given the army of powerful corporations, on the one hand, and the articulate voices of the non-governmental organisations, such as the New Economics Foundation and the World Development Movement, on the other, not to mention millions of Londoners who are daily affected by these issues, for example as shoppers, the key issue for London's new Mayor is not so much which side should he or she take, or what policies to support, **but how to engage the stakeholders in a dialogue that enables them all to play a constructive part in working out the trade rules that tend to promote a sustainable world economic order**.

Which way companies ?

London is home to the head offices of many of the largest companies in the world, some with turnovers that dwarf the economies of whole countries. These businesses have far-reaching impacts. The activities of large corporations, when driven solely by the interests of shareholders who have no other connection with the company whose shares they have probably bought on a stock exchange, can be extremely destructive of both local communities and the environment. They create vast quantities of pollution and waste, including chemicals that do not break down in nature, they use great amounts of energy, they contribute to deforestation and loss of biodiversity, and they have negative impacts on local communities especially when operations are relocated or downsized.

An agenda for change

Corporate reform is urgently needed. This is another of those daunting topics normally discussed only between professionals and academics. In fact the basics are not that difficult. The agenda for reform includes the following:

Company law

Companies have no natural existence; they have been invented by law. Company law is a system that enables shareholders to benefit from the activities of the company without being in any way accountable for the misdeeds of the company – 'limited liability' really means no liability at all. It is in the nature of corporations to seek to externalise their costs (ie make sure that someone else bears them) and maximise profits. Modern conditions require a total rethink of the whole concept. The law could be modernised
◆ by making a company's compliance with measurable eco-efficiency standards a condition of limited liability
◆ by enabling companies to be wound up after a specified period[27].

Ownership

Companies are owned by their shareholders. If these people have no connection with the company's business, its customers or the communities where it operates, and if the directors have to give priority to the interests of their shareholders, which is currently the case, then whenever there is a conflict between the interests of shareholders and those of, for example, the company's employees, the shareholders must come first. Companies like John Lewis, which are owned by the company's employees (the shares in John Lewis are held in a complicated form of trust for the employees), avoid this conflict. When you next shop there, see if you can pick up the sense that the staff have a stake in the enterprise.[28] All moves towards 'stakeholder' share ownership are constructive.

Size!

Size is closely related to ownership because the bigger a corporation grows the greater the gulf between the owners on the one hand and the employees and communities it serves on the other[29].

Regulation

The activities of business are for ever being more heavily regulated, over an ever-widening range of issues. This is a product of the old problem-solving approach that is the only approach the current political system seems capable of. It does not tackle the structural defects of the system. A more effective role for government (in addition to company law reform) is to adjust market conditions through taxation (e.g. taxes on energy and materials use instead of on labour), currency control, international agreements etc, to ensure a level playing field enabling all businesses operating in the market to do so in a socially friendly and environmentally useful way.

Self regulation

Given the right corporate structures and market conditions companies will be able to carry out activities that are good for their owners, good for their employees, good for local communities and good for the environment. How they do so is best left to people's enterprise and market forces.

These could be some of the pathways for London's business community. There could be many advantages for business people as well as for local communities and the environment.

These pathways and the pathways for reforming money converge and proceed in parallel. For example, local currencies are re-invested locally in productive activities carried out by small or medium-sized companies. These pathways for corporate reform also link up with renewable energy: in future locally owned companies producing local energy can be much smaller than the giant corporations needed to extract fossil fuels from underground and transport them huge distances. There are also links with the pathways for fair trade.[30]

Meanwhile...

Unless and until business structures and market systems have been radically reformed, business people have to do the best they can in an imperfect world. It is important to bear in mind that business people are no more responsible for the imperatives of the 'growth economy' than are their customers. In questioning the gospel of 'economic growth' I am not attacking business people any more than I am attacking their customers. The changes we are looking for are changes in the **systems that will enable business people** and their customers to operate without the adverse impacts, on the environment and people, that we are currently experiencing

The current situation poses profound strategic challenges for business; and many business leaders are making valiant efforts to take on board the implications of sustainability. Even oil companies are taking the issues seriously. Following brushes with public opinion over Brent Spa and Nigeria, Shell has now adopted the 'triple bottom line', which means that social and environmental performance are ranked alongside economic performance. Consultants SustainAbility agreed

---

The knowledge economy

One of the fastest growing sectors of the London's economy is the new 'knowledge economy': information technology, telecommunications and the media. The environmental and social benefits of the new economy are possibly great: there is a potential for e-communications to reduce resource use, to increase participation in numerous spheres, to aid learning and even to allow communities to exist in a new way. But there are also risks: a new 'information underclass' is in danger of being created, and some would argue that new media can increase individual alienation rather than collective contentment. The knowledge economy is already becoming a powerful force; great care must be take to ensure that the benefits of the new technology are available to all. There is an opportunity for the Mayor to work actively with the communications industry to this end.

to work with Shell to develop the implications of this approach for their operations notwithstanding that "a sustainable oil company is a contradiction in terms".[31]

London companies are being encouraged and helped to move ahead with this agenda. London First, the organisation representing many of London's largest businesses, has formed a Sustainability Unit in response to companies becoming more and more aware of the challenges and opportunities raised by sustainability. "The pace of change is increasing, and it is important that, if London is to retain its competitive edge, it must lead change, not follow it."[32] Numerous non-governmental organisations and consultants are active in this field. Pressure is being applied by shareholder movements and by consumer campaigns and boycotts, often inflamed by the media[33].

Companies are becoming more transparent, with an increasing number of firms reporting on their environmental and social performance using a rapidly developing array of Indicators; and companies can now have environmental or social audits undertaken as well as the more

traditional financial variety. Many companies are also improving their actual performance on social and environmental criteria as well as their disclosure of information.

There are endless opportunities for business processes to become more 'eco-efficient', requiring less material input and energy use, and producing less waste, to make the same product. "Ultimately, business must restore, sustain and expand the planet's ecosystems so that they can produce their vital services and biological resources even more abundantly."[34]

The many inspiring developments in this field are brilliantly described in Forum for the Future's magazine *Green Futures*.

Shareholders are people too

We have hitherto been rather assuming that all shareholders are only interested in income and growth. Fortunately this is far from the case: the growth of socially responsible investment (SRI) funds and bank accounts in the last 15 years has been meteoric. I again declare an interest: the whole of my pension fund is invested in National Provident Institute's Global Care Fund which is proactively managed for sustainability and has done brilliantly! Ethical investment funds are now the fastest growing sector of the unit trust market, with over two and a half billion pounds in the retail investment market now invested according to an ethical policy of some kind. Since the time of the first ethical unit trust in the UK (the Friends Provident Stewardship Fund, launched in1983 and still the largest ethical fund in the UK), many new entrants, including larger life assurance players such as Standard Life, have set up ethical funds. The Government's new system of stakeholder pensions will have SRI options. Nevertheless, sadly, ethical investment is still a minute part of the investment market.

The spread of SRI is likely to be helped by the Government's decision to introduce a new disclosure regulation for all pension funds. Under the new regulation, from July 2000 the trustees of all occupational pension funds will have to disclose the extent to which they take into account social, environmental and other ethical criteria in selecting investments and in decisions on how company shares are to be voted. This will awaken fund managers to the concept of SRI and provide opportunities for lobbying; but what a pity that the Government has not gone one step further and given all trustees power, indeed imposed on them a duty, to take sustainability into account in making investment decisions.

Ethical bank accounts are also available at, for example, the Cooperative Bank. The Ecology Building Society offers 'green mortgages' for property purchases that meet their environmental criteria, whilst Triodos Bank offers savings accounts specifically aimed at investing in environmentally and socially beneficial projects.

Insurance companies with large shareholdings could play a major role in bringing influence to bear on companies to achieve the radical shifts in corporate behaviour that are essential if ecological limits are accepted and the needs of future generations accommodated[35].

Local is beautiful

Increasingly, due to the 'growth economy' and expanding trade, going shopping is a global experience, with many manufactured goods, which could perfectly well have been made in the UK, coming from as far away as Japan or China. A lot of the things we purchase, particularly services, are by their nature very local – the plumber, the hairdresser, the window cleaner. There are many more things, especially food, that used to be made or grown locally but are now transported vast distances and are sold in supermarkets offering the same products throughout the country: bad for the planet, because of all the fossil fuels used in transport, bad for local distinctiveness and for personal service.

The local economy has been described as "a critical and enormous part of the fabric of life for all London's citizens, and so for its future health". Most businesses in the local economy are privately owned. That is true of the three shops I use most often, all situated within a couple of hundred yards from where I live. I appreciate them, not only for the things I buy from them, but as an important part of my daily social life.

Another important part of the 'local economy' is local 'social capital': "the ability of people to work together for common purposes in groups and organisations".[36] One of the ways in which people can work together is by running a 'community enterprise'. 'Community enterprises' are part of the local 'social economy'. Three defining features distinguish a 'community enterprise' from a private sector business:

◆ it is owned and controlled by the local community
◆ it aims to serve the interests of that community rather than generate private gain
◆ any financial surplus it produces is for community benefit, not distributed as private property.[37]

Like private sector businesses, community enterprises are involved in commercial activities, directly or indirectly producing goods, or services such as financial services, for which they charge, the resulting revenue being their main if not only source of income. They comprise trading organisations, community financial services such

as credit unions and LETS (Local Exchange Trading Systems), and community organisations with a wider remit such as development trusts.[38] I was once involved in establishing a village housing trust which built six homes for older villagers who could no longer manage their houses and who would otherwise have had to leave the village where I was then living. That I suppose would be counted as a 'community enterprise'.

Successful community initiatives are often the creations of 'social entrepreneurs' – people who find innovative solutions to local problems, who have the same vision and drive as commercial entrepreneurs but are motivated by a desire for social justice rather than profit[39]. That description would fit the group of us who founded and ran the village housing trust.

Local trading and local currencies

These are beautiful pathways to the future. For example **organic box schemes** are increasingly popular In London[40]. With growing concern about the quality of food and a rapidly rising demand for organic produce, they offer an affordable weekly supply of fresh, organic fruit and vegetables. Delivery is often free[41]. **Farmers' markets** bring local farmers into London's urban village centres to sell direct to the public: the idea comes from the USA where there are now over 3,000 weekly farmers markets selling over $1 billion of produce. There are now four in London[42].

LETS (Local Exchange Trading Schemes) are a form of trading system that enables people to both sell their skills to others and buy goods and services from local people, all without spending sterling. They operate by inviting all members – who will be in a locality – to say what they can offer and what they need. So, for example, you may be brilliant at accountancy but be totally lost when it comes to putting up shelving. In a normal barter system, you would need to find a DIY expert who needs his books auditing. But within a LETS scheme, a local currency unique to that scheme enables you to pay for the service in that currency. There is no interest payable, so you can afford to get into debt; within the scheme, debt simply amounts to a commitment to provide services to others[43].

A **credit union** is a savings and loan cooperative whose members share a 'common bond' – usually local residence or a common employer. People can save at a level to suit themselves and borrow at a reasonable rate of interest. Every credit union is owned and controlled by its members. Nationally, their number has grown from under 50 to over 500 since the mid-1980s. "This has been an outstanding success story of how both self-help and mutual aid can rise again ... The success of disadvantaged people to organise and provide each other effective financial services through people power rather than through financial power, as the key asset, speaks volumes about what may be possible if the cooperative spirit is endorsed more by us all."[44]

Local employment bonds are zero-interest loans repayable in (say) five years, used to tackle local unemployment. Sheffield has launched a local employment bond scheme with the assistance of the Relationships Foundation in Cambridge. This would be ideal for London – perhaps it could be part of the London Rebuilding Society project described below. It would provide a satisfying way for Londoners with money to spare to use some of it.[45]

More jobs, better cities

Prof. John Whitelegge of Liverpool John Moores University states that "Strong environmental policies are necessary in cities to create jobs. The history of British cities over the last 40 years has been characterised by a progressive loss of jobs and deterioration of the environment in terms of noise, air quality, green space and access to basic goods and services. This coincidence of two negatives is not accidental. It has been missed by most politicians and policy makers [but not by most ordinary members of the public! Ed]. The relationship between environment and jobs can be used to throw this process into reverse. Simply by improving the urban environment to the highest possible standards safe, secure, well-paid jobs can be created with all the attendant social and economic spin off, including dramatic reductions in health, social security and 'defensive' environmental expenditure (ie that incurred in dealing with the impact of environmental damage, eg health damage)" and he cites formidable evidence in support.

Source: e-mail from j.whitelegge@lancaster.ac.uk

New pathways waiting to be created include

- local produce sold in local supermarkets and high street stores
- local businesses sourcing their products and service needs locally
- local developments emphasising use of local labour, and
- local loyalty schemes to encourage people to use their local shops through offering discounts and other incentives.

With all these tools available, the future could hold "the long term construction of a web of alternative micro-economies, operating if possible within a macro-economic strategy that values the creation of healthy micro-economies".[46]

Green business is good business

Jobs in improving the environment

It is a mistake to regard environmental considerations as a brake on economic activity. It is this kind of thinking that has led to the still fashionable idea that a balance must be maintained between environmental considerations and economic development. This arises in part from the interest driven growth system that, as we have seen, makes it profitable for developers to disregard the environment and future generations. But even before we have moved away from this system, there is a huge potential for economic development which respects the environment.

Forum for the Future's Sustainable Wealth London (SWEL) group has identified[48] the following sectors as having a strong potential to create sustainable jobs[49]

- Resource use / waste management (implementing the reduce, re-use, recycle policies)
- Energy (reducing energy use, eg by insulating dwellings, and producing renewable energy)
- Transport (eg increasing high street retail business by pedestrianisation[50])
- Land use / construction (eg local developments for local needs)
- Pollution control (polluting industries can limit or block other economic activity)
- Urban food growing.

The London Rebuilding Society

The need

The term 'financial exclusion' is used to refer to the difficulties some people have in obtaining finance for themselves or for their business. It is very difficult for people who have nothing to offer by way of security to obtain a loan. There is often no source of funding for social enterprises in London's most deprived neighbourhoods. Of the 321 wards in Inner London, 115 had no local bank branch in 1990 and the figure had risen to 134 by 1995[47]. It's the same old story: the system benefits the rich and not the poorest: and it's getting worse.

The Credit Spectrum for Enterprise and Regeneration

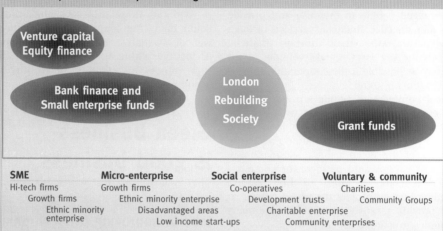

SME	Micro-enterprise	Social enterprise	Voluntary & community
Hi-tech firms	Growth firms	Co-operatives	Charities
Growth firms	Ethnic minority enterprise	Development trusts	Community Groups
Ethnic minority enterprise	Disadvantaged areas	Charitable enterprise	
	Low income start-ups	Community enterprises	

A proposal to meet the need

The London Rebuilding Society (LRS) is an initiative of a new partnership called the London Community Reinvestment Partnership (LRCP). The Partnership is led by New Economics Foundation and includes NatWest, Greater London Enterprise, Social Enterprise London, Charities Aid Foundation, Local Investment Fund, Black Regeneration Forum, London Boroughs Grants, London Voluntary Sector Training Consortium and North London Leadership.

LRS will provide loan finance for the 'social economy' in London. The idea is to obtain grants from public funds and use these to create a revolving loan fund. Other local community finance initiatives will be developed as and when opportunities arise.

LRS members will consist of investors and borrowers and will include:

♦ voluntary organisations delivering contracted out services
♦ non-profit bodies with a growing level of trading activity
♦ community enterprises and cooperatives
♦ voluntary organisations and small businesses attracted by the energy saving loans
♦ existing community loan funds needing capitalisation.

LRS will also seek to be a continuing source of innovation and a catalyst for the development of local community finance initiatives. Initially there will be three funds

♦ Social Enterprise Fund – the core fund for social enterprises
♦ London Ecology Action Fund (LEAF) — for energy efficiency and environmental sustainability
♦ Community Economy Enterprise Development Fund (CEED) – a micro credit service for small community organisations.

LRS will also provide support for organisations through the LRCP partners or directly – business advice etc as well as post-lending support.

What a brilliant project! This is just the kind of innovative, systems-changing multi-purpose initiative that London needs. **Contact:** New Economics Foundation.

SWEL's research is still 'work in progress' (and must be developed at local level) but an interesting point has emerged which applies to the whole agenda of achieving the 'double dividend' of environmental protection and increased employment: the changes needed are fundamental. **"More jobs will flow from the investment, innovation and increased labour intensity associated with transforming sectors, rather than from modifying them"**[51]. Once that transformation is made, a cascade of potential business opportunities is released, jobs in production, repair and renewal, jobs in enabling techniques such as design and materials science, and jobs in management[52].

Small businesses

We have seen that small businesses are generally better for us than big ones. The reason that in a free-for-all market big businesses oust smaller ones, is simply that they have more clout. Business delivers the goods, but is fighting a seemingly endless battle against an economic system (usually represented by the bank) which moves forward inexorably with the momentum of a steamroller and which has the unquestioning loyalty and support of governments. Small businesses and self-employment are all pathways to the future. London has about 180,000 businesses employing fewer than 25 people. In 1994 there were 450,000 self-employed workers. There is a strength and diversity here that should be cherished and supported.

Procurement policy

This refers to an organisation's policy for purchasing goods and services. It is another area where the Mayor can take a proactive stance, pushing ahead of central government, which has been very slow to include sustainable development in its procurement policies.[53] As well as procurement for the new Greater London Authority itself, London's new Mayor can network with other bodies in London and elsewhere to create critical mass for new goods and services, e.g. zero-energy vehicles and photovoltaics.

An economic strategy for London

These are exciting times because, not only is London about to have its own government again, the Greater London Authority (GLA), but it is also to have a new economic development agency, the London Development Agency (LDA). This is one of the new regional economic development agencies being established all over the country, London's being unique in being under the direct control of a locally elected authority, namely the GLA. One of the strategies that the Mayor is required to produce is a strategy for the LDA (see chapter 5). Moreover this strategy is required to contribute to the achievement of 'sustainable development' in the United Kingdom. Although for reasons explained in chapter 4, the way 'sustainable development' has been interpreted is not entirely satisfactory, it is clearly important for the LDA and the Mayor to take a broad and responsible view about the development of London's economy.[54]

What then are the broad issues that an economic strategy for London should address ? The essential thing is that this question should be answered through a process that enables all stakeholders, everyone living or working in London, right from the highly paid directors of all the banks to young people in search of work, to participate in defining the issues and implementing the outcomes.

In the meantime I suggest that the issues are those we have been exploring in this book, in particular the key issues of environmental sustainability and justice. These, not 'economic growth', should provide the overriding aims. They should determine the direction in which to move forward. They should be applied to determine, for example, whether 'inward investment', which means that development is funded from outside the area, so that profits generated by the investment leave the area instead of accruing to local people, is desirable in any particular case.

Based on these principles, a strategy for London might contain the following:

1. Move away from the interest-driven growth patterns that are currently responsible for the social and environmental trends we would like to reverse; and promote zero interest or low interest forms of finance to support economic activities that contribute to our vision of the future by reducing inequality and restoring the environment.

2. Reduce activities that damage the environment and increase those that are environmentally friendly, with strong commitments on energy and waste.
3. Move towards greater self-sufficiency for Greater London (and for its sub-regions and local centres) in terms of energy, food, manufacture, and finance, with less commuting[55], less motorised transport, fewer imports and more jobs for those currently unemployed.
4. Strict control of all inward investment to ensure that it will leave a beneficial legacy[56].

It is important to appreciate that this is an agenda, not for stagnation, but for enterprise and regeneration. It is also important to see a strategy for London as something much of which needs to be implemented at the local level, where local people decide what to do. Closure of the docks ripped the heart out of the Thames Gateway area of East London. The shining towers of Docklands (which swallowed up a lot public money) have done little to help those communities left high and dry and lacking the necessary skills to find work in the financial and media companies which have grown up out of the docks.

Forum for the Future's Sustainable Wealth London group has said it all in one sentence: "we need to create an economy to serve us, our social needs and our environment, rather than the other way round".

The challenge for London: Learning to do business without growth

I hope that I have said enough to show that, in the world of money, trade, corporate development and investment, where we thought that there was no alternative to the existing monolithic system which dictates that the single bottom line must be the ultimate arbiter of everything, and that we had to do our problem-solving against that background, there are in fact numerous pathways out of this predicament waiting to be explored. The world does not have to be like it is. We can go places. (And, if we don't, we will be taken somewhere else by forces we could have controlled.)

There may be some who will say that to change the world would need international agreement to create the new level playing fields. Whilst there certainly is much that can be, and is being, done at this level,[57] it must be admitted that the efforts of the international community to act effectively against powerful interests has been one of the great failures of the 20th century. It is not enough for London to wait to be told what to do by governments or international bodies, which are themselves controlled by governments and often dominated by the least responsible[58]. London, if it had the structures and processes to enable it to do so, could and should seek to take charge of its own future. It may well be easier for London to develop the necessary capability than it would be for the international community.

On many issues it will be both possible and wise for London to go it alone. On others, crashing existing systems would be counter-productive: there, the strategy will be for London to lead, or to use its enormous influence in support of, a global process of transition from a 'growth economy' to an economy tending to promote justice and environmental sustainability. Choosing between leaps and crawls forward towards a vision of a sustainable future will not be easy: it calls for the sorts of leadership and participation processes discussed in chapters 4 and 6 of this book.

The challenge for London's financial and corporate community is for the City to become the home base for sustainable financial and trading systems – sustainable money, sustainable currency systems, sustainable financial markets, sustainable trade, sustainable companies, and sustainable investment – systems that enable an economy to contribute to true wealth, for ourselves, for others and for future generations.

The challenge for Londoners generally is to join in supporting the local businesses and providing the local services we need; and to help create the financial systems that these activities require. Many projects (some of the projects described in this book) are starting to make it happen already. But 99% of them are working against the grain of the current systems. For the transformation to occur, we must first learn to **think** differently: only then can we change the systems.

Together we can then build an economy that really does tend to promote economic activities that satisfy human needs fairly, without destroying the natural environment.

Chapter 3
Notes and References

1. For a short and spirited introduction, see *The Ecology of Money*, Schumacher Briefing No 4 by Richard Douthwaite. *Living Lightly with Positive News* Spring 1999 contained some easily readable articles and a useful book list.
2. *Which World?* p 75.
3. Martin Khor of the Third World Network has estimated the flow of money from poor to rich countries at US$400 million annually, made up of debt repayment, adverse trade terms, depressed commodity prices, the brain drain, internal transfer pricings within transnational companies and the payment of royalties on intellectual property. It is hardly surprising that the gap between rich and poor countries is widening.
4. *Which World?* at pp 79, 80, 84.
5. See *Factor Four* and *Natural Capitalism*.
6. *F.I.A.S.C.O.* by Frank Partnoy gives a brilliant account of just how unattractive these activities are.
7. London accounts for almost 60% of all international trading in equities. Daily foreign exchange turnover in London exceeds the combined totals of New York and Tokyo.
8. *The Growth Illusion*, R Douthwaite, Lilliput Press 2000, p 5 and chapter 9.
9. For example in the last seven years the UK financial services sector has shed over 85,000 jobs and one quarter of all bank and building society branches have closed.
10. Articles by George Monbiot in *The Guardian* 24 September 1998 and 12 August 1999.
11. The case is supported by other writers some of whose works are listed in the bibliography. A recent publication is Robert U Ayres *Turning Point: The End of the Growth Paradigm*; and see his article in *World Review* Volume 3 No 4.
12. The UK's financial services industry contributed £32.9bn to Britain's economy in 1998: both service earnings and investment income rose during the year. "The long-term growth of these overseas earnings will be linked to the ability of financial institutions to gain and keep these overseas markets" BI Chairman Lord Hurd *CityView* December 1999.
13. *Interest and Inflation Free Money*, Margrit Kennedy. See also article by Ann Pettifor and Andrew Simms in *New Economics* Winter 1998.
14. Stock markets create other growth drivers due to the competition between companies and between whole sectors to outperform each other.
15. *Interest and Inflation Free Money* Margrit Kennedy.
16. *The Growth Illusion* p 322.
17. Interest-free banks exist in Sweden and Denmark.
18. See paragraph on LETS post.
19. *Funny Money: In Search of Alternative Cash* by David Boyle describes a whole range of new kinds of local money. And see David Boyle EG vol 6 no 2 Feb 2000 p 11.
20. *The Ecology of Money*, pp 49-51. See James Robertson's web site at www.ecoplan.org/tp2000. A bill making a start in this direction, the State and Local Government Empowerment Act (HR1452) is before the US Congress.
21. *Living Lightly with Positive News* Spring 1999. The EU is currently supporting four experimental currencies: see article in New Economics Winter 1998.
22. *Post-Corporate World*, chapter 2.
23. Allen Hammond in *Which World?* p 30.
24. George Monbiot's article in *The Guardian* 16 December 1999.
25. Be careful to distinguish 'Ethical Trade', a new initiative of a partnership between supermarkets, NGOs and trade unions to ensure that goods meet basic standards on labour rights, but not environmental ones. Martin Wright, in an article in the Summer/October issues of *Green Futures* sees the failure to recognise the inextricable links between the welfare of people and that of the environment on which they depend as a fundamental flaw: he fears that the scheme may attract attention from the true fair trade. Barry Coates of WDM, one of the NGO's behind the scheme, hopes to add in the environment once the scheme has got going.
26. See Fairtrade Foundation post p 120.
27. New Economics Foundation suggest, less dramatically, a Corporate Responsibility Act requiring companies to reveal their social impact. And see *Power and Accountability* Monks and Minow N.Y. HarperCollins 1991.
28. For a good statement of the broad reasoning see *The Post-Corporate World* by David Korten. It may well be that modern conditions call for a reinvigoration of the cooperative and mutual movements: see *New Mutualism* by Peter Kellner Sept 1998.
29. *The Post-Corporate World* p 157, 8.
30. For example the Body Shop's Community Trade Programme aims at building long-term, sustainable relationships so that people in communities in need can benefit through employment income and skill development.
31. See Shell's *Profits and principles – does there have to be a choice ?*
32. David Fell, Director of the Unit, who lists an ambitious range of proposed activities for the Unit.
33. The BBC is also playing an important role through programmes such as *Building Tomorrow's Company*.

34. *Factor Four* by Ernst von Weizsaecker, Amory B Lovins and L Hunter Lovins and the recent *Natural Capitalism* written by Mr and Mrs Lovins with Paul Hawken describe numerous ways in which companies are learning how to make better use of natural capital, the natural capital of ecosystems services, dramatically expanding resource productivity many times over, and producing zero waste. A key recommendation is for manufacturers, instead of selling their products, to provide services, for example, providing illumination rather than selling light bulbs.

35. See *Capital Punishment: UK Investment Companies and the Global Environment* FM Research and FoE.

36. James Colemen, US social ecologist quoted by Simon Zadek and Ed Mayo in an article in *New Economics* Spring 1997.

37. See same article. And see *Community Works* New Economics Foundation.

38. *Community Enterprise Good Practice Guide* DETR May 1999. Interest in this whole agenda is growing across Europe: see the Social Investment Forum's newsletter Autumn 1999.

39. See *Practical People Noble Causes* by Stephen Thake and Simon Zadek, New Economics Foundation.

40. In the UK there are over 35,000 members of box schemes linked to 800 farms. For more information, contact Sustain: the alliance for better food and farming, 94 White Lion Street, London N1 9PF; Soil Association, Bristol House, 40-56 Victoria Street, Bristol, BS1 6BY, e-mail – info@soilassociation.org ; Web site: www.soilassociation.org

41. Green Adventure, operating in a number of deprived south London boroughs, runs a box scheme called Green Ventures: see post p 128.

42. In Southwark, Islington (see post p 129), Swiss Cottage and Notting Hill Gate. For more information on Farmers' Markets, contact London Farmers' Markets Ltd, 6 St Paul Street, London N1 7AB, 0207 704 9659; Web site: www.LondonFarmersMarkets.com Harriet Festing, Wye College, Wye, Near Ashford, 01233 812401; Web site www.wye.ac.uk/FoodLink

43. For the potential for LETS in low income communities see *LETS On Low Income* NEF. For more information on LETS contact LETSLink London, post p 120.

44. John Matthews, British Agency of Settlements and Social Action Centres (BASSAC) in his Foreword to *A Commitment to People and Place* Pat Conaty and Ed Mayo, NEF. This report says everything about the future of Credit Unions. *Credit Union It's for You*, Association of British Credit Unions, tells everything about their present.

45. Contact Development Manager on 0114 273 1765. An alternative scheme to enable people to invest in neighbourhood development is the ICOF Community Capital scheme where shares take the place of bonds. ICOF Community Capital Scheme, 115 Hampstead Road, Handsworth, Birmingham B20 2BR.

46. Part of the vision described by Alison West of the Community Development Foundation in *Regional Studies Association Annual Conference Papers* 1997.

47. Financial Exclusion in London, Kaur, Lingayah and Mayo, NEF 1996.

48. Partly based on Friends of the Earth's discussion paper *Working future ? Jobs and the Environment*.

49. Defined as jobs which contribute to sustainable development with decent pay and conditions; jobs that offer either long-term employment or skills training which acts as a springboard to future employment opportunities.

50. See Friends of the Earth report *Less Traffic, More Jobs*.

51. Draft report by Sustainable Wealth London.

52. *Natural Capital* gives numerous examples of these activities being profitable under existing commercial conditions; but it would be idle to suggest that the market will deliver them without government action and local leadership.

53. British Government Panel on Sustainable Development, Fifth Report dated February 1999 page 18.

54. It was disappointing that the first draft of a strategy for the London Development Agency prepared by its shadow body the London Development Partnership ignored sustainable development entirely. This omission is now being rectified by instructing Ian Christie of Demos to draft suitable wording to incorporate sustainable development into the draft. A good example of how not to go about creating a strategy!

55. 670,000 people commute into London daily, while around 400,000 remain unemployed.

56. Inward investment is still being pursued as a strategy for regeneration in some areas, such as Thames Gateway, Lea Valley and White City (where LB Hammersmith and Fulham has granted permission for a vast retail development with car parking for some 4,500 cars). The erection of luxury flats in tower blocks by the Thames allowed by LB Wandsworth is another disgraceful example. Inward investment should be refused where it has negative impacts on the environment, the local economy or the local community.

57. London is the home of FIELD (Foundation for International Environmental Law and Development), the world's leading non-governmental group of international layers working at this level.

58. That US governments are dominated by big business is well known. The same charge is made about our own government in *The Prawn Cocktail Party – the Hidden Power of New Labour*, by Robin Ramsay, Vision Paperbacks, in which the author describes "the rise to power of the City of London in the post World War 2 period, its manipulation of the Heath and Thatcher governments, Mrs Thatcher's failed attempt to resist it and the Labour Party's progressive collapse before its power, which climaxed with the election of Tony Blair as party leader and front-man for it".

Chapter 4

Steps towards sustainable communities

There are many initiatives to enable people to have more say in the decisions that affect their lives. They currently lack sufficient political support, as does the current response to the 'sustainable development' agenda initiated by the 1992 Rio Earth Summit.

In the first three chapters of this book we have looked at some really big issues – the increasing gap between rich and poor, the damage we are doing to the planet's life-support systems, the suggestion that the 'growth economy', to which our economic system is firmly wedded, far from offering a means of reversing these trends, is actually responsible for them; and the further suggestion that zero-interest currencies and other 'new economics' systems do offer a constructive way forward. Given that the 'growth economy' has the active support of our democratically elected government and that of other industrialised countries, I imagine that at this point you are likely to be saying to yourself: suppose I agree with all this, what on earth can I do about it ? How can anyone influence a system that, however destructive, is strongly entrenched in our democratic society ? How, in particular, can we, as Londoners, make a difference ?

That is the question that is addressed head-on in chapters 6 and 8. This chapter 4 and chapter 5 are intended to prepare you for those chapters. In this chapter, I firstly describe various current initiatives for community involvement in decision-making; I then outline the background about 'sustainable development', 'Local Agenda 21' and the *London 21 Sustainability Network*; thirdly I refer to the use of 'indicators', mediation and the Internet; finally I draw attention to important proposals for reviving local democracy by establishing 'Community Assemblies'. Chapter 5 describes the machinery Parliament has established for the new London Government.

Engaging citizens and other stakeholders

It will be seen that whilst current initiatives, to enable people to have more say, do represent a trend towards a more participatory society, there is still a very long way to go before this becomes the dominant political culture. Local Agenda 21 has been around for many years, but in most boroughs is not recognised as a serious political process.

Other initiatives, like New Deal for Communities, are still only at the pilot study stage. They could all do with a massive in-jection of credibility, funding, legitimacy and professionalism. They urgently need the championship of the new Mayor of London: the genuine participation of all London's citizens and stakeholders in shaping a strategy for a viable future for London should be the new Mayor's number one priority.

Two very positive things do however emerge from this chapter:

◆ Processes for genuinely participative decision-making have been developed and there is a pool of experienced practitioners available.
◆ There is widespread public disenchantment with the existing decision-making processes of local government, due to their failure to engage with local people: this is soil in which change can flourish.

What, no protest ?

In view of the emphasis in this book on the need for radical change, readers may wonder why it contains no account of protest movements in London[1]. Many protest movements are based here. Some, like *critical mass* — the tide of cyclists, which surges up West End streets on the last Friday evening of every month — belong to London. Many others, like The Land is Ours[2], have conducted high profile protests in London, for example the occupation of the Pure Genius site in Wandsworth in 1997. Many national organisations have strong local groups in various parts of London.

I readily acknowledge that protest movements have been inspirational in calling for "an alternative vision of human progress and development based on social justice, ecological sanity, equality and human rights. People in the protest movements of today are advancing much needed ideas that will be considered orthodox a further hundred years on. Green activists' challenge to the Great God Growth – still so heretical for politicians the world over – is the clearest current example, but it is not the only one. Our resistance and idealism have made a difference to the twentieth century – and it must make an even greater difference to the twenty-first".[3]

Protest in the form of peaceful, direct action attracts media attention to the issues and has often won massive public support. It has been important not only in what has been achieved for society but also in providing at least some outlet for the idealism and creativity of the people engaging in protest. As Peter Melchett has written "Active citizens taking peaceful, direct action, and assuming full personal responsibility for it, is an essential part of a healthy democratic society".[4] It will no doubt continue to be all these things and will very probably grow in power.

The reason why this story has not been told here is that this book suggests a different approach — that of **changing the way the mainstream political system works**. I believe that this approach is vital because neither the existing political system nor the protest movement have been effective in preventing the trends described in chapters 1 and 2 from occurring, nor is there any prospect of their doing so. We have seen that the 'growth economy' is apparently the basic fault in the system. Decades of protest have failed to grapple with its basic assumptions, still less dent its momentum. It continues to hold complete power over the political leaders of the wealthiest countries.

Protest movements are part of a trend towards single issues politics. The growth of single issue campaigning organisations, which tend to translate complex issues into simplistic ideological gesturing, is a symptom of social alienation and atomisation: it is a force likely to impede the emergence of more holistic politics.

The alternative to protest is to bring about change through 'co-creation'. I believe co-creation offers a pathway to change. What it means is described in chapter 6. The confrontational tactics of protest have won great victories and might even win a war. They are not however capable of building a new order in place of the existing one. I believe co-creation is. Only a — usually very small — minority get involved in protest. Co-creation involves everyone.

Co-creation does however require the leaders to lead in the way that co-creation requires. Until we have such leaders, protest will indeed continue to be a necessary force for bringing major issues to public attention.

Community involvement

What does it mean ?

We referred in chapter 1 to the emerging planning model described by the Evans/Guy/Marvin trio as "Negotiative Planning and the Reflexive City". It was characterised by these features:

- The problem is actually very serious, a recognition that there is a crisis.
- Responsibility for finding a solution lies not solely with the local authority but relies on networks and partnerships involving a wide range of groups.
- The vision of the city is a reflexive one, aware of its consequences and with users, employers and many other agencies involved in defining problems and developing solutions.

This is going in the right direction. The World Health Organisation's definition of community involvement takes it a step further:

"Community involvement is a process by which people are enabled to become actively and genuinely involved in defining the issues of concern to them in making decisions about factors that affect their health, in formulating and implementing policies, in planning, developing and delivering services and in taking action to achieve change".

The vital addition here is that **people are involved right from the start**: they are not presented with a problem the authority would like their help in solving: **they actually help define the issues.**

To achieve community involvement requires 'participation processes'. These are contrasted with 'consultation' where the community is accorded a strictly subsidiary role in the decision-making process. This is illustrated by Sherry Arnstein's 'ladder of participation':

Community involvement – the current state of play

Community involvement is now being actively promoted in the fields of local government and regeneration. It is strongly recommended by Government for use throughout the delivery of public services[5]. What is not yet clear is exactly what the Government understands by community involvement. It speaks of "local government keeping fully in touch with the needs or aspirations of local people" and "partnership with other local organisations"[6] but it does not appear to have

Ladder of participation

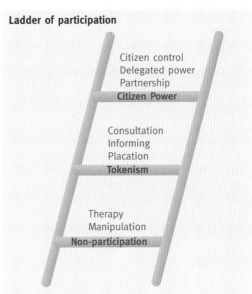

Citizen control
Delegated power
Partnership
Citizen Power

Consultation
Informing
Placation
Tokenism

Therapy
Manipulation
Non-participation

grasped the full implications of community involvement. Government is feeling its way towards making a distinction between a local authority's role as a service provider and its role in community leadership and governance, where it becomes, as in many parts of Europe, "the embodiment of the community governing itself".[7]

The recently passed Local Government Act empowers local authorities to promote the economic, social and environmental well-being of their areas. It was disappointing that Parliament did not go further and make this a duty, not just a power, and couple it with a duty to promote sustainable development. But it is a step in the right direction.

The main point I make is that unless and until the relevant authority in any particular situation does fully adopt the implications of community involvement, exercises involving the public are pointless and can easily do more harm than good by raising expectations which are not met,

leaving a sense of betrayal that does nothing to improve the relationship between the authority and the local community.

It cannot be too strongly emphasised that genuine participation processes represent a revolution in the processes of democracy. Instead of decisions being taken by an elite and legitimised through the structures of political parties, elections, agendas and committees, these processes seek to involve everyone and to be open to people raising any issue; they are about having all the stakeholders 'in the same room' and addressing all the issues. It sounds impossible but, far from that, it actually works. Whilst it does require the elected councillors to play a new kind of leadership role, it is not in conflict with existing structures.

Moving from 'consultation' to 'participation' is not just a matter of doing more of the same. It requires politicians and their professional advisers to think about the nature of democracy, citizenship, leadership and accountability. Not surprisingly, the development of community participation in London has been slow. This is unfortunate because, from a systems point of view, it is only through the genuine participation of all stakeholders that we can hope to address the issues to which we have drawn attention in this book.

Participation methods

I use two case studies to illustrate two methods and to draw some conclusions for London.

Choices for Bristol

Choices for Bristol distributed 7,000 copies of its Discussion Guide as a supplement in the Bristol Evening Post. Ideas came partly from groups using the Guide and partly from Vision Bristol Roadshows at libraries, health centres, supermarkets and so on. People came up with 2032 ideas for improving the city.

Two *Vision Bristol* meetings for adults and for young people turned the ideas into achievable goals and six vision statements.

The statements and ideas were published in February 1997 under the title "Your Ideal Bristol ? Let's Make it Happen" and displayed over five days at a 'vision fair'. People were invited to join action groups. *Choices* has taken the lead in establishing action groups on four issues: waterways; the wider community use of libraries; music in the city; and the potential for an interfaith centre.

Imagine Chicago

During 1991 and 1992, Bliss Browne, a priest and banker, planned a pilot to:
◆ discover what gives life to Chicago
◆ provide significant leadership opportunities for youth.

1993-94 saw both city-wide and community-based pilots. City-wide, 50 young people were recruited and trained as interviewers. They developed a series of questions designed to discover the best of the past as a basis for dreaming what might be in the future. Here are some of those questions:
◆ Thinking back over your Chicago memories, what have been real high points for you as a citizen of the city ?
◆ Why did these experiences mean so much to you ?
◆ Close your eyes and 'imagine' Chicago as you most want it to be a generation from now. What is it like ? What do you see and hear ? What are you proudest of having accomplished ?

They interviewed about 140 citizens, identified as 'Chicago Glue'. The interviews were then summarised for three public events.

Since 1995 the appreciative approach has been seeded, by forming partnerships, into over 100 community organisations, schools, communities of faith and cultural institutions. An example is the Urban Imagination Network: six state schools and five Chicago museums are working to improve student reading comprehension.

Conclusions for London

1. Many of the best methods, like Imagine, work well at different scales, from the neighbourhood to the city.
2. Good processes combine two stages. The first is to reach out to as many people as possible. *Choices for Bristol* used the Discussion Guide

to do this, *Imagine Chicago* used the interviews. The second stage is to bring people together to develop a shared vision of the future and a sense of momentum. In Bristol, the Vision Bristol meetings and the Vision Fair did this.

3. Encourage diversity and bring together people who do not normally meet. *Chicago* did this by getting younger people to interview older people.
4. Acknowledge every individual contribution. *Choices for Bristol* published a booklet containing all the 2032 ideas they received.
5. Find ways of including both ordinary people and decision-makers. *Choices for Bristol* found the first easier than the second. *Imagine Chicago* used the partnerships to include decision-makers.

Occasions for community involvement

Community involvement processes are currently being used in several contexts, the main ones being 'Local Agenda 21' (this is covered separately below), 'New Deal for Communities', 'Community Planning', regeneration and health. There is also huge scope for community involvement in the planning system (see boxes on pp 64, 65, 66; see also p 75 post).

Another part of the Government agenda for placing more emphasis on people's views and involvement is 'Best Value' which is a government requirement for local authorities in relation to the delivery of a wide range of services and which also applies, for example, to housing associations (involving tenants in setting the agenda and assessing the quality of services). Here again there is scope for genuine community involvement.

Who does the public trust ?

Responses to the question: *"who would you trust for information about the environment?"*

Expert	Percentage (%)
NGO scientists	75
Government scientists	46
Industry scientists	43

Source:
MORI (1998) Business and the Environment Annual Survey

New Deal for Communities

This Government programme attempts to learn from the failure of earlier programmes aimed at benefiting those living on run-down estates by paying for physical improvements: the estates concerned had tended to revert back to their previous condition because underlying social and economic problems had not been effectively tackled. The Government has realised that a more holistic approach is needed, tackling social and economic problems as well as improving the physical environment. Funding is being provided for 17 pilot neighbourhoods three of which are in London: in Hackney, Newham (this is the subject of the very interesting Social Enterprise Zone project described on page 110) and Tower Hamlets. The money can be spent on such things as multi-purpose health centres, family centres providing community-based social work, the community use of schools for a variety of activities such as homework centres, breakfast clubs, summer schools and adult education. However, it is doubtful whether even now the Government has taken a sufficiently systematic approach, offering hands-off support to enable local people to develop a healthy community. I am sure the people working on the SEZ in Newham will provide clear evidence of what local people are really capable of. The lessons learned will be applied elsewhere in London.

Community Planning

Community Planning is a new Government initiative requiring councils to bring together statutory agencies (for example, the local health authority, the police) the business sector, voluntary and community organisations and local people, to agree a set of aims and objectives for the locality. Properly conducted, and given the full political support of the council, Community Planning could be a really useful exercise. "It should be taken to represent processes of building a shared understanding of:

◆ the problems, opportunities and aspirations of diverse communities
◆ the contributions of different stakeholders
◆ the resources available both to and within communities
◆ strategic direction"[8].

Sadly, it is not a requirement of Community Planning to take into account global factors or future generations, nor does it demand an integrated approach to social, economic and environmental wellbeing[9]. There is however no reason why it should not do so.

What is generally lacking for Community Planning to be really effective is political leadership. If however the Mayor of London were to give that lead – and the obligation to promote sustainable development written into the Greater London Authority Act provides the perfect legitimacy for the Mayor to do so – all Community Planning in London could take these elements on board and we would then have a consistent pattern of community planning across London.

Regeneration

Community involvement will be a vital feature of all future regeneration schemes in London, as the following reports show.

◆ The London Planning Advisory Committee's *Good Practice to Community Planning and Development* written by Michael Parkes

shows that local people and their organisations can successfully be involved in planning and developing regeneration of their neighbourhoods and that this has far better results than either laissez-faire policies or the paternalism of the public sector. The report advocates the use of community development trusts.

Planning for sustainable development

Over the last ten years there has been growing concern as to how the planning system should respond to the challenges of sustainable development. DETR Guidance *Planning for Sustainable Development Towards Better Practice* [13] brings together much of the latest thinking and practice. The report emphasises the need to start by defining the vision or objectives which the plan is there to serve. See for example paragraph 2.1.4: "Plans should be developed from a strategic vision of what existing urban areas [in our case the area of Greater London] should be like in about 25 years' time, when they are inherited by the next generation. This vision should indicate what development should occur and where [in our case this will be limited to London-wide strategic objectives] and how this could contribute to a re-shaping of towns and cities [ie Greater London] to make them function more sustainably. The future of urban areas [Greater London] must be seen positively, the aim being to create more sustainable patterns of development, and to restructure existing urban areas to make them more sustainable. They are not just receptors of new housing and other forms of development pressure."

Chapter 6 of the Report makes suggestions on the methodology for integrating sustainable development into the plan. It suggests an iterative four-stage process (adapting that envisaged in *Development Plans: A Good Practice Guide* DOE (1992)):

◆ Stage 1 Clarifying issues and objectives
◆ Stage 2 Identifying indicators and targets
◆ Stage 3 Developing and testing strategic options
◆ Stage 4 Formulating policies and proposals

Features of the process emphasised in the Report include the following: the need for "effective involvement of a wide range of parties in the process – through consultation and partnership" (para 6.1.8). In particular "the views of as wide a range of interests as possible should be included" in Stage 1 (para 6.2.10). Examples are given of Local Agenda 21 processes, Round Table formats, working parties, Issue Reports and "other creative consultation and participation processes" (para 6.2.8).

Planning for Sustainable Development, Towards Better Practice DETR, Oct 1998

The Joseph Rowntree Foundation's *Developing Effective Community Involvement Strategies* advocates government funding to help local organisations in deprived areas build capacity prior to bidding for regeneration funding: "to develop visions and action plans for their neighbourhoods; provide smaller scale funding for confidence building start-up projects; and provide residents with access to initial training, leadership development and consultancy services". Several other JR-funded studies give valuable advice on neighbourhood regeneration.

The London Study's *Sustainable Urban Regeneration* report (part of the *London Study* carried out in 1997 by the Association of London Government with European Union money) recommended a model of regeneration partnership using the subsidiarity principle which met five objectives. These included

"Greater inclusiveness to enable all of London's social partners to participate fully in regeneration. Subsidiarity will not be achieved if partners with key competences (such as the community and voluntary sector and small businesses) are marginalised in the partnership process".

It is good to see the principle of subsidiarity being taken right down to the level of local communities and small and medium sized businesses. However this whole report has a terribly top-down tone and, whilst the importance of the role of local communities is

---

Charrettes

There is a much stronger tradition of using participation processes in the USA than there is here. A process commonly used there is the Charrette.

This is a process to achieve workable long-term visions and solutions for specific neighbourhoods or for a whole community. A series of visually engaging, interactive and collaborative public workshops, focus groups, field-condition inventories and design sessions is held over a period of (say) five days. These offer opportunities for friendly, informal discourse among community citizens. Charrettes turn planning from a reactive into a proactive process. Essential principles include:

1. All visions are based on a 20 year future outcome.
2. Vision comes before planning.
3. All groups need to be part of the visioning process.
4. All citizens and residents will be impacted by these decisions.
5. Proactive planning needs to take place before anything is built.
6. Reactive planning is futile and leads to muddled, senseless places and unhappy people.
7. Every business and every citizen of every age and ability is considered in the outcome.

Description based on text by Greenway Development Group dburden@aol.com

---

emphasised, and the past failure to involve them as equal partners is acknowledged, if in fact public funds are to be handed over to the sort of regeneration partnerships envisaged in this report, a very great deal more work would need to be done to ensure that this recommendation is not a dead letter.

This impression is confirmed by the *London Study Executive Summary* which advocates funding procedures, firstly, favouring existing partnership organisations enjoying widespread support, and secondly, on how rigorously community consultations have been carried out. I fear that this may only reflect the attitudes of consultants much closer to the culture of corporations than to the needs of local communities.

Pathways to the future

Health in London

In London, the importance now being attached to community involvement is illustrated by London Voluntary Service Council's insistence that "a commitment by all agencies to community development, capacity building and participation is essential to ensuring health improvement in London. This should therefore be integral to the London Health Strategy and its components and to other London-wide and local strategies which impact on health. These include, for example, economic development, social exclusion ... The London Mayor and Greater London Authority should incorporate this approach in all their strategies which impact on health, and promote it with other agencies that they work with."[10]

Planning

Land-use planning is in the hands of the borough councils, with guidance currently coming from the Government Office for London (GOL) and London Planning Advisory Committee (LPAC). The key process in each borough is the borough Unitary Development Plan (UDP): it guides the council when making decisions about proposed developments or change of use. The public is given opportunities to contribute to the preparation of the UDP, but in practice few do so. When developers apply for planning permission they are often in a much stronger position than local people. Many grossly inappropriate developments have been allowed to proceed. There is widespread dissatisfaction with the system.

Under the new Greater London Authority (GLA) regime, planning will continue to be in the hands of the borough councils but the Mayor will have a Spatial Development Strategy (SDS)[11] dealing with strategic matters; and the boroughs will in due course have to amend their UDPs to accord with the SDS. If past precedent is anything to go by, the preparation of both the SDS and the UDPs would be likely to be planning officer-led: in the case of the GLA this doubtless means the former LPAC staff, who have built up an portfolio of strategic policies[12] and have shown some understanding of many of the implications of sustainable development. As with the Mayor's other strategies, the legislation does not provide for a vision-led approach, let alone a process enabling the public to contribute to creating the vision. The general public and the voluntary and private sectors do not get a look in until near the end of the process laid down in the Act (by which time it will be too late.)

There is however plenty of evidence that a vision-led approach, with input from all stakeholders, works best (see boxes on this and two previous pages) and it is our contention that only through such an approach can London address the challenges of the 21st century. It will be up to the Mayor to insist on this being adopted.

Reinventing planning

A complete overhaul of the planning system is called for by the recent report of the Town and Country Planning Association Inquiry into the future of planning *Your Place and Mine, Reinventing Planning*. Principles include:

◆ adopting sustainable development as the focus for managing change
◆ positive planning based on sustainability criteria
◆ new participatory processes to create visions and strategies
◆ new structures to enable local needs and global priorities to be actively reconciled, including community planning at all levels.

Recommendations of the report include:

◆ a duty to promote sustainable development
◆ the creation of community visions and agreement on strategies for sustainable development through collaborative and inclusive processes
◆ the development of powerful new monitoring and evaluation systems which review and assess progress towards objectives
◆ community planning at all levels – a new structure of strategies and action plans at national, regional, borough and neighbourhood levels
◆ partnership trusts for areas of particular needs or opportunities.

Sustainable development, Agenda 21 and Local Agenda 21

What does 'sustainable development' mean ?

The phrase 'sustainable development' was brought to world attention by the 1987 United Nations report known as the Brundtland Report, where it was referred to as:

"development which meets the needs of the present without compromising the ability of future generations to meet their own needs"[14].

The Report pointed out that:

"sustainable development is not a fixed state of harmony. But rather a process of change in which the exploitation of resources, the direction of investments, the orientation of technological development, and institutional change are made consistent with future as well as present needs."[15]

The Brundtland Report was produced by the World Commission on Environment and Development chaired by the former Norwegian Prime Minister Gro Harlem Brundtland. The Commission was established by the United Nations in 1983 in response to "the widespread feeling of frustration and inadequacy in the international community about our own ability to address the vital global issues and deal effectively with them", with a brief to formulate "a global agenda for change"[16]. The Commission made wide-ranging recommendations and called for

"a common endeavour and for new forms of behaviour at all levels and in the interests of all. The changes in attitudes, in social values, and in aspirations that the report urges will depend on vast campaigns of education, debate and public participation.

To this end we appeal to citizens' groups, to non-governmental organisations, to educational institutions, and to the scientific community. They have all played indispensable roles in the creation of pubic awareness

and political change in the past. They will play a crucial part in putting the world onto sustainable paths, in laying the ground work for Our Common Future"[17].

The Commission's recommendations included the following on the urban challenge

"Good city management requires decentralisation – of funds, political power and personnel — to local authorities, which are best placed to appreciate and manage local needs. But the sustainable development of cities will depend on closer work with the majorities of urban poor who are the true city builders, tapping the skills, energies, and resources of neighbourhood groups and those in the 'informal sector'."

Whilst the Commission may have had 'developing world' cities primarily in mind, this passage is equally applicable to London.

The 1992 Earth Summit and Agenda 21

The Brundtland Commission requested that its report be transformed into a UN Programme for Sustainable Development and this led to the Earth Summit held at Rio de Janeiro in June 1992 when world leaders signed up to Agenda 21 – an agenda for the 21st century.

Agenda 21 and its sister document the Rio Declaration[18] are generally regarded as the key guides to action towards sustainable development. They contain a wealth of useful material. Three principles stand out:

◆ an emphasis on meeting the needs of those whose basic needs are not currently met
◆ safeguarding the natural environment
◆ equity, both as between people now living and as between generations.

Whilst the Brundtland Report and Agenda 21 are thus important landmarks on the path towards a more equitable and sustainable future, the fact is that they have not succeeded in reversing the trends they were meant to address[19]. Why is this ? We believe that it is because they failed adequately to analyse two key aspects of the existing systems:

◆ the effects of economic growth and the role of transnational companies[20]
◆ the capacity of the existing political systems and processes to bring about the changes required.

The UK Strategy for Sustainable Development

Central government has responded to Agenda 21 by producing a Strategy for Sustainable Development, the current version being entitled *a Better Quality of Life*[21]. This answers the question "What is sustainable development?" as follows: "At its heart is the simple idea of ensuring a better quality of life for everyone, now and for future generations to come"[22], then quoting the Brundtland report as cited above. The strategy document contains some excellent statements of intention (for example "The Government is putting sustainable development at the heart of every Government department's work"[23] and "Over time the Government will reform the tax system in ways that deliver a more dynamic economy and a cleaner environment: shifting taxes from 'goods' like employment to 'bads' such as pollution"[24].

There is much to commend in the Government's proposals including numerous policies under the heading of Building Sustainable Communities, referring to various Government initiatives[25]. However:

◆ Like Agenda 21 itself, the Government's strategy assumes, without analysis, that economic growth is sustainable. It is even included as one of the four principal aims of the strategy and as one of the indicators of sustainable development (see post p 73); and the Strategy says that "Trade and investment are crucial to poverty elimination. They bring resources that can help generate the growth needed to establish sustainable livelihoods"[26].

◆ It fails adequately to discuss the political processes, such as visioning, necessary to achieve sustainable development.

◆ It does not discuss the need for the UK to be a sustainable part of a sustainable world.

In short the strategy is not based on a 'systems approach' and is carefully formulated to avoid offending international money interests. The reason for these fatal flaws lies in the way the Strategy document was prepared, typical of Government practice: a consultation paper is prepared and issued for discussion (in this case it was called *Opportunities for Change*), those consulted send in their comments (in this case over 1000 responses were received) and then the Government rewrites the document taking as much, or as little, notice as it likes of the comments made. The procedure allows no dialogue, the consultants' comments are not even acknowledged. The end product inevitably rests comfortably within the limitations of the Government's permitted imagination.

Local Agenda 21 (LA21)

Careful review of Agenda 21 is said[27] to indicate that more than two thirds of its statements cannot be delivered without the commitment and co-operation of local government and local communities. Chapter 28 therefore requires every local authority to "enter into a dialogue with its citizens, local organisations and private enterprises and adopt a 'Local Agenda 21'. Through consultation and consensus building local authorities would learn from citizens and from local, civic, community, business, and industrial organisations and acquire the information needed for formulating the best strategies. The process of consultation would increase household awareness of sustainable development issues."

Most local authorities in this country responded to this; all London boroughs have now done so. The Prime Minister has stated that all local authorities should complete their LA21 plans by this year.

Many people in this country, including many in London, saw LA21 as a wonderful opportunity to help implement 'sustainable development' locally, through a process that invited the whole

revolution in the attitudes of both officers and members and the introduction of new processes. "LA 21 and its wider framework of ideas constitute one of the most striking advances in progressive politics over the last decade"[32]. Perhaps precisely for that reason, LA21 was not welcome to officials in either central government or borough councils[33]. To be fair to the political leaders, given the modern tendency for local authorities to act as mere central government agencies, the low priority most of them gave to LA21 only reflects the priorities passed down from central government; and the officers given LA21 duties cannot be blamed for not doing more with the limited budgets they had to work within.

To some extent, the future of LA21 hangs in the balance. Whether it will carry on in all its idealistic purity but as something of a side show, or whether it becomes absorbed in mainstream processes such as community planning, thereby risking being somewhat watered down, only time will show. Ian Christie in his article in the October 1999 issue of EG has strongly argued that there is already common ground ("a deep affinity", he says) between LA21 and several more

community to get involved. Much useful, and very varied, work has been done in London boroughs under the LA21 umbrella. Many local residents have put a lot of time and trouble into meetings, events and local projects. Numerous plans have been made and numerous small projects have been inspired or assisted. Most councils admit to LA21 having had some influence[28]. SLT has collected two boxes of impressive documents supplied by various boroughs, easily enough material for a whole book on the achievements of LA21 in the 32 boroughs. There have been important initiatives not related to any particular borough; for example, the National Federation of Women's Institutes has resolved to promote it through its member groups.[29] Moreover, because the LA 21 process is vision-led and values-based and does involve people in a bottom-up way, it has probably resulted in more useful initiatives and changes of behaviour than are recorded or credited to it[30].

However, the tremendous potential of the novel process called for by Agenda 21 has not been realised because in the vast majority of London boroughs the process has not received the backing it requires at either political or senior officer level.[31] The idea that a local authority should have a dialogue with and seek to learn from local people is completely foreign to the culture of London boroughs! Taking LA21 seriously would have required a complete

What the Government's own advisors say

The Government has been made well aware of the gravity of the situation by its own advisers, the British Government Panel on Sustainable Development. For example in their Fifth Report, February 1999, in their advice to the Prime Minister on sustainable development and employment, they wrote "Sustainable development means radical change in our society. It involves social and economic as well as environmental factors. The problem is not how to tinker with things as they are, including present patterns of employment, but how to achieve a fundamental culture change by bringing together the three aspects of sustainable development, with respect to employment, across society as a whole. The major global factors are well known: human population increase, damage to soils, availability of raw materials and disposal of waste, supply of fresh water, pollution generally, reduction in the diversity of life (on which we, like all other species, depend), and changes in climate and sea levels. We also have to cope with the effects of information technology, and increasing polarisation of wealth within and between countries".

Pathways to the future

strongly supported Government initiatives, including 'Community Planning' : he urges LA21 champions "to start using these affinities to win hearts and minds for sustainable development strategies — within local authorities, regional development agencies and among the public at large". This is probably good advice, especially in the London context.

Another possibility hopefully in the pipeline is that the Government might require all local authorities to put "sustainable development at the heart of all council decision-making" as urged by the RSPB (Royal Society for the Protection of Birds)[34]. This would go a long way towards removing the potential conflict between LA21 and Community Planning.

'An Agenda 21 for London'

Due to there being no London-wide local authority, there was no possibility of a genuine Local Agenda 21 process for London. However, between 1995 and 1997 the Association of London Government (ALG) — the association of the leaders of the London borough councils — on the initiative of Merton Cllr Tony Colman, established working groups to put together what was called "an Agenda 21 for London". Due to the hurried and limited procedure steam-rollered by the ALG, the resulting document has no 'ownership' beyond the desks of the officers involved. However, the working group papers (together with the later *London Study*, also led by the ALG) will provide useful background material for any process the Mayor decides to initiate. In particular, the report of a working group formed at a late stage in the proceedings to report on London's global footprint – including the impact

of the City of London – raised some important questions, some of which have been touched on in this book.

The European Union's Sustainable Cities Project (EU)

A working group set up by the EU produced a report containing a lot of wisdom – for example, thinking in ecosystems terms, emphasising the city as a complex system which is characterised by flows as continuous processes of change and development — and much practical detail. "The sustainable city process is about creativity and change. It challenges traditional government responses and seeks new institutional and organising capacities and relationships."[35]

The report provides support for some of the views expressed here – for example, the need for the commitment and active participation of the local community. It also provides valuable support for the Mayor in asking central government for greater powers: "If Europe's cities are to achieve their sustainability promise governments must allow cities maximum freedom to apply suitable tools at local level. Municipal and regional governments must be granted appropriate powers and resources, for example for taxation, subsidy, regulation and investment. ... Cities will not be able to follow different paths if the socio-economic system is too open, or if their powers are arbitrarily restricted, or if policies at other levels cut action by cities. Thus the need for experimentation requires cities to have the powers to be, up to a point, closed systems – to have the power to manage resource and financial flows. This may require reconsideration of other policy goals such as free trade. These issues should be explored openly and pragmatically, no one policy objective should be taken as absolute or inviolable". London under the new Mayor will be able to take an active part in this interesting debate.

London and 'sustainable development': conclusions

The foregoing is but a summary of where the concept of sustainable development came from and how it is being used. What is its significance for our future ?

Some would dismiss it as too vague and ambiguous a concept to be of any practical use. I disagree. It is certainly capable of being abused and I consider that governments are indeed abusing it by refusing to recognise that sustainability requires them to question some of the cornerstones of their own positions, such as the desirability of 'economic growth'.

The value of 'sustainable development' is that

◆ It is based on a recognition that the world is set on a disastrous course: see the Brundtland Report. So one does not have to start from any kind of spiritual, ethical or political position, which others might not agree with: sustainable development is boringly sensible, crucial, practical, common sense.

◆ Whilst expressing much idealism, for example about human rights and the status of women, it has the legitimacy and authority of having been endorsed at the highest level by the biggest ever get together of world leaders – the Earth Summit.

◆ It provides a space in which a wide range of so-called 'single issue' voluntary bodies, those dealing with poverty and human rights/social justice issues, the environmental lobby and others can come together to question the current political and economic systems which are damaging both the environment and the world's poor[36].

◆ It assumes a 'whole systems' approach, looking at global trends and recognising that everyone is involved and affected. It provides a short-hand expression for a global change of direction, the way to a sustainable future, for the whole world and for every part of the world.

◆ It is applicable to governments at every level, to international arrangements, and to local and city government, and also to corporations, organisations and individuals. Sustainable development requires London's strategies to be linked to national and international strategies and it also provides a framework for links between the London-wide strategic level and the borough level through Local Agenda 21.

Finally, Agenda 21 recognises that the way in which sustainable development should be applied at any particular level is something that should be worked out by the people concerned at that level. What it means to you is a matter for you. What it means for London is a matter for London to decide for itself.

This leads on to the question of process. How can London decide ? What processes are needed to ensure that, in relation to London as a whole, sustainable development and Agenda 21 can realise their true potential ? This is the question which we address in chapters 6 and 8. In the meantime, what possibilities exist for horizontal networking between people involved in building more sustainable lifestyles ?

The London 21 Sustainability Network

Local Agenda 21 (LA21) has been proceeding in the 32 London boroughs quite independently. The council officers concerned meet together periodically but there is no regular meeting place for the hundreds, if not thousands, of non-council people taking part in LA21 meetings and activities in their various boroughs. People were finding it difficult to find out what was going on in other boroughs and it was felt that the whole movement would have more impact if links could be made.

The *London 21 Sustainability Network* ('London 21') was formed in 1998 to meet this need. Anyone concerned with sustainability issues in London is welcome to make use of it. By using the Network, people can

◆ easily find information about organisations active in their field of interest

◆ make contacts for mutual support, discussion or other purposes.

Non-governmental organisations, voluntary action and community enterprise have a vital role in achieving the changes needed for London to

become part of the solution to the world's problems. For community-based groups and initiatives to become more effective, horizontal (ie cooperative) partnerships and networks are being developed to work alongside the vertical, centralised and departmentalised (ie hierarchical) structures that characterise the public sector. *London 21* is part of this horizontal activity but it can also provide a useful conduit for communications between the new Greater London Authority, its members and officers and community groups and others.

Work on establishing the Network started in 1997. In April 1998 at the *Gathering for Change* held at Goldsmiths College over 300 people endorsed the need for the Network. Since then, volunteers working with the support of the Sustainable London Trust have established a board of trustees to administer the Network; and much skilled work has gone into the development of the web site launched in August 1999, comprising a directory of organisations with various ancillary online services.

London 21's mission

The Network's mission is to assist London's communities and all those engaged in personal and community-based action for sustainability in the Greater London area to

◆ find mutual support
◆ link their work with the actions of others who have similar goals
◆ take part in creating a Greater London Authority that is democratic and sustainable
◆ contribute to the strategies of the new Authority.

The Directory

Thousands of organisations are concerned with various aspects of sustainability in London. The Directory points users of the Network in the right direction and gives useful information on the organisations held.

Details of the first 900 organisations to register can be accessed on the *London 21* web site www.London21.org. Various search engines allow users to find the information they need. The site offers links to over 300 other web sites: links to other UK-wide and international sites will be added.

Joining the Directory and accessing it via the internet are completely free. The site can be used in schools, colleges and public libraries and from home as well as from within the organisations listed on the Directory. It aims to become the first port of call for anyone concerned with sustainability issues.

A paper version of the Directory will be produced annually.

Other online services: conferencing, mailing lists and chat

The web site includes advanced user-led features such as shared and private spaces for groups to communicate via e-mail, store and share small files, publicise their work and generally network with other users and the public.

London 21 is also able to offer professional help with web site development.

Measuring progress towards sustainability: 'indicators'

"Now, as we approach the next century, there is a growing realisation that real progress cannot be measured by money alone" the Prime Minister.

Tony Blair

That quotation is taken from the Prime Minister's Foreword to *A Better Quality of Life – a Strategy for Sustainable Development for the United Kingdom*[37] in which the Government has set out how to measure progress by a system of 'indicators'. The most important if these are called 'headline indicators' and will be measured annually.

The quotation raises a number of issues:

◆ Who **decides** what 'real progress' is ? For the UK as a whole this is a matter for the Government. But it will be for Londoners, led by the GLA, to decide what 'real progress' means for London. It is for London to decide **how** to contribute to sustainable development in the UK[38].

◆ What **is** real progress ? The Government answers this for the UK in *A Better Quality of Life* by setting out the aims, priorities and guiding principles for its strategy for sustainable development[39]. Sadly, one of the Government's four aims is "maintenance of high and stable levels of economic growth and employment". As we have seen, high levels of economic growth are undesirable and indeed unattainable. But there is no reason why London should make the same mistake. For London, a world city, a place to live, however you think of London, 'real progress' might look very different from the national government's view of 'real progress' for the UK.

◆ "cannot be measured in money alone". This takes us back to the discussion in chapter 3 about GDP and ISEW. If we do not use money, or GDP, to measure 'real progress', how can it be measured ? Various answers have been suggested. One, as we have seen, is ISEW, which is produced by starting off with GDP and adding or subtracting for various factors[40]. 'Indicators' are an alternative way of measuring progress. "Sustainable development objectives are broad. To deliver them, we must focus on specific issues. One way to do that is through indicators. They help to identify areas for action and connections between them."[41] The Government has selected a list of 150 indicators for the UK strategy.

◆ "cannot be measured in money **alone**". Given that economic growth is one of the government's aims in defining progress, it comes as no surprise that one of the headline indicators in the Government's list is GDP[42]. The Government has been advised by its own advisers to reconsider this[43]. Let us hope that it heeds this advice. London, of course, must not make the same mistake.

Indicators for London

As long ago as 1995 the London Planning Advisory Committee saw the need for London to monitor its impact on the environment world-

wide, its use of natural resources and the local environment[44]. LPAC is now about to publish the second update of the State of the Environment Report with a revised list of 92 indicators. For example, under Global Sustainability five criteria are listed, Transport Energy Efficiency, Traffic Demand and Management, Energy Efficiency and Conservation, Carbon Dioxide Emissions, and Natural Habitats and Species Diversity. Under the first of those heads, five indicators are listed. The indicators will be used in the Mayor's Annual Report and the four-yearly State of the Environment Reports to measure London's progress (see chapter 5). From the look of the draft list these indicators will need a good deal of explaining — which may be a good thing if it gets people thinking. But it does include some quite simple ones like "total energy use in London" and "carbon dioxide emissions" which everyone will be able to understand.

Indicators and public involvement

In addition to their usefulness as benchmarks in measuring 'real progress', indicators are also relevant to the whole topic of public involvement in deciding what would be 'real progress' or 'sustainable development' for London. The Partners for London Vision project (see chapter 8) may be an opportunity to involve the public in choosing some indicators for London.

Indicators are frequently used in Local Agenda 21[45].

Lichen as biomonitors of air quality

In the London Borough of Brent lichens growing on stone or wood are being used as natural indicators of air quality. A-level students working with local members of the London Wildlife Trust and experts from the British Lichen Society are carrying out field surveys to establish a data base of species which will be fed into a Geographical Information System (GIS). The patterns of species distribution will be linked to sources of pollution. The project is led by the Brent Parks Ranger Service supported by the local Agenda 21 team.

Contact Tav Kazmi LA21 Team,
LB Brent, 3rd Floor, Brent House,
349 High Road, Wembley Middx HA9 6BZ
Tel 020 8937 5316 Fax 020 8937 5310
email tav.kazmi@brent.gov.uk

Mediation

The trend towards participatory democracy is part of a wider movement away from top-down decision-making. We have seen it in the growth of ethical investment, where shareholders want a say in how their money is used, we see it in a revival of the cooperative movement where workers become part-owners of a business, we see it in the new management style in the business world where directors have a more facilitating and less managerial role. A closely related trend is happening in the world of dispute resolution. Ian Haywood has provided the following text — another already well-trodden pathway to the future.

Mediation is a process of bringing together parties who are in dispute so that they can mutually resolve their differences. It is based on a belief that decisions which are jointly arrived at, *and therefore jointly owned, are likely to be better and more just decisions than those which are imposed by an external body.*

Mediation forms part of a larger process known as Alternative Dispute Resolution (ADR) where an independent person is brought in to help untangle the issues and help the parties find a way forward. There are five types of ADR and the differences between them are largely attributed to the degree of intervention the independent person or 'facilitator' has in the process. They can be characterised as:

◆ **Conciliation:** the facilitator actively guides parties toward a settlement which the mediator has identified as likely to produce agreement.
◆ **Adjudication:** the involved parties appoint a facilitator to determine the issue.
◆ **Early neutral evaluation:** the facilitator undertakes an expert review of the case and provides an assessment of what the outcome would be if it went through dispute resolution.
◆ **Structured facilitation:** the facilitator negotiates between a number of parties to reduce or resolve the range of disputed issues.
◆ **Mediation:** the facilitator encourages and stimulates the parties to come up with their own solutions to settling the dispute.

Any ADR decision may or may not be binding, depending upon how it is set up, but mediation is seen as being a win-win situation in that involvement is voluntary and decisions are not imposed but arrived at through an agreed settlement.

Pressures to adopt mediation in the UK

Mediation has been a feature of civil law cases in the USA since the 1960s and is familiar in the United Kingdom through the ACAS processes, which have been in operation for over 20 years. Mediation has been a part of the land use planning system in New South Wales since 1991.

But the real impetus for change in the UK came from the 1996 Woolf report which recommended improving the efficiency, efficacy and speed of the civil justice system by considering the adoption of alternative dispute resolution into the civil justice system. The immediate objective was to see if cases could be settled out of court and thus reduce costs, delays and the risk of one party being penalised through the imposition of a court decision.

Further pressure for local government to consider mediation as part of a more open system of decision making has come from central government in a wide range of consultation papers and advice including recent innovations such as Best Value, Beacon authorities and the need to gain Charter Mark status.

Mediation in the planning process

As part of central government's general concern for improved and more open decision making in the planning system, the then Department of the Environment issued a consultation paper 'Planning Appeals' in 1997 which included an invitation to comment on the possibility of mediation being introduced into the planning system. As a result of the responses to this consultation paper the Department of the Environment, Transport and the Regions and the Planning Inspectorate have commissioned a study to establish the viability of introducing mediation into the planning process in order to speed up decision making, and reduce the pressure on public funds and the number of disputes which might otherwise go to appeal.

London and the Internet

There is a danger that the new GLA leaders might assume that the place for ordinary people to be involved is at the local level, that they are not capable of contributing at the 'strategic' level, leaving the floor to big business and the policy community elite to influence the Mayor. Nothing could be further from the truth than that assumption or more dangerous than that result. This topic is taken forward in chapters 6 and 8. Here we look at some of the possibilities offered by the Internet.

The Internet – a new space for meeting new challenges

"The internet is a manifestation of the information age and is the escape from traditional forms of control of information. A

breakthrough has occurred and a space has been created which is uncontrollable, unlimited and where information can manifest, where we can operate in many different paradigms in parallel." Bernard Lietaer[46].

I do not think that we have yet really woken up to the potential implications of the Internet for the development of democracy. I believe that in due course many other ways will be developed for using the Internet for public involvement in strategic decision-making and London's response to the challenges of the 21st Century generally.

Audience participation

850 of 4000 residents of the Woodlands near Houston subscribe to its cable TV system. Home viewers can register their reaction to programmes through their channel selector. For example, before a community meeting is televised, they are told that channel 2 means 'approve', 4 means 'disapprove', 6 means 'talk faster, provide less detail'. The audience response is shown every 5 – 10 minutes on a screen at the meeting itself.

Direct Democracy

Keith Patton, who has been largely responsible for creating the London 21 Sustainability Network web site has provided the following text on the subject of 'Direct Democracy':

> *"...who can be the general of a mass so excessively large?"* (Aristotle [47])

We currently elect leaders who are then expected to take all the decisions for us until the next election some years in the future. This is democratic because we have some say in who governs us, and representative because we vote for those whom we think will best represent us. However today's electors are much more opinionated and informed than they have ever been. We question our politicians more and more, and yet we vote less.

Perhaps we can do things better than this ?

> *"With direct democracy, voter apathy will vanish. People participating in their future will take place. Direct Democracy is inevitable".*
> http://www.realdemocracy.com — Direct Democracy Center (US)

It is argued here that apathy is mainly resultant from a failure of the modern political process in the UK in particular to include and involve the people adequately. Introduction of Direct Democracy will stimulate community involvement in local politics in London for example and allow a new generation to experience truly engaged citizenship for the first time.

Direct Democracy initiatives include increasing the use of referenda on all issues that affect the electorate. They would be initiated both by currently elected representatives and by the community. The main advantages of such a system are that it is inherently more democratic and more efficient and allows voters to focus on specific issues rather than on a party with whom they are unlikely to agree with on even the majority of issues.

For example, Switzerland held a referendum on the legalisation of drugs in February 1999 (the vote was 3 to 1 against). There are many issues that could be put up for vote without the need for lobbying and the parliamentary to-ing and fro-ing surrounding many important social and environmental issues.

The tools for Direct Democracy

With advances in communications technology, there is now the possibility that we can allow more direct forms of democracy using the Internet via PCs and AVM's (Automated Voting Machines).

There are two main arguments against using the Internet for voting. The first is an argument which says that not everyone has the Internet or access to adequate technology and therefore such a system would not work. It is suggested that people may (if they have access) use the Internet/Web TV at home to vote, although there should be initial investment to establish AVMs in public places, such as petrol stations, supermarkets, post offices etc. Vote results would be available almost instantaneously after votes are cast.

The second argument is of security. With stories of viruses and hackers frequently in the news, the consequences of security breaches in voting systems raise serious issues. Overcoming security concerns will perhaps be the biggest hurdle that implementation of direct democracy using electronic systems has to face. Ensuring that systems are secure and stable will be an issue for business and government to ensure and there should be wide and ongoing publicity to build public trust of a revolutionary approach to voting in the 21st century. If financial transactions can be made secure using ATMs (Automated Transaction Machines) and online banking, then given the political and public will, the same future should be available for secure online voting systems.

Conclusions

It is suggested that the implementation of direct democracy using modern communications technology is a desirable and achievable objective for the UK and in particular for London. There are hurdles, mainly issues of access, investment and security, but these can and should be overcome[48].

Boroughs and neighbourhoods

The present London boroughs were formed in 1965 by combining groups of the old much smaller Metropolitan Boroughs. Their big handicap is that they are too large. They have not succeeded in winning the respect, trust and cooperation of Londoners. Their size has created difficulties for officers, many of whom have never even visited parts of the borough and who cannot hope to develop working relationships with more than a handful of the inhabitants and businesses. It has made the task of elected members equally difficult: their wards are too large for them to know most of their electors; and their responsibilities are often, with all due respect, beyond their capabilities. It is almost impossible for local people to regard the council as anything but the 'them' in an unhappy 'them and us' relationship.

In addition to their actual size, these London boroughs suffer, to a greater or lesser extent, from the fact that each of them is a slice of a much larger cake. Many of them do not have a clear centre to which its parts relate.

As a result, the state of democracy in many, if not all, boroughs is highly unsatisfactory. Electoral turnout is low. There is little incentive for members of the public to participate in any way. The level of apathy is high.

> ### Vision-led and neighbourhood based
>
> Nicky Gavron, Haringey Councillor and Chair of LPAC, is a leading exponent of a vision-led, neighbourhood based democracy. "I believe we need neighbourhood plans ... In terms of the GLA, iterative (bottom-up) is the nature of its proposed spatial development strategy and decisions will be made at the most appropriate (lowest) level with only a limited number of applications being referred to the Mayor. The introduction of a neighbourhood tier of plans would mean a simplification of the unitary [borough] level. Detailed proposals would be dealt with at the neighbourhood level and the UDP would concentrate on principles and criteria.... Neighbourhood plans should be holistic in scope and prepared with the participation of local communities, businesses and voluntary organisations".

These are not promising frameworks for the development of community involvement.

Community Assemblies for London

The London Community Alliance[49] proposes that each London borough might contain some fifteen community assemblies, each with around twenty members. The Alliance's manifesto explains what the assemblies would do:

Every local community could have its own public meeting place, supporting and facilitating local voluntary initiatives. Members of the community assembly could deal with planning applications, with appeals to the new Greater London Authority. Street cleaning and refuse collection could become a local responsibility. Agenda 21 could become a truly local responsibility. Local communities could be given a special say in the introduction of local traffic management measures.

This would bring into public life in London some 14,000 new elected councillors, each representing about 500 residents.

Does not this look like a promising pathway ? It is a pathway primarily for the extension of representative government; but it could easily be combined with the use of participatory processes by the new community councils.

Chapter 4
Notes and References

1. See *Gathering Force, DIY Culture, Radical Action for Those Tired of Waiting* by Elaine Brass and Sophie Poklevski Koziell, Big Issue 1997.

2. The Land is Ours has an office in Oxford. Its new magazine will look at international land rights issues, inviting discussion and encouraging networking amongst different groups worldwide.

3. Chris Brazier in *The New Internationalist* Jan/Feb 1999.

4. *The Rambler,* Winter 1999.

5. Article in *Urban Environment Today* 7 January 1999 by Miffa Salter, a member of Lord Rogers's Urban Task Force Secretariat and Senior Consultant at the Office of Public Management. And see the Social Exclusion Unit's report *Bringing Britain Together: a national strategy for neighbourhood renewal* Cm 4045, London: HMSO. The Prime Minister's introduction included these words "... experience shows that success depends on communities themselves having the power and taking the responsibility to make things better". See also Hilary Armstrong, Minister of Local Government & Regions's article "Dealing with Social Exclusion" in New Ground Winter 1999/2000.

6. Government white paper *Modern Government: In Touch with the People* and Hilary Armstrong's Foreword to *Community Governance, community leadership and the new local government* by Michael Clarke and John Stewart, 1998, Rowntree Foundation.

7. *Community Governance* (see previous note): very useful background reading for anyone following the current Government programme for reform of local government.

8. *Community Governance* (see note 6)

9. See article by Lynn Wetenhall in *EG* September 1999 Integrating Community Planning and Local Agenda 21: what's in a name ?

10. LVSC paper *London Health Strategy.*

11. Greater London Authority Act 1999 ss 334 – 344. This is rather different from a development plan for London: it provides a spatial development setting for the Mayor's other strategies: see *London Calling! Summer 1999* the Royal Town Planning Institute London Branch, reporting the conference with Vision for London held on 26 May 1999.

12. *Planning for Greater London, a Guide to LPAC's Strategic Policies* LPAC Ref ADV44.

13. Guidance *Planning for Sustainable Development Towards Better Practice* DETR October 1998.

14. *Our Common Future* (the Brundtland Report) – Report of the 1987 World Commission on Environment and Development. OUP 1987. p 8. Stephen Wheeler in his introduction to the chapter on *Planning Sustainable and Livable Cities* in the *City Reader* Second Ed suggests that the best approach is a relatively simple process-oriented definition emphasising long-term systemic welfare: "sustainable development is development that improves the long-term health of human and ecological systems".

15. Our Common Future p 9.

16. Our Common Future p ix.

17. Our Common Future p xiv.

18. For the text of the Rio Declaration and an abridged version of Agenda 21 see *Earth Summit 1992* Regency Press.

19. See chapters 1 and 2 ante, and see *Report on Earth Summit II, The UN General Assembly Special Session to review outcomes from the Rio Summit,* UNED-UK 1997.

20. In the *Growth Illusion* at p 303 Richard Douthwaite points out that the Brundtland definition of sustainable development is economic growth that has somehow been made more equitable and environmentally careful. "However, as growth itself is not sustainable, the concept is a dangerous contradiction in terms".

21. *A Better Quality of Life A strategy for sustainable development for the United Kingdom* DETR May 1999, available from the Stationery Office.

22. ibid p 8.

23. ibid p 25.

24. ibid p 26.

25. *a Better Quality of Life* chapter 7, p 50.

26. *a Better Quality of Life* p 90.

27. Sustain*ability – turning sustainable development into practical action in our communities* Environ 1996 p 4.

28. LGMB survey reported by Jane Morris in EG April 1999.

29. WIs – Pathways to the 21st Century LGMB LA21 Case Study 4.

30. See article Learning Community Learning – 2030 by Shirley Ali Khan LGMB local visions.

31. There are many exceptions including some in London, for example Southwark and Sutton, to take one inner and one outer London borough. Outside London, Bradford and Leicester have made strong use of LA21 in contrasting ways. IRIC (Environment and Resource Information Centre), University of Westminster is working with the IDA (Improvement and Development Agency, formerly Local Government Management Board), the DETR (Department of Environment, Transport and the Regions) and the LGA (Local Government Association) and Forum for the Future to develop a process of evaluation.

32. Ian Christie, writing in EG October 1999.

33. See The Future of Local Agenda 21 by J Gary Lawrence UNED Millennium Papers Issue 2 in which he explains why planning professional feel threatened by LA21. See also article by Timothy O'Riordan The Environmentalist 15, 233at p 238 (1995) for another view on what is lacking to enable LA21 to flourish.

34. See Habitat, August/September 1999 the Environment Council.

35. European sustainable cities Report by the Expert Group on the Urban Environment EU March 1996. Passages quoted from pp 96, 7. See also A review of urban sustainability ed. David Cadman, School of Public Policy and Jackson Environment Institute.

36. See eg The Politics of the Real World Michael Jacobs, Earthscan, supported by 30 of the UK's leading voluntary and campaigning organisations.

37. See note 21.

38. See chapter 28 of Agenda 21 and GLA Act 1999 s 30 (5) which expressly provides for the GLA to contribute "in the way it [ie the GLA] considers best calculated to contribute to the achievement of sustainable development in the UK".

39. See A better quality of life, p. 3.

40. Another is Adjusted National Product which starts from GNP, then adds and subtracts for various factors: the concept is discussed in detail by Christian Leipert in The Living Economy by Paul Ekins, New Economics Foundation 1986.

41. A Better Quality of Life para 3.2. See also "Planning for Sustainable development" DETR para 6.3.3.

42. A Better Quality of Life p 36.

43. The British Government Panel on Sustainable Development, in its Fifth Report dated February 1999 informed the Prime Minister: "Whilst welcoming the Government's consultation paper on targets and indicators, the Panel is doubtful of the value of GNP/GDP as measures or indicators of sustainable development". The Panel advised that "Work on new, alternative measures for sustainable development, including a better and more comprehensive definition of economic growth, should be initiated as a matter of urgency".

44. State of the Environment: Report for London, 1995 LPAC.

45. See Sustainability Indicators Research Project LBMB 1995 describing pilot projects one of which was in LB of Merton. And see Sustainable local communities for the 21st Century, LGA, LGMB, DETR, para 4.7 stressing that the local community should be involved in selecting the indicators. This is easier said than done in the current climate: see Public Perceptions and Sustainability in Lancashire Lancaster University Centre for the Study of Environmental Change March 1995 which stresses the difficulty created by the public's "pronounced degree of fatalism and even cynicism towards the country's public institutions, including national and local government". And see the article by Yvonne Rydin and Florian Sommer in EG Nov/Dec 1999, describing practical difficulties in the LB Southwark, and which also lists other useful publications including Communities Count (1998) New Economics Foundation, NEF London.

46. Bernard Lietaer, designer of the ECU and lecturer on money and sustainability, writing in Living Lightly: Bernard Lietaer can be contacted on blietaer@earthlink.net/money

47. Aristotle: Politics 1326b3-7.

48. For more information on direct democracy and examples of its implementation in Europe and the USA see the following sites:
http://www.directdemocracy.com
    National Voter Outreach (US)
http://www.realdemocracy.com
    Direct Democracy Center (US)
http://www.polemic.net/nzeet.html
    New Zealand Electronic Electoral Trial.

49. Legislation will be required to realise the London Community Alliance's proposals and it was sad that the Government did not think fit to take advantage of the opportunity offered by the Greater London Authority Bill for this purpose. The LCA has a lot more information available and may be contacted at 18 Victoria Square, E2 9PF.

Pathways to the future

New Democracy for London

Whilst it is obvious that the agenda contemplated in part 1 of this book involves major change – reform of the way we live and work, reform of the economy, reform of the political system – 'transformation' might be more apt – this should not deter London: this city is well used to change, having experienced many radical changes over the last 1000 years.

London has negotiated them all with remarkably little conflict. This capacity for change will be a critical strength in the years to come.

To meet the challenges presented by the current situation, London will need to be innovative in the way it thinks about itself. The metaphor which comes to mind is that of human self-consciousness. London has in some way to learn to be conscious of itself, to see the whole organism and its relationships. Something as radical as that has to happen for London to have the motivation for radical change.

If London is to be capable of tackling the issues outlined in this book, and others that may emerge, something more is needed than the mere extension to London of the system of elected representatives and top-down management that has failed us at both the national and local levels. For London to have the capacity to take a lead in changing the economic systems that currently dominate our world, changes that are necessary in order to reverse the trends we have identified, all sectors of society and the economy will have to be fully engaged in the decision-making processes.

For changes on this scale and of such a fundamental nature to be brought about voluntarily, efficiently and step by step, in a peaceful and orderly way, requires a politics of a new kind.

Politics of a new kind

The purpose of part 2 is to suggest what this new kind of politics might look like. What sort of politics do we need, in order to develop societies that honour our sense of justice, and to develop economic systems that enable us to live in harmony with the rest of nature?

Parliament has just produced a 476-page Act, the Greater London Authority Act 1999 which runs to 425 sections and 33 schedules (and of course it has no index!), the second longest single piece of legislation ever produced in this country, exceeded only by the Government of India Act 1934. Does this contain the answer? Probably not the whole answer, because Parliament did not start by defining the question in the way we are suggesting!

Credit must be given for what the Act does achieve:

◆ It restores directly elected government to London, thus greatly encouraging Londoners to take an interest in the affairs of their city.

◆ It puts in place a London-wide level of government, essential for tackling some issues such as transport, and undoubtedly providing a forum for addressing other London-wide issues, even if some services, such as education, are not the direct responsibility of the new Authority.

◆ The Act also calls for a far higher degree of integration between some, at least, of London's public services, with tough obligations applying across all these services, in particular as to 'sustainable development', the health of Londoners and equal opportunities.

Where the legislation is weak is in providing opportunities for public participation, the "by the people" part of Lincoln's famous definition. The stated intention of the legislation was more promising: it was "to create a new style of politics for our capital city, more inclusive, less confrontational and focusing on the issues that matter…" and to "meet the demands of Londoners for a real say in the affairs of their city, how it is run and who it is run by".[1] The provisions of the Act are outlined in chapter 5. There is little in the Act itself to achieve the aims of a more inclusive, less confrontational style of politics, or of enabling Londoners to decide how London is run.

I believe however that the Act has created a huge space ready to accommodate the additional, complementary processes that are necessary to enable all stakeholders to join in defining London's problems and opportunities, and in creating the pathways to the future. The Mayor has been directed to get many things done, but, apart from being provided with a few officers and the Assembly to scrutinise the Mayor's actions, the Mayor has in effect been given a wide discretion as to how London government is conducted.

To occupy this space effectively, it will not do for the Mayor to follow the lead given by officials and experts, do deals with big business and attend meetings with central government, whilst incidentally engaging with Londoners in some exercises in 'tokenism', to use Sherry Arnstein's justly emotive term. A new kind of democratic paradigm is called for. Chapter 6 is an attempt to describe how this differs from the current model.

The leadership role of the Mayor.

This is vital. We have seen in chapter 4 that participation techniques have been developed and that there is a pool of knowledge, skills and experience available, but that the political support, **without which these practices are meaningless**, has generally been lacking. The big question for the future of London will be the priority the Mayor and Assembly give to promoting and resourcing community/stake-holder participation on the scale needed to meet the formidable challenges.

Partners for London Vision, described in chapter 8, have been considering how the new style of participatory, inclusive governance can be introduced on a London-wide scale. The Mayor is required by the new Act to prepare various strategies for London's future. Partners for London Vision have been considering how all Londoners could be given the opportunity to take part, jointly with the Mayor and other leaders, in creating an inspiring vision of the future of the city which can be incorporated into the various strategies proposed by the Act and new forms of partnership. This initiative arose out of an experimental series of meetings run by the Sustainable London Trust described in chapter 7.

The restoration of directly elected London-wide government offers London a unique opportunity to push forward the agenda of participatory democracy at all levels of government and throughout the whole economic and social system. It's London's chance to leapfrog from having no city-wide democracy at all, and only very unsatisfactory systems at borough and corporate levels, to being the most democratic city in the world.

> The role of the Mayor and Assembly will be to lead – to lead us
>
> in making the new pathways the making of which will change us and our destination

References

1. See the Deputy Prime Minister's foreword to the Green Paper *New Leadership for London* introducing the proposals.

A little history

The Greater London Council (GLC), formed in 1965, was abolished in 1986 as a result of bitter disputes with central government. It had an awkward mixture of functions – education, strategic planning, housing, main roads, refuse disposal, fire, ambulance, transport. There were also difficulties in defining the boundary between its functions and those of the boroughs. It is claimed that towards the end of its life the GLC was in advance of its times in assisting people to devise their own solutions.[1]

Since the abolition of the GLC in 1986 London has been without a government of its own. Even so, in many ways, it has continued to flourish. People still love to live and work here.

On dissolution of the GLC its functions were scattered in various directions. Some were given to the 32 boroughs or the Corporation of London (the local authority for the City of London), some were taken over by Whitehall. There were various quangos and certain bodies run by the Boroughs, including the London Planning Advisory Committee (LPAC), the London Research Centre (LRC) and the London Ecology Unit (LEU) each of which continued to perform vital London-wide functions. Later a number of new bodies were established in an attempt to coordinate certain policy areas: the Government Office for London (GOL) brought together some of Whitehall's responsibilities and the Association of London Government (ALG) was formed by the Boroughs, though without any statutory powers of its own.

The result was that very few people, if any, really understood how London was governed. Also, Londoners wanted their own government. The inadequacies of the system and popular demand led New Labour's election manifesto to propose "a new deal for London, with a strategic authority ... to take responsibility for London-wide issues, economic regeneration, planning, policing, transport and environmental protection". A green paper *New Leadership for London* was followed by a white paper *A Mayor and Assembly for London*. The Greater London Authority Bill passed through Parliament and became the Greater London Authority Act 1999.

The Mayor and Assembly

The structure, powers
and duties of the new
Greater London Authority (GLA)

The GLA: structure

On 4th May 2000 Londoners will launch an extraordinary experiment in city governance by electing a Mayor and an Assembly of 25 members. This novel set-up gives whoever is elected as Mayor a unique opportunity to engage Londoners in taking part in creating London's future.

Let us look at the main provisions of the legislation setting up the new authority, to see how the Mayor could do this.

The Mayor and the Assembly

Labour has been keen to avoid being seen as 'bringing back the GLC', and so the new GLA will look very different. Instead of the standard local government and Parliamentary system in which there is an administration which depends on getting the support of a majority in the council or in the Commons, the new Authority will consist of the 'Mayor of London' and the 'London Assembly', together called 'the Greater London Authority' (GLA). The Mayor will be elected completely separately from the Assembly Members. This means that the Mayor won't need the support of a majority in the London Assembly to get his or her policies through: the Mayor will be able to go ahead on the basis of being directly elected. Even if one party has an absolute majority of Assembly Members, it is easily possible for the Mayor to be from a different political party. In the event of conflict between Mayor and Assembly, it is basically the Mayor who will have the power and whose wishes will prevail.

The elections

The Mayor will be elected every four years using the Supplementary Vote System (SV) under

The London Study

This study, led by the Association of London Government, was carried out in 1998 in anticipation of the introduction of a new London-wide authority. The conclusions of the study formed the basis of the first draft of the Mayor's strategy for the London Development Agency (see ante p 55).

which a voter has two votes: if no candidate wins more than half the first choice votes, the two leading candidates go through to the next count, when the second choices of the other candidates are added and whoever then has the most votes becomes Mayor.

The 25 Assembly members are also elected every four years. 14 will represent large constituencies consisting of two or more boroughs each, using the first-past-the-post system, the other 11 being drawn from London-wide lists provided by political parties[2], these seats being allocated between the parties in proportion to the votes cast for each party, subject to a 5% threshold.

This electoral system is likely to have two main consequences: it will be difficult for any party to gain an overall majority in the Assembly because it is difficult for any party to achieve over 50% of the votes of Londoners, and it will be much easier for a small party like the Green Party to get candidates elected than it would be under a first-past-the-post system of constituency seats with no 'top ups'.

The Mayor and Assembly members will take up office on 3 July 2000.

The Mayor's position

The Mayor does not have an entirely free hand to do whatever he or she likes. The 32 London boroughs and the Corporation of London remain in being and their functions remain the same – for example, they include education, over which the GLA has no direct powers; and they have numerous functions, such as planning and local transport, where they will have to cooperate closely with the Mayor. The powers given to the new Authority – primarily to the Mayor – are mainly powers which have been exercised by central government during the inter-regnum since the demise of the Greater London Council in 1986. Central government retains many functions and massive power: the Government Office for London (GOL) will accompany London on its journey into the future, albeit carrying a lighter briefcase.

The Mayor's functions

The Mayor will have functions of two distinct types:

The Mayor's Functions

The Mayor	
LEADERSHIP FUNCTIONS	**SERVICE PROVISION** (via separate 'functional bodies')
Planning for the future	Transport for London (TfL)
Mayor's Strategies	London Development Agency (LDA)
Co-ordinating actions	Metropolitan Police Authority
Appointing to key bodies	London Fire and Emergency Planning Authority[4]
Representing London	

Transport for London (TfL) will
- manage the Underground, buses, Croydon Tramlink & Docklands Light Railway. The Mayor will thus have a say over fares, commuter railways, new services and ticket systems.
- manage important roads – the 'GLA road network'
- regulate taxis and minicabs
- run London River Services
- help co-ordinate Dial-a-Ride and Taxicard schemes for people with mobility problems
- have responsibility for traffic lights
- prepare London's Local Transport Plan – Boroughs will prepare implementation plans

London Development Agency (LDA) will
- prepare London's economic development and regeneration strategy
- promote London's competitiveness, market London as business centre, and coordinate inward investment, facilitate investment in projects as part of Public-Private Partnerships, advise Government on regional grants
- tackle problems of deprived areas, reclaim and prepare sites for economic development
- improve skills base, promote innovation, promote technology transfer, work with business links to improve support and advice to small businesses

Metropolitan Police Authority
- Annual policing plan after consulting local communities
- Setting targets and reporting progress

London Fire and Emergency Planning Authority
- Fire Brigade and assist boroughs with emergency planning

The total budget for the services over which the Mayor will have control is currently about £3.3 billion per annum. The GLA itself will cost an estimated £20 million for administration, mostly provided by central government but topped by an addition to council tax. Government literature states that for a Band D council tax bill, for example, this will amount to about three pence a week. "This contribution", it says, "will give Londoners a direct financial interest in the efficiency of the GLA"! What world are these people living in ?![3]

The Mayor's Cabinet and Office

The Mayor is allowed to appoint two political advisers and may have a cabinet. The Mayor is allowed to appoint 10 members of staff.

The GLA Staff

Three bodies with a London-wide brief will be absorbed into the GLA

◆ London Planning Advisory Committee(LPAC)
◆ London Research Centre (LRC)
◆ London Ecology Unit (LEU).

As we go to press staff from these three organisations, together with those working for the Greater London Authority Transition Team, have started working together on all eight of the Mayor's Strategies (see post). An officers working group called the GLA Sustainable Development Forum has been formed to bring together prospective GLA staff and staff from the four functional bodies and other agencies in relation to 'sustainable development'. I have always wondered whether I would live to see 'joined-up government' actually happening: at officer level I believe this is it!

The Assembly

The 25 Assembly Members will have significant influence. They will be like backbench MPs in Parliament. They will be able to investigate the Mayor's strategies and decisions, conduct inquiries into issues which concern them or which they believe concern the public in London, try to get publicity and support for the conclusions of their inquiries, and thereby put pressure on the Mayor to go in the direction the Assembly wants. In some cases, this will be a matter of convincing the Mayor that he or she will become unpopular if they don't adopt the Assembly's policies.

It will be interesting to see what role the Assembly manages to play.

◆ The Assembly's committees will need to get themselves out and about in London to conduct real investigations, rather than wait for written papers to be sent to them. They will need to seek out a wide range of views, not just those of large well-connected and well-funded organisations. There will be two early tests of this: whether the Assembly's committees employ staff with responsibility for 'outreach' work of this sort, and whether the Assembly draws up a firm set of rules to control the activities of lobbying companies.

◆ Another key early test for the sustainability agenda will be the appointment of members to the board of the London Development Agency: will it represent simply business interests, or a wider range of concerns and experience ? And in the longer term, will the Assembly be successful in holding to account the four functional bodies, especially the LDA and TfL ?

How can a mere 25 people possibly represent the vast diversity of London's communities ? Some may be well represented, others not at all.

The GLA: purposes, duties and strategies

The Act gives the GLA three 'purposes', which are quite flexible, and imposes on it three duties, which are likely to be much more significant. It then requires the Mayor to prepare eight 'strategies', which are capable of becoming the focus for wide participation in policy making and implementation. Together these provisions offer a framework for the new kind of politics advocated in this book.

'principal purposes'

The GLA is given power "to do anything" to further any of the principal purposes of the new Authority. These are to promote

a) *economic development and wealth creation in Greater London*

b) *social development in Greater London*

c) *the improvement of the environment in Greater London.*[5]

Comments on the purposes

As to a), note that the Act says "economic development", not "economic growth". Everything suggested in chapter 3 is well within the concept of 'economic development'. Moreover 'wealth creation' must include all those many forms of 'wealth' that do not consist only of money.

As to b), "social development" is a useful phase, leaving the Authority with a good deal of scope as to what kinds of social development it seeks to promote. It could well (and, I say, should) make greater equality a goal of social development.

As to c), it is good to see a positive emphasis on improving the environment, as opposed to merely protecting it. Whilst it is a pity that the environment referred to here is confined to the area of Greater London, this may not matter too much, because, as London's economic and social development is so dependent on the health of the global environment, policies that have regard to wider environmental impacts will be legitimate under (a) and (b).

The 'balance' fallacy

True to conventional, but misguided, thinking, the Authority is required to have regard to the desirability of securing "over a period of time, a reasonable balance between furthering each of its principal objects".[6] The idea that the three purposes are somehow separate and that one could place each in the scales and balance them up is really a nonsense. It is misleading because it obscures the true relationships between people, their activities and the Earth. The whole-systems approach advocated in this book requires all strategies, policies and projects to treat social, economic and environmental issues not as competing, but as inter-linked design elements; and the kinds of economic development this approach would favour (some of which were mentioned in chapters 1-3), are good from all three angles.

Purposes or just a framework ?

In laying down the principal 'purposes' of the Authority, Parliament may have been trying to tell the Mayor what he or she should try to achieve. But the co-called purposes are really little more than subject categories. It is clearly left to the Mayor to decide what to do in the specified fields of economic and social development and environmental improvement. The Mayor will be free to formulate objectives in all three fields. As these categories are so wide, the Mayor, and indeed the Assembly, will not in practice be prevented from getting involved in any issue they consider to be of importance to the future of London.

Devolution, 'but...'

The Mayor's power "to do anything" to further any of the 'principal purposes' is carefully circumscribed. In addition to detailed provisions to avoid duplication of powers already belonging to other public bodies, and forbidding the Authority to provide housing or education, social or health services, the Secretary of State is given power

a) to issue 'guidance' to which the Mayor must have regard[7] (but not necessarily follow!) and

b) to make orders preventing the Authority from doing "anything … specified in the order" or imposing spending limits.

Parliament, although embracing devolution (graciously granting London what should be London's right anyway) and going to all the trouble of producing one of the longest ever Acts to give back directly elected government to London, has evidently still not quite learned how to 'let go'! One wonders if Parliament has broken the addiction to centralisation acquired during the Thatcher years[8]. However the "power to do anything", even when so severely restricted, has a symbolic and psychological importance: it bolsters the idea of the community governing itself[9].

The GLA's extra, overarching duties

In exercising its powers the GLA is required to promote or have regard to the health of Londoners, the achievement sustainable development in the UK and equality of opportunity for all people.[10]

Comments on the duties

◆ **'health':** the GLA is not the Health Authority for London, but the Act recognises that the health of Londoners is largely determined by economic, social and environmental factors. There is no requirement for the Mayor to have a strategy on health but London needs one. A group of organisations led by the NHS Executive London Regional Office is already preparing one – the London Health Strategy. LVSC is pressing for a commitment to 'community involvement' to be written into the strategy[11].

◆ **'sustainable development in the UK'.** The direction for the GLA to promote sustainable development in the UK is possibly the most powerful and useful thing in the whole new set-up. This provision catapults London into the forefront of thinking in terms of sustainability and integrated policy making. Comparable cities around Europe generally limit their activity in this regard to the development of a Local Agenda 21 process. London is probably the first European or indeed world city to submit all the work of its government to the sustainable development test, yet this is what the GLA will be doing. From being notably absent from the European discourse on urban sustainability policy, London will find itself in the vanguard of thinking.

◆ The reference to sustainable development in the UK evidently refers to the UK Strategy for Sustainable Development, the current version of which is *A better Quality of Life.*[12]

◆ **'equal opportunities'** this important provision is buttressed by a duty to publish an annual equal opps. report.[13]

The Mayor and Assembly

The Mayor's strategies

The Mayor is required to have the following strategies

◆ *an integrated transport strategy*
◆ *a strategy for the London Development Agency*
◆ *a biodiversity action plan*
◆ *a municipal waste management strategy*
◆ *an air quality strategy*
◆ *an ambient noise strategy*
◆ *a spatial development strategy*
◆ *a culture strategy.*[14]

There is no requirement for the Mayor to have an energy strategy, but London clearly needs one to work out how to curb global warming emissions. The omission is another sign of the 'problem-solving' approach behind this Act: most of the subjects listed are 'problems' calling for a strategy to solve them. Only when oil prices go through the roof will we need an energy strategy!

Comments on the strategies

1 **All "available" policies and proposals to be considered**

After specifying various matters to which the Mayor must have regard in preparing or revising all the strategies[15] all of which are pretty obvious (further evidence of a reluctance to "let go"?), there is an interesting provision imposing on the Mayor a positive duty to include in any strategy "such of the available policies and proposals relating to the subject matter of the strategy as he considers best calculated to promote improvements in the health of Londoners and contribute towards sustainable development in the UK".[16]

This looks like an invitation, whether or not intended, to non-governmental organisations to make policies and proposals "available" for consideration by the Mayor.

2. **Targets and Indicators.**

The Mayor must set targets for measuring implementation of the strategies, having regard to any targets set nationally and any performance indicators set by the Secretary of State[17]. The LPAC indicators referred to on page 73 will provide a starting point.

3. **Preparation of the strategies.**

There are special provisions as to how the various strategies are to be prepared.[18]

4. **Consistency between the strategies.**

The strategies must all be consistent with each other[19]. This is a serious attempt to facilitate joined-up government: it "is both novel and challenging. It offers a real opportunity to break down the compartmentalisation of functions which has for so long been a barrier to sustainable development within many local authorities".[20] However the Act does not explain how it can be achieved. The GLA Sustainable Development Forum mentioned above is a response to this challenge at officer level. The Partners for London Vision project described in chapter 8 is designed to enable the general public to take part in creating a unifying vision.

5. **A 'whole systems' approach**

Although the Act does not say so in terms, it is vital that all the strategies should adopt a 'whole systems' approach: they should not be confined to the particular powers of the Mayor, but should be strategies for London as a whole. This follows necessarily from the GLA's strategic function and the Mayor's leadership role. From it follows the absolute necessity for all relevant stakeholders to be fully involved from the outset in preparing the strategies.

The Spatial Development Strategy

This is more than a land use strategy for London. It is a new concept originating in the EU (the European Spatial Development Perspective) which, in addition to the more traditional function of providing the general policies for the development and use of land which the boroughs will have to follow in their UDPs, is meant to provide the spatial development setting for the Mayor's other policies, such as transport.[21] This seems to give it a degree of precedence over the other strategies. The officers preparing the first draft intend to have this ready by the end of 2000.

The GLA: consultation and accountability

Public Consultation

The mayor must consult "such bodies or persons as the Authority may consider appropriate in a particular case". The bodies which the Authority must consider consulting include

(a) voluntary bodies
(b) representatives of different racial, ethnic or national groups
(c) representatives of religious groups
(d) representatives of business.[22]

Comments on public consultation

1. **Arrangements for facilitating consultation.** There is a useful provision enabling the Mayor to make arrangements with any of the above or "such other bodies or persons as it may consider appropriate" for the purpose of facilitating consultation.[23] This would enable the Mayor to make such arrangements with, for example, the London 21 Sustainability Network (see p 71) for the purpose of facilitating consultation.

2. However these provisions refer only to 'consultation', not positive involvement of people in the voluntary, community or business sectors in the formulation of any policies or strategies: they do not get beyond the 'tokenism' rungs of Sherry Arnstein's ladder (see p 61). Moreover, in the case of the Mayor's strategies, the Mayor is specifically instructed to consult with the Assembly and functional bodies **before** consulting anyone else.[24] By the time the public is consulted, the strategies are likely to be well advanced and difficult to change.

Therefore, to ensure that the Mayor's strategies have the benefit of public involvement **in their preparation**, arrangements outside the provisions of the Act will need to be made. As to this see chapters 6 and 8.

The accountability of the Mayor

The scheme of the Act is to give the Mayor executive authority subject to various 'checks and balances':

◆ all the Mayor's actions will be closely 'scrutinised' by the Assembly through a monthly report and question time
◆ numerous organisations have to be 'consulted'
◆ targets have to be set and progress towards them measured by Indicators
◆ an annual public State of London debate
◆ a twice yearly People's Question Time.

In addition, the GLA, and also TfL and the LDA, will be subject to scrutiny by the Audit Commission.

The whole agenda of scrutiny by the Assembly, consultation and accountability in a way misses the point. All those things are part of the language and thinking of democracy-as-was. Whilst they still need to be in place, the new democracy is more about working with Londoners. A vital role of the Mayor will be to insist that the Mayor's own staff and those of the functional bodies, the boroughs and the central government agencies operating in London cooperate with and support business people and organisations in the voluntary and community sectors, making sure that they are involved from the start of any initiative, indeed that they can take the initiative.

The evolution of Democracy

In *Reinventing Democracy* [3] edited by Paul Hirst and Sunil Khilnani, Anthony Barnett's article The Creation of Democracy offers a fascinating insight into the nature and history of representative democracy. His conclusion that "One of the most extraordinary historical achievements of this form of government is the way it has transformed itself. Its elasticity, its capacity for some degree of 'openness', its adaptability ... " encourages the hope that it can now be transformed to adopt the disciplines of co-creation called for by the circumstances of the 21st century. Will London lead the way on this journey of discovery?

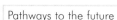

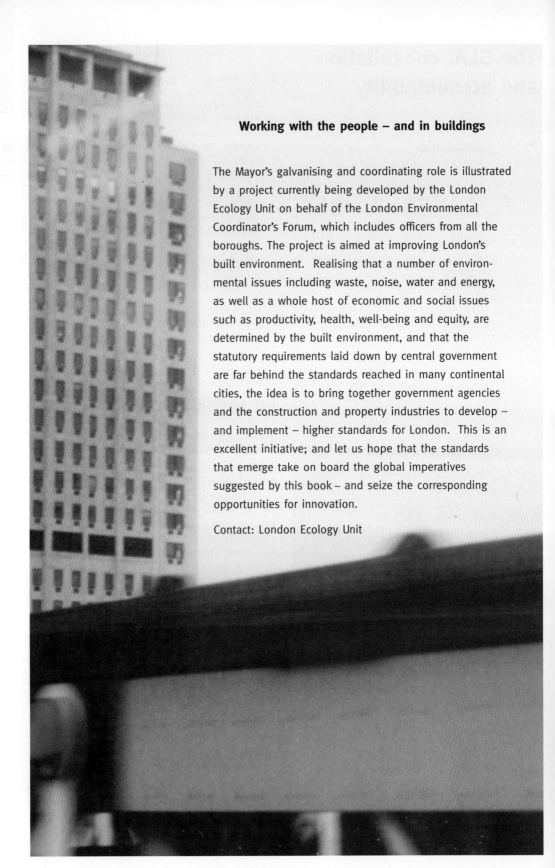

Working with the people – and in buildings

The Mayor's galvanising and coordinating role is illustrated by a project currently being developed by the London Ecology Unit on behalf of the London Environmental Coordinator's Forum, which includes officers from all the boroughs. The project is aimed at improving London's built environment. Realising that a number of environmental issues including waste, noise, water and energy, as well as a whole host of economic and social issues such as productivity, health, well-being and equity, are determined by the built environment, and that the statutory requirements laid down by central government are far behind the standards reached in many continental cities, the idea is to bring together government agencies and the construction and property industries to develop – and implement – higher standards for London. This is an excellent initiative; and let us hope that the standards that emerge take on board the global imperatives suggested by this book – and seize the corresponding opportunities for innovation.

Contact: London Ecology Unit

The London Civic Forum

The 'Third Sector'

The existing structures of the 'third sector' – London's innumerable and immensely diverse voluntary and community organisations, clubs and networks – have a vital part to play in making the pathways for London's future. In the past these have too often been left out of account by the tendency to see expansion of the private sector as the alternative to failing government services. They are too often treated by local authorities as inferior partners. These attitudes are now beginning to change. The potential of this sector as an instrument to deliver the changes London needs cannot be under-estimated.[25]

The creation of the GLA prompted the London Voluntary Sector Council (LVSC) to propose a complementary body to be known as The London Civic Forum. This will be established early in 2000 to bring together all the main participants in civil society in London – the private sector, faith communities, black and minority ethnic groups, educational establishments and the voluntary and community sectors.

The purpose of the Civic Forum is to enable London's civil society bodies to:

- scrutinise the strategic plans of the Greater London Authority and its agencies
- examine the GLA's budget proposals and their impact on London communities
- initiate its own research and develop policy ideas
- generate cross-sectoral solutions to London's problems
- ensure continuity between GLA policy and those who will implement it.

The Civic Forum will expand the limits of civic engagement by:

- establishing a London citizens panel/citizens juries
- assisting in setting up a London Youth Council to ensure direct consultation with young people
- exploring electronic means of involving Londoners and their organisations in dialogue about major issues
- working closely with Black Londoner's Forum.

Membership of the Forum will be open to any organisation in London. Once or twice a year there will be large plenary meetings, one of which will have an address from the Mayor. The Forum will be managed by a Council elected through electoral colleges of the membership. Most of the work will be carried out by open Working Parties whose conclusions will need to be endorsed by the Forum Council to become Forum policy.

The Forum is being established by a Development Team. The team sees the Civic Forum as performing a number of important functions:

- reviving democracy and promoting good governance in the capital
- balancing an inclusive social purpose with effective political action
- informing and educating citizens of the new structures of London government
- providing a civic-focused counter-balance to personality driven politics
- contributing experience, innovation and enterprise to government in the capital.

The launch date for the Forum is expected to be in March 2000.

The Development Team (John Griffiths) can be contacted at LVSC (see page 111).

Chapter 5
Notes and References

1. Sheila Rowbotham, co-editor of the newspaper of the GLC's Economic Policy Group, *Red Pepper* Dec 1999 / Jan 2000.

2. What a pity that the Government did not take this opportunity to ban party politics from London government. In Seattle, in addition to the elected mayor, there is a 9-member council not allowed to declare any political affiliation.

3. *Factsheets on Greater London Authority Bill* Factsheet 5 *Spending and Costs* DETR

4. A fifth quango will be set up with a role which is more to advise the Mayor than to implement the Mayor's policies. This is the Cultural Strategy Group for London, which seems likely to consist of the managers of the main arts and culture institutions in London – defined to include sport, libraries, and tourism.

5. GLA Act 1999 s.30 (1) and (2).

6. GLA Act 1999 s.30 (3) (b).

7. GLA Act 1999 s 31 (7) and (8).

8. See *Accountable to None – the Tory nationalisation of Britain* Simon Jenkins, 1995 Hamish Hamilton, London; and the Democracy and Local Government chapter by John Stewart in *Reinventing Democracy* 1996 Political Quarterly Publishing Co, Blackwell Publishers.

9. *Community Governance, community leadership and the new local government* Michael Clarke and John Stewart, Rowntree Foundation, describing the dominant European model of the local authority as the corporate manifestation of the local community (*collectivise locale*): "The power of general competence and the idea of the local authority as the community governing itself, albeit within the national framework of legislation, are interdependent".

10. GLA Act 1999 s 30 (4) and (5) which imposes on the GLA a duty when exercising its general powers to "do so in the way it considers best calculated (a) to promote improvements in the health of Londoners and (b) to contribute towards the achievement of sustainable development in the United Kingdom", s.33 and s 42 (4) and (7).

11. The LVSC input is coordinated by Jane Belman who is looking for "the development of an over-arching London-wide strategy for community development, capacity building and participation, which all key agencies, including the GLA would subscribe to".

12. *A better Quality of Life, A strategy for sustainable development for the UK*, The Stationery Office.

13. GLA Act s.33 (2).

14. GLA Act s.41 (1).

15. GLA Act s. 41 (4),(5) and (6).

16. GLA Act s. 41 (7).

17. GLA Act s. 41 (9).

18. GLA Act s. 41 (1) refers the reader to the relevant section for each strategy.

19. GLA Act s. 41 (5)(b).

20. Dr David Goode, Director of London Ecology Unit, writing in *Nature's Place* December 1999.

21. GLA Act s. 334 (4).

22. GLA Act s. 32 (3).

23. GLA Act s. 32 (4).

24. GLA Act s. 42 (5).

25. See Lindsey Colbourne *EG* Feb 1999 and the reports of the *Bridges to a Sustainable Future* project run by Projects in Partnership and LVSC, available from Projects in Partnership (see p 127).

Chapter 6

Governing Differently

Contrasting the problem-solving government of the 20th Century with the 'systems-thinking' government needed for the 21st Century.

Towards the systems paradigm

Joseph Tainter and Dietrich Doener have written major books[1] on the differences between governance that is based on the 'problem-solving' paradigm and that based on the 'systems-thinking' paradigm.

Roy Madron has combined their work with his own ideas as a participation and leadership consultant to produce the comparative models for 20th Century Governance (based on the 'problem-solving' paradigm) and 21st Century Governance (based on the 'systems-thinking' paradigm) which you will find on the next two pages.

Both models have five main active components:
◆ The basic paradigm
◆ Purpose
◆ Leadership
◆ Process
◆ Implementation.

The thrust of Madron's argument is that we will never be able to achieve sustainable societies unless we re-model the policy-making processes and institutions of government on the basis of the 'systems-thinking' paradigm rather than the 'problem-solving' paradigm.

Within the systems-thinking paradigm, processes for citizen and stakeholder participation play a crucial role, since it is they who, collectively, `know' the whole system in its current state, and it is they who will have to implement the new system that will achieve the purposes of justice and sustainability.

To achieve such a transformation will require political leaders who have a clear understanding of the need to re-orientate governance to ensure that 'systems-thinking' replaces 'problem-solving' in London governance.

There is no shortage of skills, experience or innovation in the field of citizen participation. The multitudinous benefits of *properly led*, designed, conducted and *sustained* processes of citizen participation, says Madron, far outweigh any immediate costs.

I believe Madron is right; and I believe that this approach is going to be crucial to London's

future. I base that judgement partly on my own knowledge and experience of citizen participation – from having read books on how well these processes have been found to work, both for large companies and also in civil society, albeit mainly in the USA[2], and from having taken part in professionally run events, which have been both enjoyable and fruitful – partly on my

perception of the abject failure of democracy as currently practised, and partly on my logical mind which tells me that this makes sense (see below under Self-regulating systems, Eco-feedback and Understanding the whole).

The Mayor and Assembly Members will have available to them both the tools and the resources for effective stakeholder participation in London

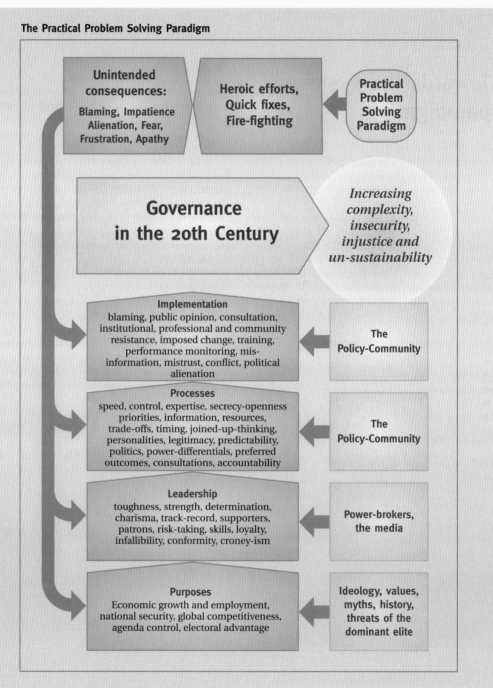

The Practical Problem Solving Paradigm

Unintended consequences:
Blaming, Impatience Alienation, Fear, Frustration, Apathy

Heroic efforts, Quick fixes, Fire-fighting

Practical Problem Solving Paradigm

Governance in the 20th Century

Increasing complexity, insecurity, injustice and un-sustainability

Implementation
blaming, public opinion, consultation, institutional, professional and community resistance, imposed change, training, performance monitoring, mis-information, mistrust, conflict, political alienation

The Policy-Community

Processes
speed, control, expertise, secrecy-openness priorities, information, resources, trade-offs, timing, joined-up-thinking, personalities, legitimacy, predictability, politics, power-differentials, preferred outcomes, consultations, accountability

The Policy-Community

Leadership
toughness, strength, determination, charisma, track-record, supporters, patrons, risk-taking, skills, loyalty, infallibility, conformity, croney-ism

Power-brokers, the media

Purposes
Economic growth and employment, national security, global competitiveness, agenda control, electoral advantage

Ideology, values, myths, history, threats of the dominant elite

governance – the knowledge and understanding of how to design and facilitate participation processes and a pool of skilled practitioners. It will be for the Mayor, with the support of the Assembly and the Civic Forum, to provide the missing ingredient needed for the GLA to lead London in the 'co-creation' of just and sustainable societies. **The missing ingredient is the necessary political and/or executive leadership, 'liberating' leaders, people who regard such processes as essential for their purposes and strategies.** This is the ingredient the Mayor and Assembly can supply (and only they can supply), by themselves, and through the appointments the Mayor makes to the functional and other bodies[3].

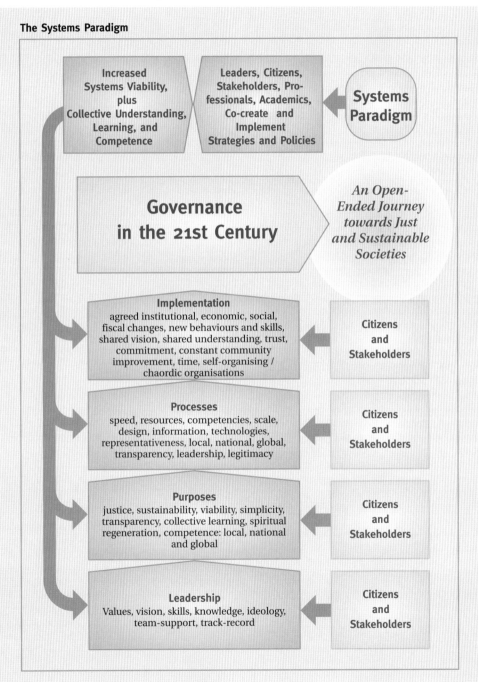

The Systems Paradigm

Increased Systems Viability, plus Collective Understanding, Learning, and Competence

Leaders, Citizens, Stakeholders, Professionals, Academics, Co-create and Implement Strategies and Policies

Systems Paradigm

Governance in the 21st Century

An Open-Ended Journey towards Just and Sustainable Societies

Implementation
agreed institutional, economic, social, fiscal changes, new behaviours and skills, shared vision, shared understanding, trust, commitment, constant community improvement, time, self-organising / chaordic organisations

Citizens and Stakeholders

Processes
speed, resources, competencies, scale, design, information, technologies, representativeness, local, national, global, transparency, leadership, legitimacy

Citizens and Stakeholders

Purposes
justice, sustainability, viability, simplicity, transparency, collective learning, spiritual regeneration, competence: local, national and global

Citizens and Stakeholders

Leadership
Values, vision, skills, knowledge, ideology, team-support, track-record

Citizens and Stakeholders

Governing Differently

Pathways to the future

Co-creation through the use of participation processes

In the 21st Century model there is a real sense in which the strategies and policies are 'co-created' – they are the product of processes in which all stakeholders have had an opportunity to be involved, at all stages in the 21st Century model. They are processes based on the same principles as those described in Chapter 4 (and see the bibliography). 'Co-creation' envisages participation in identifying issues such as the malfunctioning of economic systems, even where these are not being questioned by the Government. **'Co-creation' involves everyone in every aspect of creating the pathways to the future.** To bring about the changes London needs to achieve, peacefully and coherently, will require deliberative, transparent, fully participative processes; this is 'co-creation'.

Self-regulating systems

Ian Parker in his Introduction to the Granta *London – the lives of the City* has commented on London's 'jumble and complexity' and he mentions Samuel Johnson having referred to its 'wonderful immensity'. This is the soil in which the creativity of Londoners flourishes. Whatever new order may now be required on some levels, the creativity needed for London to meet the challenges of the future and turn them into opportunities will only flourish in the fertile soil of London's 'jumble and complexity'.

The ideal for London must be to work as numerous largely self-regulating systems: a complex web of diverse social, economic, and natural systems, all operating with the very minimum of regulation and control, all driven by their own energy and thriving on their own creativity.

It seems unlikely that the new economic systems, or political arrangements, that London needs to meet the challenges of the future will be characterised by more regulation or greater control. To my mind, they are likely to seek to maximise the benefits of self-regulation and individual creativity. I believe that this is what 'co-creation' achieves. The challenge for London under its new leaders is to create the democratic processes, and seek to create the market conditions, that will enable us all to take part in re-creating London as a sustainable part of a sustainable world economy, with the minimum of regulation and control.

Eco-feedback

Eco-feedback refers to people being given sufficient information about ecological issues to enable them to decide how to modify their own lifestyles or working practices to ensure that their actions have the best consequences for the environment. It is a key concept of systems thinking. It is a key concept for London, given London's size and complexity. It means that decision making can be done at the level where the best decisions are likely to be made, leading to greater efficiency.

Feedback Loops

Sculptor Alf Lohr is using the concept of feedback loops to enable art workshops to promote Agenda 21. "Feedback loops enable a system to regulate its own operation. Basically a system with a feedback loop is composed as a series of causally connected elements. The effect of the initial action is fed back eventually to its source, after each element has acted upon the next, in a feedback loop. This results in self regulation of the system and can be expressed simply as the conveying of information about the outcome of any activity to its source". At East Kilbride feedback loops were created through a work of art, a web site and workshops. A series of workshops were held with specialists on specific environmental topics as the basis for establishing a web site. A work of art that is visible to everyone – a landmark icon by the motorway gateway to East Kilbride – is used as a starting point to attract the attention of the community – to give people a reason to start talking. Another series of workshops was then held with the local business community, ethnic minority groups, Age Concern, community councils, the local Council for Disability and Special Needs Schools, a women's group and healthcare workers.

The theme of the workshops and feedback loops is to look at East Kilbride as an eco-system. The workshop participants become advocates to reach a wider audience in the process of making the landmark an integrated part of the cultural fabric. Informed feedback goes on the project web site. "We aim to tap into the amazing power and energy of the people of East Kilbride".

Contact Alf Lohr at: 3 East View Vale of Health, NW3 1AU tel/fax 0171 431 9315

It follows that an important function for leaders is to make sure that the necessary information is made available to all concerned, so that they can take their own decisions, rather than to tell people what to do.

Other implications include the need for all concerned to share a commitment to acting in ways that have the best consequences for the whole. Hence the need for a shared understanding of the predicament we are in. Hence the need to provide **processes** to arrive at this understanding – another function of leadership.

Understanding the whole

The idea is that, by having a greater understanding of the whole, individuals can attune their everyday actions in whatever way **they** see as being useful to the health of the whole city, be they business people, financiers, nurses, teachers, office workers, young people, the retired or elderly: it will apply to everyone because we are all part of London. **Together** we have it in our hands to change the direction in which we are going. **"The aim is to optimise the whole system. You do not achieve this by optimising each part in isolation"**: David Korten in *Natural Capitalism*. The need to optimise the whole system is why all the parts need to have their interests included in the 'bottom line'. That is why they must be involved in the dialogue to arrive at the shared understanding. That is why we need to build the structures and processes for stakeholder democracy for the city.

The spatial framework for democracy in London

At the London-wide strategic level, the GLA will now provide a framework for the 'co-creation' of strategies for London. It will be vital for the Mayor to make a positive choice to make use of the new structures in this way; because, as we have seen, the processes laid down by Parliament are quite capable of prolonging the 20th century model into the third millennium.

At the next level down from the London-wide, the London boroughs are mostly far too large for the councillors and officers to be able to relate closely to the numerous communities each borough serves; and it is difficult for members of the community to play a constructive part on local affairs. This provides a poor environment for 'co-creation'. Also, borough boundaries often do not follow the natural boundaries of town centres; and wards, the areas represented by individual councillors, often do not comprise communities or neighbourhoods. The size and shape of the London boroughs forces councils and officers, on the one hand, and the communities they serve, on the other, into relationships of corporation and customer, funding body and applicant for funding, consultor and consultee; it does not lead easily to mutually supportive partnerships; it tends to result in distrust, apathy and poor service.

And at the neighbourhood level there are generally no democratic structures at all (which is why the London Community Alliance has put forward proposals for London to have Community Assemblies: see ante page 77).

Could London develop a more effective hierarchy of democratic bodies ?

Following a 1994 study by Middlesex University[4] in April 1996 the London Planning Advisory Committee (LPAC) published *Supplementary Advice on Town Centres* which classified centres throughout Greater London as either

◆ International (Knightsbridge and the West End)
◆ Metropolitan (10 big centres such as Bromley or Ealing)
◆ 33 Major centres (such as Barking or Bexleyheath)
◆ 154 District centres (such as Chadwell Heath or Dagenham)
◆ one Regional Shopping Centre (Brent Cross, to which Lakeside at Thurrock and Blue Water at Dartford might now regrettably need to be added)
◆ and many more numerous neighbourhood and more local centres.

This was seen by LPAC as a network, a mechanism for delivering town centre policy concerned inter alia with fostering sustainability, especially in terms of reducing the need to travel, encouraging the use of public transport and protecting and enhancing the environment. It was also seen as a framework for partnerships between developers and local communities. "In more general terms, a plan-led, network-based approach to retail and town centre policy, driven by concerns to foster sustainable access to town centre services, should provide one of the most effective strategic policy mechanisms to sustain London in the next century. ... The network provides the basis around which policy is structured but is not itself a policy proposal. Associated with policy, it will help in the achievement of town centre objectives including sustainability, as well as wider objectives for London as a whole." It will no doubt play an important role in the preparation of the Mayor's Spatial Development Strategy.

Could this pattern of spatial ordering become the framework for the whole of London governance, not only in relation to planning issues about town centres and retail development, but for defining the powers and responsibilities of various layers of local authority, from neighbourhoods upwards, and for fixing ward boundaries? Barry Fineberg, an independent thinker, thinks so. "Political boundaries", he says in a note to me, "should define, not divide communities. ... This frame of reference gives energy and direction to the analysis of urban space, with corresponding social, economic and political implications for local publics. Hopefully a means of getting a

purchase on the complexities of a city and its region". Information would be crucial but, in this framework, would be more coherent: "I envisage that suitable mechanisms may be designed for the graduated and measurable handling of information. These might include indicators, controls and feed-back loops. Such mechanisms would enable the development of flexible organic potential for matching both internal and external changing environments with more local corresponding actions." Barry would elevate LPAC's network framework into **the** organising principle.

Much activity in London, the way we live our lives and much of the economy, is not closely related to neighbourhoods or centres, but for most people most of life is related to the places where they live and work: the immediate neighbourhood is crucial to where we live, our neighbours, our shopping habits, and many of our journeys. It is at this level that community works. Moreover, as we have seen in the chapter on economics, the strengthening of local economies is one of the keys to achieving a more sustainable national economy. The LPAC concept, especially if it is developed as Fineberg suggests, would make the whole thing so much easier for ordinary people to understand and make sense of.

Of course the Mayor would not have power to reorder London's entire local authority framework in this way: it would need legislative action through Parliament. But a Mayor, backed by reason and the people, could ask Parliament to make the necessary changes. A goal, perhaps, to be achieved after the next General Election.

The role of the Mayor

It has often been pointed out that the position of an elected Mayor of London will be immensely powerful. We are now in a position to draw together the strands of this book. How should this power be exercised? The 'co-creation' model of government has crucial implications. If the vision for the future of London is to be 'co-created' by the people jointly with the leaders including the Mayor, it cannot be pre-judged by the Mayor. The new kind of politics for London will be very different from national politics as now practised. For example, New Labour made it clear before the 1997 Election that they would be committed to free trade; and in chapter 3 we have seen this reflected in the Government's support for free trade as part of its strategy for 'sustainable development'. This has made it difficult for those arguing for protectionist policies to engage in

reasoned discourse with Government: their voices are confined to a lobbying or campaigning role. If London's first Mayor had made a similar commitment, for example to give priority to attracting inward investment, this would render academic any discussion of the underlying issues; it would provide a basis for the Mayor to enjoy the same sort of relationship with the City of London as that now enjoyed by the Government and by the same token it would create distrust between the Mayor and those parts of London's society and economy seeking a higher priority for other policy options. This would be to follow the 20th Century model of government.

In the 21st Century model the commitment required from mayoral candidates is a commitment to the active promotion of 'co-creation' processes leading to strong action to implement the policies that emerge. In this role the Mayor has an immensely important and powerful part, far more exciting and demanding, I would have thought, than that offered by the 20th century model. The 'co-creation' processes will have enabled fundamental issues – such as those aired in the first three chapters of this book – to be explored in the course of building the strategies; they will have ensured that the strategies are based on clear principles and on values which have come from the hearts of Londoners, they will have ensured that the strategies are consistent with each other, and that they comply with the obligations regarding sustainable development, the health of Londoners and equal opportunities.

When the Mayor comes before the Assembly to present, for their scrutiny, the strategies prepared in this way, he or she will be doing so on behalf of Londoners, not just because they have voted in the mayoral election, but because they have had a say in the preparation of the strategies and in creating the vision on which they are based. And when it comes to implementation, often involving many other bodies and individuals – the 'stakeholders' – the fact that they will have been parties to the 'co-creation' of the strategies will be immensely helpful.

The Mayor and the City of London

I have explained why it is contended that the current economic system is driving us towards ever greater inequality and environmental destruction; and I have suggested that this – the whole way in which the economic system works – should be an item on London's agenda, in spite of the fact that the current UK Government, for whatever reason, purports to base its policies on the assumption that there is little that governments can do against the power of transnational finance.[5] If I am right in seeing the reform of the global economic system – the search for sustainable economic systems – as a huge opportunity for London as a whole and, ultimately, for the City of London in particular, the relationship between the Mayor and the City will be crucial. Much of what goes on in the City at present simply feeds on the existing system. On the other hand, if, as writers such as Richard Douthwaite have argued, the system is doomed, no one has a greater interest in its reform than those currently on board the doomed ship. The Mayor would not be anti-city: **in promoting a debate about the fundamentals, the Mayor would be advocating the holistic approach, a vision of London becoming the most responsible financial centre in the world, for the long-term benefit of the city, even if this meant massive changes for the Square Mile.** I would not be surprised if there are many in high places even in the City who would be happy to be invited to even join such a debate; I sense that there are few who are entirely happy with current trends, or, for that matter, with the lifestyles that the current systems impose on those engaged in this sector.

The great thing is that the Mayor should make a clear break from old style politics, avoiding alliances of all sorts, whether with the Square Mile or any other sector, so as to be able to represent the whole of London. The Mayor needs to be a skilled and trusted chair-person, only human, of course, with his or her own passions and

subtle effects on our humanity to that of apartheid in South Africa. "In one way or another, as a supporter, as a perpetrator, as a victim, or one who opposed the ghastly system, something happened to our humanity. All of us South Africans were less whole than we would have been without apartheid. Those who were privileged lost out as they became more uncaring, less compassionate, less humane and therefore less human; for this universe has been constructed in such a way that unless we live in accordance with its moral laws we will pay a price. And one such law is that we are bound together in what the Bible calls 'the bundle of life'. Our humanity is caught up in that of all others. We are human because we belong. We are made for community, for togetherness, for family, to exist in a delicate network of interdependence. Truly, 'it is not good for man to be alone': Genesis 2:18." So Archbishop Desmond Tutu described the effects of apartheid in his book on the South African Truth and Reconciliation Commission *No Futures without Forgiveness*.

I consider that something similar is happening here in London and indeed all over the world, as the heartless power of the growth economy, the rule of the single 'bottom line', extends its inexorable power over people. Just as good white Christians collaborated with an essentially evil system, and good blacks turned to commit crimes as horrible as those of the whites, so today the effect of the economic system is to corrupt our humanity. Where money is the main currency for human dealings, where wealth defines status, we are a divided, separated society: that is a less human society. **Pathways to the future are pathways for people.**

enthusiasms, but above all impartial, never taking sides. This is not merely a suggestion by the author, based on the concept of 'co-creation': it is also the consequence, I would argue, of the Authority's power to do anything to promote its 'principal purposes' and its duties with regard to 'sustainable development', the health of Londoners and equal opportunities, and to prepare strategies for London on the various topics required by the Act, all of which must be consistent with each other. These obligations negate the concept of a Mayor coming along with a briefcase full of policies and strategies. The need for an examination of the fundamentals of the economic system, as a basis on which to pursue sustainability and equality, is no more than a matter of economic reality.

A Movement for Change

The various proposals put forward in this book add up to something greater than the sum of the parts. And yet they are only one contribution to a greater whole. This greater whole is a movement for change. It has a dynamic of its own. It is of a different order from the various components we have suggested – for example, new forms of public involvement, lobbying for legislative action by Parliament, the reform of corporate structures – each of which may be a major item in itself requiring acute departures from the 'business as usual' agenda. The movement for change of which all these things will be part is something else: it is a global movement, which has already begun and is bound to gain momentum.

The way in which the 'growth economy' exercises power over London is comparable in its

1. *Getting Down to Earth* and *The Logic of Failure* by Joseph A.Tainter and *Why things go wrong and what we can do to put them right* by Dietrich Doener.

2. See post p 135

3. Roy Madron and the sources he cites are not alone in asserting that leadership is the key issue: see, for example, *Implementing Holistic Government* David Wilkinson and Elaine Appelbee, Demos, The Policy Press 1999; and see Tom Heuerman's web site http://amorenaturalway.com.

4. *Leadership Place and Local Identity – A Study of factors in Local Spatial Identity* Middlesex University 1994.

5. Robin Ramsay in *The Prawn Cocktail Party* calls this 'the powerlessness thesis'.

Chapter 7

The Mayor's Strategies for London events

Describing a series of events in 1999 to enable people to contribute their own ideas to the strategies for London's future

The media coverage, through 1997 and 1998, of the proposals for the return of directly elected government for London were largely confined to the novel arrangement of a mayor and assembly, burning issues such as traffic and the underground, and the trouble the two main political parties were having in choosing their candidate for the post of mayor.

Another novel feature of the proposals – the requirement for the Mayor to prepare eight strategies on specified subjects[1] – covering different aspects of London's future development – went largely unnoticed. And yet these strategies are going to be crucial in deciding the policies or programmes that will affect people's lives. The content of the strategies is of far more real significance for Londoners than how to finance improvements to the underground system or the shenanigans of party politicians. That is why the Sustainable London Trust felt that Londoners should have an opportunity to contribute their own ideas to the various strategies.

We therefore ran a series of evening meetings between March and November 1999 to enable participants to join in making proposals for the various Mayor's strategies. Each event was attended by about 60 people from different backgrounds, including politicians, government officers, campaigning organisations and local activists. Alan Baxter Associates kindly lent us *the Gallery* in Farringdon for the meetings.

Hatching the idea of holding these events, finding a venue and inviting the participants was the easy part. Preparing the background information for the series, and for each event, was also something that SLT could do with the help of one or two volunteers. The difficult part was how to enable 60 people to contribute their, often divergent, ideas for a strategy on, say, transport in London, in the course of one evening. Or so it seemed to SLT until we got in some 'participation' experts – Roy Madron and a team from the Environment and Society Research Unit (ESRU) at University College London[2], to help design the process to be used. These participation practitioners have been doing this

kind of thing for years; it is not so difficult after all, if you have the know-how and the skills; and experience helps.

Before the participation people came on the scene, we had envisaged inviting half a dozen experts to each event to start a discussion at a high level. But no, that would have placed everyone else in a lower class. Instead we worked throughout the evening in groups of about 10, each with one of the participation people as a 'facilitator' and another as a flipchart writer, and with the 'experts' taking part in the groups like anyone else – applying the principle that experts should be 'on tap, but not on top'. It worked. And the experts probably learned as much from the events as anyone else.

The basic formula which we developed in the course of these events was to divide the evening into two halves. In the first session the groups worked on some fairly general question – in the transport event the groups brainstormed two questions about the importance of transport on the quality of life in London and how the Mayor could improve the sustainability of London's transport. The ideas that came up were analysed during the interval and collated into themes which then became the subjects for newly formed groups to work on in the second session; the purpose of these was to identify the actions and policies needed for that theme. Finally there was an opportunity to vote for the five most important points.

For example at the event on the Mayor's transport strategy the themes that emerged from the first session, and which were the subjects of the second session, were

◆ Challenging the 'car culture' – how do we do it ?

◆ What policies are required to improve public transport ?

◆ How do we make our public transport system fairer ?

◆ How do you reduce the need to travel ?

◆ How do we achieve an integrated transport system ?

The point is that these were the questions that the participants in this particular event proposed as being the key questions. In the second session the groups sought answers to the questions the participants themselves had set. This kind of process contrasts with surveys, where the questions are pre-set, or local authority 'consultation' exercises, where the proposed policies have all been worked out by officers or consultants before the public is approached. The kind of process we used is much more satisfying for the participants: it allows them to be part of the decision-making process from the outset.

We began the series with a general 'visioning' event, starting with a brainstorming session to complete the sentence: "Dear Mayor, our vision for a sustainable London is…". In SLT's introduction to the Report of this meeting we suggested the following reflection based on the outcomes set out in the report, including the voting:

"Dear Mayor, We see tremendous potential for a sustainable London: it demands a challenging agenda for change, **combining** social justice and environmental responsibility, and calling for major economic and political reform. It's a long-term project. It involves:

◆ **Political change:** bottom-up community politics, more local democracy and direct participation for people of all ages.
◆ **Societal change:** ethnic and racial equality and justice.
◆ **Economic change:** restructuring London's economy to serve the ends of justice and environmental sustainability.
◆ **Infrastructure change:** transforming the city's transport, resource use and waste disposal systems.
◆ **Cultural change:** integrating principles of sustainable living with London's wealth of heritage and diversity".

The outcomes from the first six of these events have been analysed by the ESRU team: copies of the Analysis and of an executive summary of it are available from ESRU on request.

At the seventh and last of our events we invited people to say what the series had meant to them and how they would use the experience and the material that had emerged. The response left us in no doubt that the events had been worthwhile in terms of the experience of having taken part: the events had been enjoyable and people had benefited not only from the sharing of views but also from experiencing the processes that had been employed at the events. Everyone felt that the events would be useful in their own work: the main direct legacy of the series may well materialise through the individual work of the participants in their many different roles in London, in true 'self-regulating system' fashion.

Around 300 people took part in these events. They did not pretend to be a representative group. Their views can be forwarded to the Mayor but they are of no more importance than those of any other gathering of Londoners. The Mayor will need a participatory process that enables **all** Londoners to contribute. That is the challenge that has led to the *Partners for London Vision* initiative described in the next chapter.

Notes and References

1. See ante p 88.
2. Those taking part included Prof Jacquie Burgess, Marie Cann, Dr Kevin Collins, Tamsin Cooper, Caroline Davies, Dr Gail Davies, Charlotte Fry, Dr Carolyn Harrison, Kersty Hobson, Tomoo Machiba, Prof Richard Munton, John Murlis, Bronwyn Purvis, Mary Tatman Dengler. Sally Mullard and Jane Hobson worked with SLT for these events.
2. ESRU may be contacted on tel. 020 7387 7050, esrulist@geog.ucl.ac.uk.

Chapter 8

Partners for London Vision

Enabling all the people of London to join with their leaders to create an inspiring vision for the future of their city to stimulate action through incorporation in the Mayor's strategies and new forms of partnership.

On 4 May 2000 Londoners will be able to elect – how many of them will actually do so is another matter – the Mayor of London. He or she will have immense authority. At the same time Londoners will elect 25 members of the London Assembly. Thereafter all other Londoners, except for a small minority of activists prepared to campaign, lobby and attend the occasional meeting, will have virtually no say in the future of their city.

That is unless we, all concerned Londoners, insist on the Mayor giving all Londoners the chance to have a say.

If we can find a way for all Londoners to have a say, there could be immense benefits, for London, and not least for the Mayor. Instead of the Mayor's authority resting solely on the election, the Mayor will be able to relate his or her programme to the expressed views of Londoners. This should strengthen the Mayor's authority both in dealing with central government and other outside bodies and, perhaps more importantly, in dealing with Londoners. People have got totally disenchanted with politicians who think they know best and merely 'consult' them, possibly after they have already made up their minds.

But, realistically, what kind of a say in London's future could **all** Londoners have ? There are 7 million of them. Surely, you may think, the idea that they could all have a say in these difficult, strategic, London-wide issues must be a pipe dream. We think not. There are many different ways it can be done. The techniques and the technology exist[1]. They have been found to work, mainly to improve business performance and in community regeneration, never perhaps on quite this scale, but why should not London be the first to do this on this scale ?

Chattanooga, Bristol and O.R.A.K.E.L. in West Germany

A well-known example of city-visioning is Chattanooga, USA. In 1969, Chattanooga was the worst polluted city in the USA. In 1990 it was recognised as that country's best turn-around story. In 1984 all members of the community had been invited to envision what they wanted their city to be like in 2000. Sustainable community development emerged from a shared vision of what citizens wanted for the future. Affordable housing, public education, transportation alternatives, better urban design, parks and greenways and neighbourhood vitality were on top of people's agenda. Following this exercise, the energetic collaboration of government agencies, manufacturers and citizens resulted in successful initiatives to clean up the air and revitalise a city in decline. Several eco-industrial parks were established to rebuild the city's economic base, proving that economic development and environmental stewardship can be achieved together. This was a smaller city in very different circumstances. But what stands out in the story of Chattanooga is the determination of all parties, based on the all-inclusive visioning process, to set in motion a comprehensive, interrelated and strategic process for sustainable development[2].

A more recent example nearer to home is the *Choices for Bristol* project described in chapter 4.

A different kind of process was used in the West German O.R.A.K.E.L. project in 1971. West Germany's Second TV channel and the Heidelberg Systems Research Group used network TV to engage millions of viewers in a rigorously objective process for 'co-creating' a national policy on the issue of pollution in West Germany. The broadcast on the first of two evenings featured a 20-minute film and a panel of viewers discussion; proposers then put forwards three options; viewers voted on the options; and on the second evening these were developed towards more concrete policies.

There are other examples. London does not have to follow any of them exactly. We can learn from their successes and from their mistakes; and design a process that suits London.

Other technologies are also now available, especially the Internet. Since not all Londoners have access to this, it could only be part of a process to enable ALL Londoners to take part; but it enables forms of interactive communication hitherto impossible; and it provides an attractive way of persuading young people to take part.

Partners for London Vision's proposal

London's size, situation and character is unique and highly complex; we need to design a process tailor-made to suit London. Partners for London Vision is an initiative bringing together a group of people many of whom participated in the Mayor's Strategies for London series of events. The group has defined its objective as being to secure the design and adoption of

a process to enable ALL the people of London to join with their leaders in creating an inspiring vision of the future of their city, which will stimulate action through incorporation in the Mayor's strategies and in new forms of partnership.

Note that the process we envisage is not simply to enable Londoners to contribute. The process itself will involve the 'leaders': it is a process whereby people join with their leaders, in other words it is a kind of 'co-creation' process, which I have argued is the new kind of governance required in the 21st century.

Making it happen

It can only happen with public support and the leadership of the Mayor. The Partners for London Vision group will collaborate closely with other organisations and the officers responsible for preparing the Mayor's strategies in order to ensure that this opportunity for the public to participate in creating a vision for London's future can be, and will be, incorporated into the Mayor's strategies. It is envisaged that the process might be started a few months after the Mayor has been installed.

What it could achieve

In addition to providing the vision needed to link the various Mayor's Strategies (how else can the Mayor comply with the statutory requirement for all the strategies to be consistent with each other ?) we think that a London-wide visioning process of this kind could have enormous benefits in terms of people beginning to think constructively about the future, increasing their understanding of the potential for London's future and the reality of its present. People who had been invited to help create the vision to be incorporated into the strategies would be more likely to have the commitment to play their part in implementing them. The process could also lead to the unlocking of talents, creativity and resources currently unused due to people's current disengagement with authority and cynicism about their power to contribute to a better future.

A process of this kind can only improve the quality of the Mayor's decisions and people's satisfaction with them. It is bound to raise the level of trust in, and respect for, the Mayor and Assembly Members.

Above all, this process would help to promote a fundamental shift in the processes of London government of the kind called for in this book, so that, right from its inception, the new London government accepts participative partnership as the norm for the governance of London, partnership not just with the powerful interests with whom governments already work, but with **all** the people of London.

This process would put London at the forefront of international good practice in urban governance. It offers the new Mayor an exciting way of engaging Londoners in making the pathways, the making of which will change London and London's destination.

"There needs to be a vision-led framework of strategic direction with which Londoners can identify and which must resonate with the values of the opinion-makers of the future. The challenge for London's new leadership and local authorities is to build a new trust and enthusiasm for a form of government that is inclusive and consensual, not government by edict, but by partnership and participative democracy so that people have a stake in the process of planning London's future."
Nicky Gavron, Haringey Councillor and Chair of LPAC, speaking at Planning Aid for London's *Our Future London* conference in September 1998

[1.] See chapter 4, pp 62-64, bibliography on page 135 and *RAC Foundation Civilised Cities Project, Civilised Cities, City Visions and Indicators* Ben Tuxworth and Ann Garrett, University of Westminster.

[2.] Best Practices Database, UNCHS, Nairobi. A fuller account is available from the New Economics Foundation, Centre for Community Visions, Tel 020 7407 7447, *info@neweconomics.org*

Curitiba – closing the loop

The story of Curitiba, in Brazil, is often quoted as an inspiring example of a city that has made real progress towards sustainability. The authors of Natural Capitalism devote a whole chapter to this remarkable city. "Though starting with the dismal economic profile typical of this region, in nearly three decades the city has achieved measurably better levels of education, health, human welfare, public safety, democratic participation, political integrity, environmental protection, and community spirit than its neighbours, and some would say than most cities in the United States".

London's situation and problems in 2000 are very different from Curitiba's in 1970, so the actual projects carried out there, although inspiring (the chapter in Natural Capitalism is a joy to read), might not be appropriate for London. What is transferable is the design approach that has enabled Curitiba to achieve success. "It has done so not by instituting a few economic megaprojects but by implementing hundreds of multi-purpose, cheap, fast, simple, homegrown, people-centred initiatives harnessing market mechanisms, common sense, and local skills. It has flourished by treating all its citizens – most of all its children – not as its burden but as its most precious resource, creators of its future. It has succeeded not by central planning but by combining farsighted and pragmatic leadership with an integrated design process, strong public and business participation, and a widely shared public vision that transcends partisanship. The lessons of Curitiba's transformation hold promise and hope for all cities and all peoples throughout the world".

Curitiba was fortunate in a succession of mayors, most notably the architect, town planner and humanist Aime Lerner who was appointed mayor in 19971 and has since held office three times. But "Curitiba is not a top-down mayor-dominated city; everyone respects the fact that, while it is served by its leaders, many of the best ideas and most of their implementation come from its citizens. It encourages entrepreneurial solutions". A key player has been the Curitiba Research and Urban Planning Institute (IPPUC), of which Lerner had been president before he became mayor. "Having such a base for institutionalising the continuous improvement of the city's strategy has proven invaluable. Now 200 strong, this independent non-profit think tank has served as a vital incubator and reservoir of creativity, training three mayors and many of their senior advisors".

Curitiba's government has regularly faced many challenges. "The process by which it seeks to overcome them, however, through persistent application of whole-system thinking, is far more important than particular successes". Finally, the authors of Natural Capitalism write "Teasing apart the strands of the intricate web of Curitiban innovation reveals the basic principles of natural capitalism at work in a particularly inspiring way. Resources are used frugally. New technologies are adopted. Broken loops are reclosed. Toxicity is designed out, health in. Design works with nature not against it. The scale of the solutions matched the scale of the problems. A continuous flow of value and service rewards everyone involved in ever-improving efficiency. As education rejoins nature and culture to daily life and work, myriad forms of action, learning and attitude reinforce the healing of the natural world – and with it, the society and its politics. ... as Lerner insists 'If people feel respected, they will assume responsibility to help solve other problems'. Closing the broken loop of politics, this principle recycles the poor and the hungry, the apathetic and illiterate, into actively contributing citizens".

People making paths

When I and my fellow trustees of the Sustainable London Trust decided to produce this book, we wanted to bring together, in one volume, both some of the ideas that challenge us all to 'think differently' and some of the stories that offer hope for the future. Parts 1 and 2 have been concerned mainly with trends, systems, structures and processes. Part 3 describes some of the things people are already doing in London to build a better world.

As Daisy Froud has written "London is packed with groups of people who are working, in their own way, to develop a more sustainable city. From small networks of friends clubbing together to set up a car-share scheme or to organise a virtual bus to take their children to school, to huge community centres which welcome thousands of visitors through their door each year, these initiatives share a common objective: to use their energy and creativity, not to mention their time, to take responsibility for the well-being of their neighbours and themselves, to make London a better, fairer place to live".

Inevitably, the selection is a personal one, based on my own experience and contacts – being involved here in Camden in Local Agenda 21 and through the work of the Sustainable London Trust. Many initiatives I wanted to include have had to be omitted. For organisations not mentioned here, reference should be made to the Directory on the London 21 web site *www.london21.org* currently holding details of nearly 1000 organisations. **That** list will eventually be comprehensive: please help make it so by adding to it, following instructions on the web site.

My selection omits altogether various categories that are well illustrated elsewhere. There is, for example, very little about 'green consumerism', for the very good reason that this whole subject is fully covered in the excellent *Green Guide to London* listing some 2000 businesses, educational resources, campaign groups and contact organisations. And see *www.greenguideonline.com*

I have omitted many national organisations with which readers will already be

Part 3 gives you a glimpse of some of this activity, plus short descriptions of some of the organisations involved. The list is impressive even though there is room here to mention only a tiny fraction of the organisations and activities that could have been included.

familiar. The reader is also referred to the list of periodicals and bibliography at the end of this book for further reading on other subjects.

Even so, the selection featured here is enough to underline two big points made in this book –

about the 'growth economy', and about government by 'co-creation':

◆ the organisations and activities that are contributing to a sustainable future do not depend on a 'growth economy'; on the contrary, in many cases the conditions they seek to alleviate have, if the argument in chapter 3 is right, been brought about by the 'growth economy'; and

◆ the number and variety of the organisations and groups active in London, whether at a local or more strategic level, are such that it is only through co-creation processes that they can take part effectively in the governance of London.

Some of the material in this part of the book also helps to bring out the power of ideas – the way in which a new idea, if followed up, has immense potential, like an acorn growing into an oak tree. The starting point is learning to 'think differently'.

Finally, Part 3 colours-in my point about the future of London being about people rather than money – people who have ideas and follow them through with action.

The stories and organisations are listed under a number of heads and I hope that this grouping will make this part of the book easier to read. However I would like to emphasise that most of the organisations featured could have been listed under several heads. If the book is used, as I hope it will be, as a resource for reference purposes, the index on page 136 may be found useful.

I regret that space has severely limited the information given for each organisation and hope that readers will not hesitate to contact any of the organisations listed for further information.

Pathways to the future

People making paths

Health and community

Brixton On-Line – a community networking web-based project with a difference – was set up as a non-profit company by two local businesses, an on-line communications company and a database application developer, together with representatives from the Brixton Community Forum. Its web site provides useful local community information and focuses on the development of training and skills in internet technologies. It has developed an innovative on-line learning network *www.brixton.co.uk/learning* that combines with its learning centre in Brixton to provide training and learning for local people and small businesses.
PO Box 17619 London SW2 1WN
Tel 020 7274 2888
Info@brixton.co.uk
www.brixton.co.uk.

The Bromley by Bow Centre is less a 'community centre' than a centre-point for a number of communities: see feature opposite.
1 Bruce Road, Bromley by Bow, London E3 3HN
Tel 020 8980 4618 Fax 020 8880 6608

Camden and Westminster Citizen Advocacy is a registered charity and voluntary organisation with four paid staff. It seeks to ensure that people with learning difficulties have a voice in planning their own lives and are involved in their local community. Two staff recruit, train and support volunteer citizen advocates linked to individuals; the other two are employed as formal or short term advocates.
380 Harrow Road, London W9 2HU
Tel 020 7289 5051 Fax 020 7289 5510

The Centerprise Trust Ltd. is a multi-purpose community and arts centre in Hackney set up to encourage initiative, self-development, and pride-in-achievement' among the youth of the area. It offers classes in reading and writing for all sections of the community; through history it revisits the movement of black people throughout the world; and it celebrates creativity and cultural diversity through the Mar de Gras – an annual festival that brings together the multicultural population of Hackney.
136-138 Kingsland High Street, E8 2NS
Tel 020 7254 9632 Fax 020 7923 1951

Communities and Homes in Central London (CHiCL) was formed in 1980 as a federation of community groups working to maintain viable communities in central London. Its membership is drawn from Battersea, Covent Garden, the Docklands, Fitzrovia, Hammersmith, Kings Cross, North Southwark, Spitalfields and Waterloo. CHiCL works with local groups to ensure that planning policies and local development proposals support rather than threaten the life of each neighbourhood.
6 Southwark Street, London SE1 1TQ
Tel 020 7378 8300 Fax 020 7378 9393

The Kings Fund was launched in 1897 by the future King Edward VII to support the great voluntary hospitals of London. Today it is concerned with the whole pattern of London's health services and with the health of its immensely varied population. It has published a series of significant reports and books, most recently *Health and the London Mayor*, 1999, which seeks to define a role for the new Mayor in relation to the needs of Londoners and their health.
11-13 Cavendish Square, London W1M OAN
Tel 020 7307 2400 Fax 020 7307 2801
http://www.Kingsfund.org.uk

The Public Health Alliance, promotes and defends public health through publications and lobbying and by organising seminars and conferences.
12 Eastwood Road, London N19 1NL
Tel 0121 643 7028 / 678 8842
Pha@ukonline.co.uk

A lively community

The centre's story began when the dwindling elderly congregation of Bromley-by-Bow agreed to offer the neglected church buildings to the community. The first inhabitants were local artists who gave art classes for locals in exchange for rent free studio space. Over the next 15 years a succession of dynamic initiatives has grown from this seed, built around the five 'pillars' of Health, Art, Education, Environment and Enterprise. Today, the centre is used regularly by 1,500 people – 23% of local households have at least one member who visits on a regular basis. The ethnicity of the staff (80% of whom live in Tower Hamlets or the neighbouring boroughs), volunteers and users matches that of the remarkably diverse local population: nearly fifty languages are spoken within ten minutes walk of the centre. This social and cultural diversity appears to be the source of a special sense of energy which has fuelled a series of collaborative projects. Although the church is still the heart of the centre, a principle of inclusiveness operates and religious festivals are shared. The Harvest Festival, for example, is a community celebration in which both Bengali and Christian members participate.

Inclusiveness and integration are key principles of all the centre's activities. It is felt that innovation springs from the connections that can be made when people from different backgrounds and a variety of ages come together. It is the centre's philosophy that everyone has something to contribute to community life, and that people rather than structures are the bricks of sustainable urban regeneration. Local people are accordingly encouraged to try out new ideas and to learn how to make things happen for themselves: to become 'social entrepreneurs'. A number of local business enterprises have evolved with the centre's support, some flowering into independent businesses and others remaining within the centre programme.

The Pie-in-the-Sky Café, which nourishes the 75 centre employees as well as hundreds of visitors, is one of the centre's more remarkable enterprises. Another is its Healthy Living Centre, an initiative which takes an integrated and holistic approach to treatment, offering complementary therapies and art in health activities alongside more conventional forms of treatment. Other projects include the Multicultural Outreach Project; the Parents and Children Together Group, which brings together families from different backgrounds to create art and learn about each other, and the Youth Project, members of which have run a community radio station and designed the centre's playground equipment. There is a wide variety of art and craft classes, and opportunities to participate in sports and outdoor activities.

Pathways to the future

Community

The Association of Community Trusts and Foundations (ACTAF)

The Association of Community Trusts and Foundations (ACTAF) is the national umbrella body for 'community foundations'. These are locally organised charitable trusts, aiming to promote charitable and community activity in their area by encouraging local philanthropy and building a permanent endowment fund. They attract funds from individuals, companies, charitable trusts and local and central government. ACTAF provides a wide range of practical support and information, much of it applicable to all kinds of local groups – residents associations, voluntary organisations and community groups. There are 8 community foundations in London and ACTAF's London Unit is currently setting up a London Community Foundation Network.

2 Plough Yard,
Shoreditch High Street, London EC2A 3LP
Tel 020 7422 8611 / 020 7609 8405 Fax 020 7422 8616
London@communityfoundations.org.uk

Social Enterprise Zones

The idea of Social Enterprise Zones (SEZs) is the brainchild of a team led by David Robinson, Director of Community Links, the community centre in Canning Town (see opposite). The concept is described in the report *Social Enterprise Zones: Building innovation into regeneration* published by the Joseph Rowntree Foundation which is also supporting the creation of the first CEZ. What is more, this is based at Community Links, where Matthew Smerdon has been appointed as Research and Development Worker to get the project under way.

SEZs build on the growing movement towards greater community involvement in urban regeneration, described in chapter 4. Local communities will have more say and control over how government regeneration grants are spent. But the SEZ concept is significantly more ambitious than that: the aim is to achieve greater community control over the way mainstream public money is spent. This is a new concept; it comes from 'thinking differently', thinking in 'systems terms'.

The significance of this new departure is highlighted by the figures in Newham, part of one of the most extensive areas of deprivation in Europe, where the public sector accounts for 65 – 75 per cent of the local economy. Of the public sector, 98% is mainstream programmes, such as welfare and housing. I quote from the Development Group's document:

"Large amounts of public sector money are flowing into Newham. The problem is that it is being used to tackle *symptoms* of deprivation rather than its *causes*. Clearly, the two per cent of the budget currently spent on regeneration is not enough. But what if we could harness the potential of the other 98% more effectively? This is precisely what Community Links has been trying to do, with its pioneering work on the development of SEZs. ...

"The SEZ concept builds on the experience of the Business Enterprise Zones, introduced in the early 1980s, which tested how far industrial and commercial activity could be encouraged by removing certain fiscal burdens, and removing, or streamlining, certain statutory or administrative controls. This flexible approach was successful in the business arena, so why not try it in the social one? Currently, statutory rules and procedures governing public sector spending can prevent existing mainstream resources from being used effectively. In a SEZ a consortium of agencies and local people can seek licence to flex these rules wherever this would make a difference to social and economic regeneration. The ultimate idea is that the partners to this consortium sign a ten-year commitment to work together, not just in the management of fringe activities, but in radically reviewing and subsequently delivering mainstream programmes".

The same document then describes how the SEZ will work, starting, significantly, with these words: "A SEZ is driven by a distinctive way of working, designed to be lean and catalytic, which is totally dependent on active community involvement."

Best wishes to the Development Team!

The British Association of Settlements and Social Action Centres (BASSAC) is a network of independent, multi-purpose, urban community centres committed to social change and seeking to tackle the causes as well as the effects of poverty and discrimination. The agency leads the Pan-London Community Regeneration Partnership (PLCRC) which seeks to build the capacity of community groups to engage in regeneration partnerships – those formed to administer Government grants for local urban regeneration.
Winchester House,
17 Cranmer Road, London SW9 6EJ
Tel 020 7735 1075 Fax 020 7735 0840

The Community Development Foundation (CDF) is a public body funded by the Home Office to "strengthen communities by ensuring the effective participation of people in determining the conditions which affect their lives". It does this by
◆ providing support for community initiatives
◆ promoting best practice
◆ informing policy-makers at local and national level.
60 Highbury Grove, London N5 2AG
Tel 020 7226 5375 Fax 020 7704 0313

Community Links (CL) is an East London charity founded by local volunteers in 1977 and now running a range of local and national projects with children, teenagers, parents, pensioners and disabled people. It has pioneered new ways of tackling the problems of our inner cities and has earned a national reputation. More than 450 volunteers currently work on projects in more than 60 locations. CL has converted the old Canning Town Hall into a unique multi-purpose centre including facilities for all large groups. See the Social Enterprise Zones initiative featured opposite.
105 Barking Road, Canning Town, London E16 4HQ
Tel 020 7473 2270 Fax 020 7473 6671

The Development Trusts Association (DTA) is a membership body for development trusts. These are independent, not-for-profit organisations that are engaged in the regeneration of their area and aim to be self-sufficient. The DTA supports the efficiency, effectiveness and growth of its members, promotes their achievements, and encourages and advises on the creation of new trusts.
20 Conduit Place, London W2 1H
Tel 020 7706 4951 Fax 020 7706 8447
Info@dta.org.uk

The Greater London Action on Disability Association (GLAD) works to improve the rights, choices, and independence of disabled people. It campaigns for accessible and affordable public transport and for full and enforceable civil rights for disabled people. It supports networking across London.
336 Brixton Road, London SW9 7AA
Tel 020 7346 5800 Fax 020 7346 5810
GLAD@btinternet.com
106043.1620@compuserve.com
http://www.vois.org.uk/cdf

The London Thames Gateway Forum services an area of East London stretching from the City to beyond the M25 both north and south of the river. The Forum has a membership of approximately 500 community organisations and provides a strategic service working to support the development of inclusive partnerships in which local people have the capacity to participate effectively.
Brady Centre, 192 Hanbury Street, London E1 5HW
Tel 020 7377 1822 Fax 020 7247 5637
Docklandsforum@dial.pipex.com

London Voluntary Service Council (LVSC) strengthens London's voluntary organisations – there are over 1,000 pan-London or cross-borough voluntary organisations and tens of thousands of smaller ones – through a range of support services and by giving them a strong voice on issues that affect Londoners. The LVSC's Greater London Authority liaison project will enable the voluntary sector to understand and influence the GLA, and ensure that the GLA works with voluntary organisations in the production and revision of its strategies. The formation of the London Civic Forum, described on page 91 ante, is led by LVSC.
356 Holloway Road, London N7 6P
Tel 020 7700 8124 Fax 020 7700 8108
Lvsc-library@geo2.poptel.org.uk

The National Council for Voluntary Organisations (NCVO) was established in 1919 as the representative body for the voluntary sector in England.
Regents Wharf, 8 All Saints Street, London N1 9RL
Tel 020 7713 6161 Fax 020 7713 6300
www.vois.org.uk/ncvo

The Children's Society initiated the *Children and Neighbourhoods in London Programme* to help children and young people in 6 London boroughs to get involved in local decision making, in particular improvements to their neighbourhoods. It is now running the 'My Vote Counts Too' campaign to encourage active citizenship and participation and to give youngsters a stake in society.

St Hilda's East Community Centre, 18 Club Row, London E2 7EY

Tel/Fax 020 7613 4107

Edward Rudolf House, Margery Street, London WC1X 0JL

Tel 020 7841 4400 Fax 020 7842 4500

www.the-childrens-society.org.uk.

Green Net is part of the only global computer network specifically designed for the use of groups concerned with the environment and human rights. Its members have extensive contacts in political and social movements, as well as expertise in information technology and its applications.

74-77 White Lion Street, London N1 9PF

Tel 020 7713 1941

www.support@gn.apc.org

www.gn.apc.org

The Institute for Citizenship promotes informed active citizenship and greater participation in democracy and society. It does this by developing innovative projects in citizenship education, concentrating on practical ways in which young people can participate as active citizens. It's *A Mayor for London – involving student citizens* programme provides opportunities for students from 7 – 18 years to learn about the new arrangements, attend a hustings event and send a message to the new Mayor.

62 Marylebone High Street, London W1M 3AF

Tel 020 7935 4777 Fax 020 7486 9212

Info@citizen.org.uk

http://www.citizen.org.uk.

Internet Future in Kennington describes itself as 'the coolest Internet centre in London'. A place where people seeking to use the Internet for co-operative purposes can meet and exchange ideas, the co-op aims to empower marginalised people through information technology, to provide low-cost access to the Internet to the local community, and to provide resources for alternative views to be published. It offers free e-mail addresses and training to locals, and plays host to a number of web sites. It is now currently working on establishing internet TV stations.

42 Braganza Street, SE15

Tel 020 7582 8518

www.internetfuture.com.

London Youth Matters is an umbrella organisation for voluntary youth groups in the capital – from the Scout and Guide associations to the Woodcraft Folk to the Prince's Trust. Statutory sectors are also dealt with.

Good Shepherd Building, Pastures Youth Centre, Davies Lane, London E11 3DR

Tel 020 8558 1233 Fax 020 8558 7878

londonyouth@compuserve.com

http://www.londonyouth2000.org.uk

The 1990 Trust was established to promote good race relations and to articulate the needs of the black community from a grassroots black perspective. In addition it has set up a unique information technology programme.

Suite 12 Winchester House, 9 Cranmer Road, London SW9 6EJ

Tel 020 7582 1990 Fax 020 7582 2129

Blink1990@gn.apc.org

www.Blink.org.uk

Race On the Agenda works to eliminate discrimination and promote equality of opportunity and best practice. It provides information and researches into racial harassment, education, social exclusion, regeneration, elders, health and community care, and other issues that affect black Londoners.

356 Holloway Road, London N7 6PA

Tel 020 7700 8135 Fax 020 7700 8192

rota@rota.org uk

http://www.rota.org.uk

The East London Communities Organisation (TELCO) is a remarkable partnership of local mosques, temples, churches, gurdwarahs, tenants groups and school communities committed to working together for the common good. Launched in 1996, it covers the boroughs of Tower Hamlets, Hackney, Newham and Waltham Forest. It is funded by subscriptions paid by the 33 founding groups. It helps local people to campaign effectively, for example, for worker recruitment policies on the part of corporate developers in the area, favouring workers living in these boroughs.

1 Merchant Street, Bow, London E3 4LY

Tel 020 8983 9808 Fax 020 8983 9808

The Greenwich Young Peoples Council (GYPC)

The GYPC was set up with a helping hand from the local authority. It is run entirely by the young people of the area, guided and supported by local youth-workers. It offers genuine empowerment and a real sense of being able to contribute to important debates on issues such as racism and social exclusion. At the more specifically local level, the GYPC ran a vigorous campaign against the local authority's decision to reduce the value of school-meal tokens.

Aged between 14 and 21, the council's members, of whom there are about 30 at any time, are elected by local schools and youth organisations and are representative of all sections of the local community. The first elections were held in February 1998, after an initial six-month period during which a Shadow Youth Council set up the required structures for democratic elections and the subsequent administration of the body; and a second set have been held recently. New members receive an intensive training in communication, negotiation and team-building, along with an exploration of issues of self-awareness and equal opportunities, before taking up their posts. They are also encouraged to work towards Youth Achievement awards during their time on the Council.

The GYPC meets at least four times a year to discuss the issues affecting young people in Greenwich, but the representatives also run a wide range of sub-groups that meet on a weekly basis at the Council's headquarters (three brightly-painted rooms, decorated by the members themselves, at the top of a community centre in Woolwich.) On any night of the week one can find a lively discussion in progress, whether around the 'Youth Shout' pages in the local newspaper and on the Internet that one sub-group is responsible for; or about the Peer Education project for local schools that another sub-group supervises. Sub-groups are also involved in running advice surgeries for young local residents, promoting local democracy among young, and organising the Council's Youth Exchange, which recently sent a group to Ghana to consider the rights of young people there and to help involve them in the democratic process. The Chairs of all eleven sub-groups meet once a month as an Executive Committee to make important decisions and to respond to urgent requests for action.

The Annual Conference for Young People is one of the most striking examples of the GYPC's success. Members are responsible for organising all aspects of the event, from press and publicity to event co-ordination and troubleshooting. Speakers of all ages are interspersed with group discussions and panel debates, as well as dance, issue-based comedy and other entertainment. A video box was run at the 1999 conference, where visitors were encouraged to express what they would do if they ruled the world, and at the end of the day all participants took part in a march to the Thames where an effigy representing young people's fears for the new millennium was symbolically burnt and set afloat.

Greenwich Young Peoples Council

An Organisation Run By Young People For Children And Young People

"Voices for the future"

The GYPC is going from strength to strength. Its youth workers feel that success is due not only to the phenomenal support of Greenwich Council, but above all to the motivation, energy and ownership of the young people themselves, who give up their evenings and weekends on its behalf. As it becomes better established, the GYPC hopes to involve even more young people in Greenwich in its activities.

"I love the GYPC because to has enabled me to open my mind to every good aspect of life. It has also educated me on lots of different issues I never knew could be so relevant to my life. It has also helped me to be myself and to help others to do the same".

Melissa Knight

Contact Mark Clay at GYPC on 020 8885 4888.

Artists and performers

Art for Space is a group of three artists who work with children, making mosaics out of found objects and collaborating to enhance their surroundings. See feature below.
24 The Quadrangle, Herne Hill, London SE24 9QR.
Tel 020 7737 5752

The Art of Change is a not-for-profit visual arts organisation funded by the National Lottery and the London Arts Board through the Arts Council. It is concerned with change, and, in particular, the transformation of the urban environment. It is located in East London in an area of diverse cultures. It draws out the ideas and aspirations of those involved in its artworks. It uses the focus of Agenda 21 as the basis of a holistic approach. It uses traditional and emerging technologies and renewable energy resources, where possible, to animate, power and light artworks.
2 Brodlove Lane, Wapping, London E1 9DS
Tel 020 7702 8802 Fax 020 7702 8803
mail@artofchange.demon.co.uk
www.artofchange.com

Artsline helps disabled people access arts and entertainment in London through access guides, a multicultural project, and a youth project (14-25). It also provides a free helpline which operates between 9.30am to 5.30pm.
54 Chalton Street, London NW1 1HS
Tel 020 7388 2227 Fax 020 7383 2653
artsline@dircon.co.uk
www.artsline.org.uk

Cardboard Citizens is the UK's only professional theatre company to be run by homeless people. It performs interactive theatre that requires spectators' intervention and creates two shows each year, one for homeless audiences and one for young people in schools and youth clubs.
Tel 020 8533 4466

Heart 'n' Soul is the only professional music-theatre company for people with learning disabilities. Based in Deptford, the company tours nation-wide, with shows that reflect their unique and challenging viewpoint of the world. The skills and employment possibilities of members are broadened as the cultural and social expectations of learning-disabled people are championed. The company also runs The Beautiful Octopus Club, a cabaret and club run for and by people with learning disabilities.
The Albany Theatre, London SE8 4AG
Tel 020 8694 1632 Fax 020 8694 1532
www.heartnsoul.co.uk

Art for Space

The three artists at ART FOR SPACE use mosaic, a medium perfected by the Romans, to teach children how to reuse and re-cycle materials and then how to arrange colours and forms to decorate and tell 'stories'. Their projects characteristically have three phases. First, the children are sent on an imaginary journey, to stimulate ideas that will eventually be transferred to the mosaic. Next, they start collecting and assembling the found objects which will become the sculptured elements of the mosaic, discovering unpredictability, letting the materials take over while still working within the framework of the design. Finally, they grout, clean, and enjoy the finished work. By working in this way, the artists hope that the children will take as many of the decisions as possible. They have successfully implemented this programme in the playground of 'The Small School' Kingston. This project took five days to complete and involved members of the community as well as school-children. It admirably illustrates the several ways recycling and mosaic work is educative – it stimulates the sensory development of children through the use of diverse textures and colours, while at the same time increasing their awareness and understanding of their surroundings. They become collaborators in a project that directly enhances their local environment.

London Arts Board (LAB) is the regional Arts Board for the capital covering 32 Boroughs and the Corporation of London. It is one of the 10 regional arts boards in England and, as such, is part of the central government funding for the arts. The Board receives most of its grant-in-aid from the Arts Council of England (ACE) and the Crafts Council. Its aims are twofold: to support artistic quality and innovation throughout London; to create a climate in which the arts can thrive and make a significant contribution to the life of the capital.

133, Long Acre, London WC2E 9AF
Tel 020 7240 1313 Fax 020 7670 2400
Chrissie.cochrane@lonab.co.uk.
http://www.arts.org.uk/lab

London Bubble Theatre Company was founded as a touring theatre company in 1972 and began touring London's parks and open spaces with its own brand of innovative popular theatre. The company strives to make theatre accessible, appealing and affordable for thousands of people across London. London Bubble creates popular and exciting theatre on a year round basis. The annual programme includes promenade and site-specific theatre in unusual venues, pantomimes, school residencies, youth projects and a wide range of participatory projects which often utilise Forum Theatre, where the audience are invited to discuss and influence the events in the play. As part of its commitment to community theatre, London Bubble runs the Bubble Adult Drama Group (BAD) and the Bubble Youth Theatre (BYTe-sized Theatre and mega-BYTes) every school term. Over the course of the year, the company will be forging many new links to create community projects with young Londoners.

5, Elephant Lane, London SE16 4JD
Tel 020 7237 4434 Fax 020 7231 2366

Platform combines the creative talents of artists, scientists, activists and economists to work across disciplines on issues of social and environmental justice. It has won an international reputation for innovation and imagination. The focus of Platform's work is London and the Tidal Thames Valley. In 1992 its *Still Waters* project proposed the recovery of the buried rivers of London. That led to the *Delta* project involving sculpture, music, performance and the installation of a micro-hydro turbine in London's river Wandle. This in turn led to the creation of the largest urban renewable energy scheme in the UK – *RENUE* (see page 130). Another strand of Platform's work is *Homeland*, a commission of London International Festival Theatre, which investigated Londoners' links o producers through international trade systems. Since 1996 Platform has been working on *90% Crude* focusing on the culture and impact of transnational corporations and their dependency on oil, with particular reference to the City of London and the web of organisations that enable these organisations to function.

7, Horselydown Lane, Bermondsey, London SE1 2LN
Tel/Fax 020 7403 3738
platform@gn.apc.org

The Streets Alive Project is a theatre company of 16-to-25 year olds who have experienced homelessness, based at the National Theatre. They work with interactive theatre, meaning that the audience don't just sit there, but become involved in the 'fast, furious and totally unpredictable' action. The group tours festivals, day centres, schools and colleges. The project is currently looking for funders.

Tel 020 7583 0275
www.streetsalive.org.uk

Pathways to the future

Greener homes and neighbourhoods

BioRegional Development Group was established in 1994. It is a charity dedicated to bringing local sustainability into the mainstream. Based at the Sutton Ecology Centre, it specialises in projects that make use of the natural resources of a region, thereby avoiding importing resources from elsewhere. Local production for local needs. Unusually, it takes a market-led approach, promoting the application of appropriate technology – technology which both satisfies its green ideals and is viable economically. Its first major project was the local charcoal trading scheme featured on page 127. Other projects include the local paper for London scheme , growing of fibre for textiles and paper, and reviving lavender. Its exciting zero energy development project is featured opposite.

Sutton Ecology Centre, Honeywood Walk, Carshalton, Surrey SM5 3NX

Tel 020 8773 2322 Fax 020 8773 2878

nl@bioregional.com

www.bioregional.com

www.bedzed.org.uk

Brixton Common Land (BCL) is a registered co-op (industrial and provident society) that aims to share ownership of land and buildings for the benefit of its members and the community. Groups with specific needs are brought together to develop/share facilities that are complementary to city living, but could not be afforded individually. BCL's long term ambition is to become self sufficient, developing land and buildings, sustainably managed, at fair rents to support the life and diversity of Brixton.

89, Hayter Rd, Brixton, London SW2 5AD

Tel 020 7737 0189

Coin Street Community Builders (CSCB) is a not-for-profit public service company formed in 1984 by local residents, which seeks to improve the South Bank as a place to live work and visit. Since 1984 CSCB has created 160 new affordable homes, open space, design studios, shopping and leisure facilities as well as the annual Coin Street Festival, featured on this page.

Oxo Tower Wharf,

Bargehouse Street, London SE1 9PH.

Tel 020 7401 2255 Fax 020 7928 0111.

Coin Street: "there is another way"

This prime part of London is made up of eight sites between Waterloo Bridge and Blackfriar's Bridge where the local community has fought to redevelop the area and bring about affordable housing, recreational space, workspace, and shopping and leisure facilities for the whole community as well as its many visitors. Two bodies – Coin Street Community Builders(CSCB) and South Bank Management Services – work together to co-ordinate activities on the sites, supporting economic and social regeneration of the area. Housing sites are leased to Coin Street Housing Co-operative, established "to provide public service not for gain". The structure ensures local control and retention of the public service ethos which underpinned the community campaign from the start.

Local community groups fought a major campaign from 1974-1984 to prevent a major office development of the area. They presented alternative plans for housing, open space and light industrial workshops and in 1984 the Greater London Council gained the private interest holdings and shortly before its own demise sold the freehold of the entire site to CSCB.

Developments include the Bernie Spain Gardens and riverwalk, the Mulberry, Palm and Redwood housing co-operative developments, Gabriel's Wharf and Oxo Tower Wharf. These incorporate flats, retail design studios, shops, cafes, restaurants, public viewing and exhibition spaces, venues for dance and craft workshops and workplaces for designers. Still to be completed are a museum and further housing and mixed use development, including 59 homes for up to 350 people in housing need.

Congratulations to CSCB for proving that, yes, there is another way, not dependent on the 'growth economy'.

The Community Self-Build Agency's aim is for multi-cultural community self-build projects to become more common place so that many more people realise their potential and benefit from the satisfaction and pleasure that building your own home brings.

40 Bowling Green Lane, London EC1R oNE

Tel 020 7415 7092 Fax 020 7415 7142

Csbigloo@dircon.co.uk

The Peabody Trust, established by an American philanthropist in 1862, currently manages over 17,000 rented homes in 24 of London's 33 boroughs. In the last three years it has been striving to increase the number of new and refurbished homes for low income Londoners, and broaden the range of housing provision to fill the gap between social housing and home ownership. Peabody is now a major force in urban regeneration initiatives designing and building schemes which provide a focal point for local communities, undercutting home-lessness and giving people the opportunity of decent living accommodation, with better employment, skills and community opportu-nities. The BedZED development featured opposite is one of several Peabody initiatives to meet the environmental challenges of our time.

45, Westminster Bridge Rd, London SE1 7JB

Tel 020 7928 7811 Fax 020 7261 9187

Beddington Zero Energy Development (ZED)

Peabody Trust and BioRegional Development Group are constructing a 90 eco-home and workspace development on a brown-field site in the London Borough of Sutton. This will demonstrate best practice in urban sustainability, showing high density urban housing with zero net carbon dioxide emissions. Passive solar design combined with good insulation reduces the heating requirements of the housing and workspaces to around 10% of normal. High levels of amenity are maintained by using roof surfaces as gardens, and office space is incorporated into the shade zone of the housing.

The design was developed by architect Bill Dunster and a team including Ove Arup, Gardiner & Theobald and Ellis & Moore. The development includes local and sustainable building materials and water efficiency, for example using rainwater for toilet flushing and washing machines. The mixed-tenure scheme is the most advanced eco-community development being planned in the UK with houses which will be sold at conventional prices.

BedZED is the first development to include a green transport plan as a legally binding requirement of the planning conditions – reducing dependency on cars and promoting public transport and cycling. The developers consulted closely with the local community who welcomed the development. The environmental benefits of the scheme as a whole were regarded by the London Borough of Sutton as having so clear a financial value that this could be taken into account when the Council sold the land to the developers competitively on the open market: this is thought to have set a valuation (and valuable) precedent.

It would be great if this is treated as a model for all new residential developments in London.

Contact Nicole Lazarus at Bioregional Development Group.

Greener homes and neighbourhoods ctd

Architype Ltd is one of the leading architectural practices in the UK for low energy and environmental impact design with particular expertise and experience in consultation design, timber construction and self-help building. The practice seeks to create environments which enhance the quality of life, which are designed to suit people's needs and financial circumstances, which cause minimum environmental impact, and which are sustainable in the long term. See feature opposite.

The Morocco Store, 1 Leathermarket Street, London SE1 3HN, Tel 020 7403 2889 Fax 020 7407 5283

http://www.architype.co.uk

CIRIA (Construction Industry Research and Information Association) is helping industry members in the drive towards sustainable development by developing guides on environmental and sustainability best practice. CIRIA works with leading practitioners and policy makers to identify opportunities for and demands on the construction industry, and to develop appropriate best practice in areas such as urban regeneration, environmental management, sustainable resource use and performance measurement.

6 Storey's Gate, London SW1P 3AU

Tel 020 7222 8891 Fax 020 7222 1708

http://www.ciria.org.uk

Mile End Park – a 'Green Chain through the heart of the East End'

The Regents Canal, connecting the Grand Union Canal at Paddington with the Limehouse Cut and the river Thames, is one of London's oldest pedestrian throughways. Its buildings and the open spaces along its banks invite re-generation. In 1995 Tower Hamlets Council, the East London Partnership and the Environment Trust formed the Mile End Park Partnership to regenerate a linear space of around 90 acres alongside the canal between Victoria Park in the north and the Limehouse basin in the south. A series of 'community planning' week-ends were held to create a dialogue between the design team and the local communities which greatly influenced the development of the masterplan and emphasised the need to integrate art, sport, play, ecology, and fun. Hence there are play areas, an ecology park, art parks, terraced gardens, sports parks and adventure play parks. A futuristic Green Bridge carries walkways and a cycle path over the Mile End Rd. The project has been advanced in stages and will be completed in the course of 2000. Other activities in the Mile End Park scheme include the use of borehole water, running an electric go kart track, building earth sheltered buildings and deriving some 40% of the running costs from shops under the new Green Bridge.

Mile End Park, Freepost Lon1403 London E1 6BR, Tel 020 7377 0481 Fax 020 7247 0539

mep@envirotrust.org   www.mileendpark.co.uk.

Environment Trust Green Homes

Aware that many people cannot afford their own homes, the Environment Trust set out to provide discounted housing constructed with environmentally friendly materials. In partnership with local authorities and with funding from Government, it has been successful in creating homes with high energy and water efficiency. These are sold at well below the market price to local buyers from council housing waiting lists. The Trust's first scheme was in support of a Bethnal Green residents' campaign to build homes on a derelict site. Other schemes have been developed in partnership with local authorities. The sites were then transferred from local authority ownership to the Trust, and, having consulted with the public, building was begun.

The programme has now delivered 52 new homes each with excellent energy standards. All the new units have a National Home Energy Rating (NHER) of 10. Space and water heating costs will be between £85 and £120 per year for two-bedroom flats and three-bedroom housing. This is between a quarter and a third of the cost for a conventional house of the same size. The houses are being sold at around three-quarters of full market value and can be bought by those who could not otherwise afford home ownership. The programme aims to meet the need for affordable housing and also reduce the environmental damage associated with housing provision.

Constructive Individuals is an architecture practice that specialises in ecological design, energy & energy efficiency, water conservation, recycling systems, and the use of recycled and natural materials. It supplies ecological architectural services for private clients and community groups and support and training for self-builders. See feature on Homerton Grove Adventure Playground on page 131 post.

Buoy Wharf,
64 Orchard Place, London E14 0JW
Tel 020 7515 9299 Fax 020 7515 9737
design@constructive-i.freeserve.co.uk
http://surf.to/constructiveindividuals

The Environment Trust (TET) is a charity created in 1979 for the purpose of improving the environment in general and in Tower Hamlets in particular. See two features opposite.

150 Brick Lane, London E1 6RU
Tel 020 7377 0481 Fax 020 7247 0539
Info@environtrust.org

Greenwich Millennium Village

Up to 1,400 new homes will be built together with retail spaces, workshops, restaurants, studio offices, a school, health clinic, community centre, and a visitors centre. Innovative construction techniques are being used and the developments are energy and water efficient. An ecology park is enhancing wildlife habitats. The first homes are due to be occupied in 2000, with the project competed in 2005. A flexible tenure scheme will allow residents to move between outright ownership, part ownership and renting.

Contact Glenn Davey, English Partnerships
Greenwich Peninsula Development Office, 110
Buckingham Palace Road, London SW1 9SB
Tel 020 7730 9399 Fax 020 7730 4979
www.greenwichpeninsula.co.uk

The Centre for Understanding the Environment, Horniman Museum, LB Lewisham

"Our aim was to build an ecologically designed centre which will give visitors an opportunity to learn about life on earth. The building itself will be a green exhibit promoting awareness for ecology and conservation." Architype.

When designing the Centre, the environmental impacts of the building were considered from the outset. Energy, water use and recycling were key issues. The building collects rainwater, recycles its own grey water through reed beds for a cooling system, generates a percentage of its energy needs with photovoltaic cells, and uses sun-tracking solar collectors to heat water. The performance of these 'environmental' systems is monitored continually with computers and displayed for visitors to the site, as part of the exhibitions.

Raw materials also play a significant role in the overall ecological "footprint" of a building. Architype, chose these with care though the timber had to be imported. Ecologically-responsible paints and stains were used in the decoration and protection of the building, as much for the effect on the health of the people working in the new building as for the health of the immediate environment.

The literal footprint of the building consists of a number of holes drilled in the ground for pillars on which the building sits, without further disturbance of the site. All in all, a rare architectural achievement and an inspirational place to visit.

Pathways to the future

Business, training and new economics

Bootstrap Enterprise London Credit Union Development Agency (BELCUDA) sets up and supports credit unions (see ante page 53) in Hackney. It provides training, and gives advice & guidance to people wanting to derive benefit from credit unions.

The Print House, 18 Ashwin Street, London E8 3D
Tel 020 7254 6015 Fax 020 7275 9914
hackney-cuda@pop3.poptel.org.uk

Business in the Community (BITC) is a unique movement of companies across the UK committed to continually improving their positive impact on society, with a core membership of 650 companies, including 75% of the FTSE 100. BITC is a not-for-profit organisation set up in 1982 by business leaders concerned with inner city problems, with the HRH The Prince of Wales as President. Its mission is to inspire businesses to increase the quality and extent of their contribution to social and economic regeneration by making corporate social responsibility an essential part of business excellence. One of BITC's most useful functions is to put professional people willing to give some of their expert time in touch with a voluntary organisation in need of professional assistance.

44 Baker Street, London W1N 1DH
Tel 020 7224 1600 Fax 020 7486 1700
http;//www.bitc.org.uk

Ethical Investment Research Service (EIRIS) was set up in 1983 with the help of churches and charities which had investments and needed a research organisation to help them put their principles into practice. EIRIS provides the research into corporate behaviour needed by ethical investors, helps charities and other investors identify the approach appropriate to their requirements, publishes guides to help identify and chose between funds with ethical criteria, offers services to all types of client but concentrates purely on ethical research and does not offer financial advice or investment management services.

80-84 Bondway, London SW8 1SQ
Tel: 020 7840 5700 Fax: 020 7735 5323
Ethics@eiris.org

The Fairtrade Foundation promotes fair-trade (see ante page 49) in the UK and awards consumer labels to products as a guarantee that third-world producers are receiving a fair deal.

Suite 204, 16 Baldwin's Gardens, London EC1N 7RG
Tel 020 7405 5942
mail@fairtrade.org.uk   www.fairtrade.org.uk

The Gateway Foyer enables young people to take part in training and employment initiatives while receiving support and somewhere to live. It encourages young people to plan their education and training and make effective choices in their careers.

66 Lancaster Street, London SE1 0RZ
Tel 020 7928 7232 Fax 020 7401 8548
scott@foyer.net

The Industrial Common Ownership Movement Ltd (ICOM) is a non-profit organisation promoting and representing democratic employee-owned businesses throughout the UK. Since 1971 it has pioneered the cause of democratic employee ownership especially in the form of worker co-operatives. It is also involved in developing other forms of co-operation including an increasing number of co-operative consortiums made up of small businesses or self-employed individuals.

74 Kirkgate, Leeds LS2 7DJ
Tel 0113 246 1737/8 Fax 0113 244 0002
Icom@icom.org.uk

LETSlink London is a forum for organisers of LETS schemes in London. It serves as a public information point and training agency for individuals and groups running LETS systems. LETS are set up to facilitate the exchange of goods and services that some people may not be able to afford to buy within the money economy (see ante page 53).

12 Southcote Road, London N19 5BJ
Tel 020 7607 7852 Fax 020 7609 7112
Letslinklondon@freeserve.co.uk
www.letslink.org

The London Enterprise Agency (LentA) is a group of major companies who work together on issues of job creation and employability. It helps by providing a business development service for small businesses and enterprises of all kinds. In addition LentA sets up innovative projects covering all aspects of employability such as job schemes for young homeless, one-stop shops for new business start up and education business partnerships.

301 Central Market, Charterhouse Street, London EC1A 9LY

Tel 020 7236 3000 Fax 020 7329 0026

Info@lenta.co.uk

www.lenta.co.uk/

The Prince's Trust helps young people to develop self-confidence, learn new skills and get into work.

18 Park Square East, London NW1 4LH

Tel 020 7543 1234 Fax 020 7543 1200

www.princes-trust.org.uk

Social Enterprise London (SEL) promotes the development of self-help organisations – cooperatives, community businesses, credit unions etc (see ante pages 52-54). An example is the successful firm that runs swimming pools and leisure centres in Greenwich. SEL's work falls into three areas: policy development, capacity building and business development of trading social enterprises. Their role in delivering services in leisure, health, childcare and education in London is expected to grow: SEL has arranged for all mayoral candidates and numerous other influential people to sign a Social Enterprise Charter for London promising support for social enterprises. Good work!

1A Aberdeen Studios, 22-24 Highbury Grove, London N5 2EA

Tel 020 7704 7490 Fax 020 77094 7499

info@sel.org.uk

www.sel.org.uk

UK Social Investment Forum was launched in 1991. Its primary purpose is to promote and encourage the development and positive impact of Socially Responsible Investment (SRI). It works to bring together different strands of SRI nationally and to act as a focus and voice for the industry. The Forum is open to professional advisers, and fund managers, individual and institutional investors, community organisations and other bodies concerned with SRI, and members of the public.

Holywell Centre, 1 Phipp Street, London EC2A 4PS

Tel 020 7749 4880 Fax 020 7749 4881

Info@uksif.org

www.uksif.org

A New Path for Ethical Investment

A recent innovation in the ethical investment market is the investment fund set up by the Word Wide Fund for Nature and NPI (National Provident Institute) the life assurance company, the first such partnership between an environmental organisation and an investment company. Companies in which shares are held are selected on their merits as profitable investments, but with the added component of an assessment of the company against defined sustainability criteria. Companies can be proposed for inclusion on the fund's Approved List either on the basis of being "Industries of the Future" or for being "Best in Class" in their sector.

The fund holds profiles of all companies which lay out their environmental strengths and weaknesses; and investment holdings are also subject to a quarterly review by the fund's Monitoring Group. The entire fund is subject to a screen by the independent Ethical Investment Research Service (EIRIS) (see opposite) twice a year, and the fund also has an Advisory Committee to review criteria and selections. Companies which are not felt to have the possibility of a sustainable future are excluded from the fund altogether. This policy currently excludes companies in arms, tobacco, genetic engineering, nuclear power, pesticides and agro-chemicals, ozone-depleting chemicals, and animal testing for cosmetics (as well as the use of primates in medical testing). Companies engaging in fossil fuels, mining, certain chemicals and plastics, timber products, tourism and intensive farming are also excluded unless they can demonstrate outstanding environmental and social performance. The fund's approach is not limited to selecting investments on the basis of social responsibility criteria: once shares have been purchased in a company, the fund managers seek to use the votes to encourage the company to move in a more sustainable direction.

Contact NPI at 53 Calverley Road, Tunbridge Wells, Kent TN1 2UE

Tel 01892 515151

http://www.npi.co.uk/globalcare

People making paths

Children and international issues

The Calthorpe Project maintains a community garden for the people of Kings Cross. It provides a safe open space for children, disabled people, women, under-eights and their families, and teaches gardening to people with learning difficulties.
258-274 Grays Inn Road, London WC1X 8LH
Tel 020 7837 8019 Fax 020 7713 0321

Camley Street Natural Park is one of the 60 nature reserves managed by the London Wildlife Trust. Created nearly fifteen years ago, it continues to demonstrate how wildlife can co-exist with people in the inner city. It is an important resource for inner city school children and is visited by organisations and individuals from all over the world.
12 Camley Street, London NW1 OPW
Tel: 020 7833 2311 Fax: 020 7833 2488
lwtcamleyst@cix.co.uk

Common Ground encourages people to enjoy and take responsibility in their own locality by offering ideas, inspiration, and enjoyment. It aims to link people with the landscape through, history, conservation, and the arts.
P O Box 25309 London NW5 1ZA
Tel/Fax 020 7267 2144
www.commonground.org.uk

The Environmental Investigation Agency (EIA) uses research, lobbying, and undercover activities to investigate illegal trade in wildlife and environmental crime.
69-85 Old Street, London EC1V 9HX
Tel 020 7490 7040 Fax 020 7490 0436
eiauk@gn.apc.org
http://www.eia-international.org

FIELD (Foundation for International Environmental Law and Development) develops and formulates law through research, teaching, training and the application of law through the provision of advice and assistance. It seeks to contribute to the progressive development of international law for the protection of the environment and the attainment of sustainable development. As noted in chapter 2, FIELD lawyers have been, and are, playing a significant role in the international climate change negotiations.
University of London
46-47 Russell Square, London WC1B 4JP
Tel 020 7637 7950 Fax 020 7637 7951
Field.org@field.org.uk
www.field.org.uk

Cities for Children

This is a project launched and managed by Groundwork Hackney. It aims to give young people (children aged eight to eleven) the ability to interpret and understand their local environment, to highlight problems that the area faces, and to develop solutions for those problems. The idea was to encourage young people themselves to identify things that could be improved and if possible to involve them in that improvement. The project goes through four phases that give the children room to develop their own ideas. The first phase is exploratory. Children are asked what it might mean 'to improve the environment' and are encouraged to rethink the widely-held idea that the 'environment' is something remote from their lives. The second phase involves site visits, walks around the neighbourhood, and often some survey work on issues such as traffic or litter. Information from such surveys can be used in maths and IT classes. In the third phase the children refine both the issues and the geographical areas they see as priorities. In the final stage, Groundwork staff and teachers identify real possibilities, bring in outside experts such as landscape architects, and make drawings and models some of which have been presented by the children to wider audiences through seminars held at the Town Hall.

Millennium Young People's Congress

In October 1999 612 young people from 102 countries met in Hawaii to discuss their priorities for the 21st century. Education emerged as everyone's top priority. But not the "school that we have" said the congress report "it is a totally new kind of education that prepares us to live in harmony with our environment and with each other. We desire an education that stimulates and engages our creative energies and applies validly to our lives, not the stifling schools that imprison us within four walls. We seek outlets for our energy, creativity, love and commitment." Environment, human rights, poverty and peace came next in order. Rheillyn Valdez and Betty Behane from Maria Fidelis School in Camden attended the congress. They had a great time but as Betty said "it wasn't only about having fun but to help the world from being destroyed as well. We were preventing the world from being a harmful place and making it safer and more beautiful".

Contact: Rescue Mission Planet Earth

Rescue Mission Planet Earth empowers young people to implement Agenda 21, promotes local community Agenda 21, and encourages school courses in Agenda 21. See Millennium Young People's Congress on this page.

The White House, Buntingford, Herts SG9 9AH

Tel: 01763 274 459 Fax: 01763 274 460

Rescuemission@compuserve.com

www.peacechild.org

Groundwork Hackney is one of six local Groundwork trusts in London. These are charitable trusts seeking to help build sustainable communities through environmental action. The Groundwork vision is "a society made up of sustainable communities which are vibrant, healthy and safe; which respect the local and global environment and where individuals and enterprise prosper". See feature opposite.

6-8 Lower Clapton Rd London E5 0PD

Tel 020 8 985 1755   Fax 020 8 986 4834

Hackney@Groundwork.org.uk.

London Environmental Education Forum (LEEF) provides a forum for all whose work involves the promotion, support and delivery of environmental education in London. It publishes a newsletter, provides meetings and workshops, and responds to the needs of its members as appropriate. Its members bring with them a diverse range of backgrounds, jobs and skills, and a valuable depth of knowledge and experience.

C/o The London Ecology Unit, 125, Camden High Street, London NW1 7JR

Tel 020 7267 7944 Fax 020 7267 9334

Sl@london-ecol-unit.demon.co.uk

The World Development Movement (WDM) is London's leading campaigning organisation on world poverty. Now led by Barry Coates, WDM has been at the forefront of recent campaigns against the MAI (the threatened Multilateral Investment Agreement) and further liberalisation of world trade via the World Trade Organisation. Using reasoned argument backed by reliable information, WDM has influenced governments and companies. Its supporters include members who give money and dedicated local volunteers. Its magazine *WDM in action* is published four times a year.

25 Beehive Place, London SW9 7 QR

Tel 020 7737 6215 Fax 020 7274 8232

Wdm@wdm.org.uk

www.wdm.org.uk

In touch with Nature

BTCV (British Trust for Conservation Volunteers) is the country's leading practical environmental conservation charity. Every year BTCV supports over 95,000 volunteers in activities to promote and improve their environment. In London, BTCV runs mid-week and weekend conservation projects and training courses, and assists a network of more than 200 affiliated local groups. Increasingly, BTCV is working in partnership at local level: 12 project offices around London enable local communities to initiate and deliver sustainable environmental regeneration programmes.
80, York Way, London N1 9AG
Tel 020 7278 4294 Fax 020 7278 5095
London@btcv.org.uk
www.btcv.org

English Nature (EN) is the statutory nature conservation agency for England. It promotes the conservation of the country's wildlife and natural features. It has divided the South East Region into distinctive "natural areas" – most of London is in the London Basin are but parts are in the Greater Thames Estuary and North Kent Plain areas: see EN's report *Natural Areas in London and the South East Region.*
Ormond House, 26-27 Boswell Street, London WC1N 3JE
Tel: 020 7831 6922 Fax: 020 7404 3369
http://www.english-nature.org.uk

The Environment Agency (EA) is the public body responsible for safeguarding and improving natural water resources, flood warning and flood defence, fisheries, recreation, conservation and navigation; and also for regulating waste (London produces 13.5 million tonnes of it each year) and industrial releases to air. Its overall aim to is to protect and enhance the environment as a whole so as to contribute to the world-wide goal of sustainable development. It works through a series of LEAPs (Local Environment Agency Plans) on which it consults locally in order to produce a local agenda of integrated action. The non-statutory Thames Estuary Management Plan aims to secure widely accepted sustainable use of the estuary (see opposite). EA's *Creating a Greenprint for London* summarises the issues facing the city and points out that the GLA's task is not to find a balance between the claims of the environment, society and the economy "but to integrate the needs of all three". Its *Riverbank Design Guidance for the Tidal Thames* shows how the tidal foreshore could be greatly enhanced.
Thames Region Office: Kingsmeadow House, Kingsmeadow Road, Reading RG1 8DQ
Tel: 0118 953 500 Fax: 0118 9500 388
www.environment-agency.gov.uk

Friends of Rainham Marsh (FORM) is a voluntary group protecting and enhancing the last area of Thames tidal grazing marsh in Greater London – over 90% of this habitat was lost to development in the 20th century. FORM is working with all the major governmental and non-governmental organisations concerned with the environment to turn the Marshes into a major nature reserve – so that larks and lapwings can continue to nest within 12 miles of the Tower of London.
218 Lodge Lane, Romford RM5 2EU
Tel 01708 754 391

Making a Green Corridor

Architect Anthony Meats has launched a personal crusade against the car. His vision is for a network of great sign-posted and signalled walks criss-crossing London where pedestrians can stroll without risk of being squashed, deafened, poisoned or mugged. He has argued that there is a clear consensus that Londoners should be encouraged to get out of their cars but that they can be persuaded to do this *only if there exists a safe, convenient and enjoyable alternative which a network of priority pedestrian routes can provide.* The first of the projected walkways links Highgate to St. James' Park. It starts in Highgate Village, runs southward through Hampstead, and winds its way through Swain's Lane, Primrose Hill, Regent's Park, and John Nash's Via Triumphalis before entering St James Park. Meats believes that such a walk is *a vision of a humane and civilised London environment in which a boulevard of architectural beauty and classical green landscape is opened up, revealing attractive places.* The *Green Street* has the backing of the London Tourist Board: it encourages both visitors and Londoners to enjoy different aspects of London, in particular the capital's wealth of open spaces.

The London Cycling Campaign (Central Office) works to raise awareness of cycling issues and to improve conditions for cyclists. In collaboration with *Sustrans* it pioneered the Thames Cycle Route from Hampton Court to Dartford.

Unit 228, 30 Great Guildford Street, London SE1 0HS

http://www.kc.org.uk/lcc/

The London Transport Activists Roundtable (London TAR) is a forum of voluntary organisations concerned to end London's transport crisis. These include Transport 2000, the London Cycling Campaign, the Pedestrians Association, Friends of the Earth, etc. Its members are united in the view that without traffic reduction – as distinct from mere restraint – we shall never deal with the massive transport problems afflicting each borough and the capital as a whole. It publishes briefings highlighting transport issues and making recommendations to local authorities.

13 Stockwell Raod, London SW9 9AU

Tel/Fax 020 7737 6641

London Wildlife Trust cares for 60 nature reserves across Greater London and is involved in all aspects of nature conservation. It runs 600 free events every year, offers advice and information through leaflets and packs and visits schools and colleges. In 1998 it produced a guide to developing Local Biodiversity Action Plans (LBAPs) (see ante pages 33,4). Call for a free nature reserves guide, events listing or wildlife gardening advice. Better still, become a member!

Harling House, 47-51 Great Suffolk Street, London SE1 0BS

Tel: 020 7261 0447 Fax: 020 7261 0538

enquiries@londonwt.cix.co.uk

http://www.wildlifetrust.org.uk.london

The Pedestrians Association aims to make roads safer for all – especially the walking majority. It campaigns for (l) the provision of safe, convenient and attractive ways for people on foot, (2) more and better pedestrian crossings, (3) strict observance and enforcement of speed limits, (4) recognition that pedestrians have priority over turning traffic at road junctions, (5) the creation of pedestrian precincts and safe streets, and (6) the removal of parked cars and other obstructions from the footway.

3rd Floor, 31-33 Bondway, London EC1A SW8 1SJ

Tel 020 7820 1010

Sustrans is a charity run by practical engineers and designers who design and build traffic-free routes for cyclists, walkers, and people with disabilities. During the last fifteen years, it has built over 300 miles of traffic free paths and designed many hundreds of miles more. These routes provide practical benefits to local communities countrywide, reducing traffic fumes, easing congestion, and providing a pleasant alternative to the stress and danger of motor traffic out of London. *Sustrans* uses redundant railway lines, neglected tow-paths and derelict land and creates linear parks running right into urban areas. In London greater emphasis is placed on provision of safe crossings over busy roads, linking quiet residential streets to make safe and pleasant routes through the capital.

Main Public information line 0117 929 0888

14-16 Cowcross Street, Farringdon, London EC1M 6DG

Tel 020 7336 8203 Fax 020 7250 3022

http://www.sustrans.org.uk

The Thames Estuary Partnership brings together everyone with an interest in the area. The estuary boasts 116 species of fish and is an important breeding or feeding ground for 170,000 birds. It has eleven 'sites of special scientific interest'. It is also home to the Port of London; and many other human activities, including agriculture and fisheries, are potentially damaging to the ecology of the estuary. The need for a strategic approach to the planning and management of the area was realised in 1992, since when estuary users and managers have worked together to produce management plans. These have now been developed to form Management Guidance for the Thames Estuary, a comprehensive document which sets out guiding principles for action by all the various users and agencies in a very readable, easily understood and attractive form. Congratulations to Caroline Davis who has pulled this together on behalf of TEP which is a non-statutory partnership of all the agencies, clubs, committees, councils and other bodies concerned.

C/o Institute for Environmental Policy, University College London, 5 Gower Street, London WC1E 6HA

Tel 020 7692 5791 Fax 020 7813 5283

Local issues and local trade

The Centre for Environmental Initiatives, founded in 1987, aims to "create and sustain strong vibrant communities within a healthy environment". Projects include the development of Local Agenda 21 in Sutton, social audit of the LA21 Forum, community visioning, a farmers' market, a community orchard, a complementary health network, a solar club, Skill Swap (LETS – see ante page 52) and the Beanstalk Project, to help children grow their own food on an allotment..

The Old School House, Mill Lane, Carshalton, Surrey SM5 2JY
Tel 020 8770 6611 Fax 020 8647 0719
cei@a4u.com   http://www.a4u.com/cei

CPRE (the Council for the Protection of Rural England) have a London branch concerned with urban regeneration, and improvement in the quality of life in London with particular regard to housing, transport and open spaces. London CPRE specialise in land use planning and researches and lobbies on transport and development issues.

70 Cowcross Street, London EC1M 6EJ
Tel 020 7253 0300 Fax 020 7490 3001
London.CPRE@virgin.net
http://www.greenchannel.com/cpre/

The Environment Council, an independent charity, helps people to make decisions to improve their environments and their lives and also helps businesses move towards environmental sustainability. It does this through a comprehensive programme of membership schemes, events and training, mediation and facilitation and the provision of supportive literature.

212, High Holborn, London WC1V 7VW
Tel 020 7836 2626 Fax 020 7242 1180
Info@envcouncil.org.uk
www.the-environment-council.org.uk

The Environmental Law Foundation (ELF), a charity founded in 1992, helps people use the law to protect their environment. It provides access to specialists in environmental law for individuals and community groups. Members of the public are given support and guidance and can receive a free initial consultation with a local solicitor or technical expert to investigate how the law may be used to resolve a problem.

Suite 309,16 Baldwin Gardens, Hatton Square, London EC1N 7RJ
Tel 020 7404 1030 Fax 020 7404 1032
Info@elf-net.org
http://greenchannel.com/elf

Richmond upon Thames College Agenda 21 Programme

This life-long learning programme of courses responds to the needs of a changing society. Initiated by professionals made redundant by the closure of a British Aerospace factory, the project builds on the ideas and approaches of Agenda 21 (see chapter 4), developing ecologically sustainable ways of conducting industry and agriculture but also contributing to social and personal awareness and well-being. The College maintains links with outside agencies such as the Ecological Design Association and Robert Harris the programme coordinator keeps up to date with government thinking about ecological and environmental issues.

The programme, with courses on developing the self, complementary health, sustainable land, food and buildings, innovation and information technology, has been especially attractive to professional people made redundant and women returners, enabling many to go on to entirely new work.

Agenda 21 Course Administration Tel 020 8607 8163 Fax 020 8744 9738
courses@richmond.utcoll.ac.uk   http://www.richmond.utcoll.ac.uk

Friends of the Earth (FOE) works to protect and improve conditions for life on earth, now and in the future. In London it works through local groups and at regional level on a diverse range of social, economic and environmental issues, using campaigning, lobbying, public information and collaborative working.

26-28 Underwood Street, Hackney, London N1 7JQ

Tel 020 7566 1678 Fax 020 74900881

pauldz@foe.co.uk

http://www.foe.co.uk

The Land is Ours campaigns peacefully for access to the land, its resources, and the decision-making processes that affect them, on behalf of everyone.

Box E, 111 Magdalen Road, Oxford OX4 1RQ

Tel and fax 01865 722 016

office@tlio.demon.co.uk

http://www.oneworld.org/tlio

The London Forum helps amenity and civic societies to work together to protect and improve the quality of life in London. It represents more than 120 local societies and associated groups with a combined membership of some 100,000 Londoners. Key issues include public transport and traffic policy.

70, Cowcross Street, London EC1M 6EJ

Tel 020 7250 0606

londonforum@wayahead.demon.co.uk

Planning Aid for London (PAL) offers free and independent advice on town planning issues to groups and individuals who cannot afford to employ consultants.

Calvert House, 5 Calvert Avenue, London E2 7JP

Tel 020 7613 4435 Fax 020 7613 4452

www.plfl.org.uk

The Policy Studies Institute performs high-quality research and informs the policy-making process by disseminating its findings.

100 Park Village East, London NW3 5RN

Tel/Fax 020 7794 9661

Projects in Partnership (PiP) has been operating as a not-for-profit company and charity since 1993. It is a small organisation specialising in creating sustainable solutions through participation and partnership. In 1998 it produced a manual *Sustainability in Practice* designed to help voluntary and community organisations participate in sustainable development.

Top Floor, Tea Warehouse, 10a Lant Street, London SE1 1QR

Tel 020 7407 8585 Fax 020 7407 9555

Pip@pship.demon.co.uk

Thamesbank is an independent organisation that campaigns on behalf of the grass-roots community to ensure proper management of the Thames corridor through London. Formed by Dido Berkeley in response to the development of riverside sites by the erection of massive blocks of flats for the luxury market with little or no regard for the local community ("capitalism killing the community"), and inspired by Agenda 21 and by a vision of thriving riverside communities able to use the river as a transport artery, for recreation and for quiet and tranquil places, Thamesbank is campaigning for:

- the Thames to be given a BLUE RIBBON designation, equivalent to tougher than Green Belt status
- new developments to be preceded by Environmental Impact Assessments and an Independent Social Assessment to secure local communities' culture and heritage
- special protection of boatyards, slipways, and youth facilities or riparian sports and recreations
- provision within the forthcoming GLA for strategic and integrated management of the Thames
- co-ordinated floodplain management to be adopted by all riparian borough councils.

39 Ellerby Street, London SW6

Tel 020 7736 9299 Fax 020 7371 7202

dido@thamesbank.demon.co.uk

http://www.greenchannel.com/thamesbank/index.htm

Local Charcoal

In 1995 the Bioregional Development Group (see page 116) set up the Bioregional Charcoal Company (BRCCo) to implement a scheme whereby independent charcoal burners are brought together to supply barbecue charcoal to DIY giant, B and Q. By creating a national network, the scheme allowed British charcoal access to 75% of the market held by national retail chains and until then exclusively supplied by imported charcoal. The "Local Charcoal" scheme has shown how the green ideal of local production for local needs can be met, reducing the environmental costs of transportation, putting money back into the woodland economy, and creating local rural employment.

Sutton Ecology Centre, Honeywood Walk, Carshalton, Surrey SM5 3NX

Tel 0181 669 0713 Fax 0181 643 6419

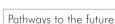

Growing food in London

Becontree Organic Growers Association (BOG) practices gardening in a nature reserve. It is reclaiming the site of a bombed church using permaculture methods.

Three Trees, 44 Gale Street, Dagenham, Essex RM9 4NH
Tel 020 8592 8941

Green Adventure (GA) was started in 1995 when two ex play-workers in Camberwell were concerned about city kids having no links with the natural world. Today Green Adventure

- runs an orchard growing fruit, herbs and flowers at Camberwell Green
- has helped local residents rescue a condemned greenhouse site in Brockwell Park and develop it as community greenhouses and possibly a future garden centre
- is developing various other garden sites
- runs an organic box scheme: see below
- runs various small recycling schemes
- organises Green Adventure Youth Action, a play scheme to "mobilise the vision and energy of youth towards sustainability".

Green Ventures Organic Box Schemes

Green Ventures distributes fresh organically grown fruit and vegetables to local people by bike and trailer. The pricing is on a sliding scale, so that people on lower incomes pay less, and those on higher incomes pay more. In addition, part of the payment can be made in the local LETS currency. People also have the opportunity to volunteer on the scheme in return for produce.

Close to 40% of the scheme members are unemployed, and nearly 40 people on low incomes have worked on the scheme. Which means that, as well as cutting down food miles, the scheme improves the health and nutrition of local people and provides them with the opportunity to get involved in a local urban food initiative.

Green Ventures Organic Box Scheme,
Tel 00171 703 1260
greenventure@safetycat.org

Spitalfields City Farm

Spitalfields City Farm is tucked away behind Brick Lane, no than 15 minutes walk from Liverpool Street station. A tiny, incredibly calm place, where the culturally diverse women of the Coriander Club meet every Tuesday and Thursday to grow organic vegetables and herbs, it is very much a part of the lives of many in its local community. Most of the women involved are from the Shylet region of Bangladesh. Many of the older women have brought traditional organic horticultural skills with them to the project. The Coriander Club has produced tomatoes, onions, runner beans, amaranthus, broccoli, cabbage, beetroot, leeks, spinach, courgette, pumpkin, loofah, chillies, peppers, parsley, chervil, sorrel, basil and coriander. Excess produce is often sold at the Sunday Spitalfields organic market and organic waste from the market is cycled over to be mixed with manure from the farm to make compost for the Coriander Club.

Weaver Street, Spitalfields, London E1 5HJ
Tel/Fax 020 7247 8762

Green Adventure strives to be an inclusive and open organisation with a strong commitment to equality of access and opportunity and to involving young people in the planning and management of projects. The composition of its Management Committee reflects these principles.

Green Adventure relies on the non-money economy. A small staff supports numerous others working voluntarily or being paid in produce or LETS currency. There is an emphasis on training and many volunteers have gone on to get jobs. Wherever possible GA looks to generate business opportunities for unemployed people.

All its projects meet community needs in a way that cares for the natural world.

Brockwell Hall, Brockwell Park, SE24 9BN
Tel 0795 7365 285
greenadventure@btinternet.com
http://www.greenadventure.demon.co.uk

Islington Farmer's Market

On the 6 July 1999 the first Farmer's Market came to London. Thanks to the energy and enthusiasm of Nina Planck, the farmer's Market in Essex Road, North London, has been selling fresh farm produce every Sunday morning since.

The unique thing about Farmers' Markets is that local producers can sell their own products locally. The consumer can ask about how produce was growth as well as how best to prepare it. The farmers' market reduces food miles, and means that food does not need to be processed and preserved for long journeys. It also preserves variety; where farmers have to accommodate big distributors and retailers, they are often required to bow to size and appearance over taste and variety.

Islington Farmers Market, Sundays 10am – 2pm, Essex Road, N1, opposite Islington Green, Angel Tube.

London Vegans was formed to educate society in the ways industrial farming methods and land use impact on health and poverty. It organises vegan food stalls at fairs and monthly meetings with information and food stalls.
7 Deansbrook Rd, Edgeware, London HA8 9BE
Tel 0207 354 8256 Fax 0208931 1904
londonvegans@onet.co.uk

The National Federation of City Farms and Community Gardens promotes and supports community managed farming and gardening. It provides information and advice and lobbies the Government on behalf of city farms and community gardens and low-income people engaged in food-growing. There are 14 city farms in London at the moment; the federation can provide a full list on request.
London Office Tel/Fax 020 7485 5001

Naturewise offers courses in permaculture stretching over eight weekends. It has also planted forest gardens where much of the course's practical work is done.
c/o Crouch Hill Recreation Institute, Hill Rise Road, London N 19 3pt
Tel 020 7281 1328

Sustain: the alliance for better food and farming was formed by the merger of the National Food Alliance and SAFE (the Sustainable Agriculture, Food, and Environment Alliance). See ante page 32.
94, White Lion Street, London N1 9PF
Tel 020 7837 1228 Fax 020 7837 1141
Sustain@sustainweb.org
www.sustainweb.org

Growing communities

The idea for Growing Communities grew out of the vision and commitment of one person. In 1994 Julie Brown joined forces with a couple of friends and started a box scheme, buying produce from an organic farm. At the time, box schemes were in their infancy, so unloading vegetables at 6am 'really felt very subversive'. But Julie wanted the scheme to be about more than supplying vegetables. She had in mind a growing community of people engaged in creating positive change through food. *Growing Communities* was officially launched in 1997. It now supplies vegetables to around 100 households who collect from five pick-up points in North London – usually people's houses. The weekly bag generally contains a mixture of seasonal vegetables as well as eggs and, occasionally, fruit, a loaf of bread, nuts or organic orange juice. Growing communities has been producing a large range of vegetables on a demonstration site in Clissold Park. A bigger site at Oaktree in Stamford Hill was transformed in 1998 from a weedy dump to a flourishing garden with raised beds, works of art, and barbecue area. There are plans to develop a plot at Springfield Marshes in 1999. All these areas are leased for nominal sums. Help is provided by volunteers, some of whom are working towards an NVQ in horticulture, along with members who join in at the regular weekend workdays.
Old Fire Station, 61 Leswin Road, London SW 11 1JL
Tel 020 7923 0412

Energy and recycling

Construction Resources is an ecological building centre, the first of its kind in the UK, promoting state-of-the-art building products and systems from all over Europe selected according to strict environmental criteria. The centre has three floors of product displays, including large-scale construction models and working demonstrations, and offers specialist advice, seminars, training and a trade-sales counter and warehouse. The products range from the most basic unfired clay bricks and renders through natural insulation materials such as flax, wool and wood fibre, to non-toxic paints 100% natural carpets with no chemical additives, rainwater harvesting systems, in-wall radiant heating, and advanced energy control systems.

16 Great Guildford Street, London SE1 0HS

Tel 020 7450 221 Fax 020 7450 2212

www.ecoconstruct.com

info@ecoconstruct.com

The Greater London Energy Efficiency Network (GLEEN) was launched in March 1999, to provide co-ordination of energy initiatives across the capital. It is a non-profit energy agency, a partnership comprising over 30 local authorities. It acts as a strategic body for London, facilitating the writing of an energy efficient strategy for the domestic and small business sectors.

Contact: Tony Rose, London Borough of Croydon

Tel 020 7633 9625 Fax 020 7620 0246

8686 4433 ext 2188

info@gleen-uk

www.gleen.org.uk

London Community Recycling Network was established in April 1997 to support the activities of London-based voluntary groups and organisations engaged in community waste minimisation and recycling. It currently has 50 members and is affiliated to CRN (Community Recycling Network).

c/o unit 3, Sumner Workshops, 80 Sumner Road, London SE15 6LA

Tel: 020 7703 5222 Fax: 020 7928 2318

http://www.chirons-s.demon.co.uk/lcrn

Work bikes

Zero Emissions promote and market a range of human-powered vehicles for freight and people transport, one of them being the christiania, a perfect means of transportation in cities, pollution free and easy to park; and the bike trailer, which like the trike, carries 100 kilos. Workbike are increasingly used in central London for courier services, taxis, delivery services and advertising. Lewisham and Hackney have set up shopping services for elderly and disabled residents using quadricycles. ZERO envisions this cost-effective and sustainable system gradually being adopted in more sectors, and that the whole urban freight infrastructure will begin to change.

66 Rossmore Court, Park Rd. London NW1 6XY

Tel/Fax 020 7723 2409

RENUE (Renewable Energy in the Urban Environment) was born when one of its founders, PLATFORM (see page 114/115), renovated a waterwheel on the Wandle and subsequently built a micro-hydro scheme in partnership with a local school. RENUE promotes energy conservation and the use of renewable energy sources along the river Wandle (boroughs of Merton and Wandsworth). Its millennium projects involve the construction of a Renewable Energy and Community Resource Centre, due to open in 2001 at Merton Abbey Mills, which will be powered entirely from the sun, wind and water and heated by burning woodchips from parkland waste. The centre will be a base for arts and environment projects and will act as a focus for other sustainable energy projects in local homes and other buildings (schools, shops, libraries etc).

1929 Shop, Unit 9,

Merton Abbey Mills, Watermill Way, London SW19 2RD

tel 020 8542 8500 Fax 020 8542 7789

cleanpower@renue.freserve.co.uk

Solar Century is a non-profit company set up in 1997 to bring solar energy to the world. It is the brainchild of Jeremy Leggett (see ante page 26), who has lobbied banks and insurance companies to see global warming, and its accompanying risk of freak weather patterns, as a threat to their business. Those companies who have signed up to the scheme have already installed solar panels at their headquarters. Solar Century functions as a consumer alliance – a sort of global buyers club. It aims to build market volume, bringing down the price of solar PV, to brand solar energy

Homerton Grove Adventure Playground

The playground building was constructed with volunteer labour and with natural and recycled materials. Photovoltaic cells provide all the energy needed, any surplus being fed back into the national grid. Simon Rix, the project manager, was assisted by Simon Clarke of Constructive Individuals and by Stephen Wade of Wind and Sun. Greenpeace published a short case study of the project in their report *Building Homes with Solar Power* (1996). Hackney Council has made a Local Agenda 21 commitment to construct fifty solar-powered houses by 2005.

Contact Simon Rix c/o Chats Palace, 42-44 Brooksbys Walk, London E9 6DF

Tel 020 8985 9202 Fax 020 8958 6878

generically in terms of an environmental imperative, and to raise a fund for investment in solar for those in need, primarily in the developing world.

Unit 5 Sandycombe Centre, 1-9 Sandycombe Road, Richmond, Surrey TW9 2EP

Tel 0870 735 8100 Fax 0870 735 8101

ch@solarcentury.co.uk

http://www.solarcentury.co.uk

Woodbank processes, researches, and redistributes waste wood for the benefit of businesses, charities, training centres, environmental and community organisations. The waste comes from a variety of sources – builders, commercial business, theatres, packaging companies and the DIY market.

92, Cranbrook Road, London SE8 4EJ

Tel/Fax 020 8691 8807

Combined heat and power (CHP)

Two blocks of flats behind Euston Station, Richard's House and Hilwood House, owned by St Pancras Housing Association (SPHA) rely on one of the most cost-effective sustainable energy technologies currently available for their electricity and heat – that is CHP, or combined heat and power, also known as co-generation. Under this system, energy is generated on site, and heat, a major by-product of almost all energy generation, is utilised as space heating in the building. The use of this major by-product, as well as reduced energy loss as a result of electricity transport and storage, allows CHP generation to achieve fuel efficiency rates of up to 90% compared with many traditional generation technologies of around half that.

110 Eversholt Street, London NW1 1BS

Tel 020 7209 9222 Fax 020 7209 9224

Wastebusters Ltd, environmental consultancy giving businesses specialist expertise and practical advice on how to green the office, resulting in costs savings. Runs Waste Alert clubs helping small businesses to reduce costs and increase efficiency through improved waste management and exchange of materials.

3rd Floor, Brighton House, 9 Brighton Terrace, London SW9 8DJ

Tel 020 7207 3434   Fax 020 7207 2051

sales@Wastebusters.co.uk

Car Free Cities Network

This network of over 70 European cities provides an ideal forum for the exchange of ideas and experience, the transfer of know-how between local authorities and the development of transnational projects to promote sustainable urban mobility.

One such scheme is car clubs, currently being tried out in Edinburgh as a joint venture by Edinburgh City Council and Budget the car rental firm. Members can call up to book a car with as little as 15 minutes notice. Research suggests that each car club vehicle replaces four to six private vehicles, and that participants' car usage tends to fall by 50%, as they tend to choose the most appropriate mode of transport for their journey, but without compromising their freedom of mobility.

Contact Eurocities 18 Square de Meeus, B-1050 Brussels

Tel +32 2 552 08 74/75 Fax +32 2 552 08 89

cfc@eurocities.be.

Periodicals

Connections
Global and national environment
and health news.
UNED-UK, 3 Whitehall Court,
London SW1A 2EL
Tel 020 7839 1784
Fax 020 7930 5893
connections@earthsummit2002.org
www.oneworld.org/uned-uk
www.uned-uk.org (from May 2000)

earthmatters
Friends of the Earth Magazine.
Friends of the Earth, 26-28
Underwood Street, London N1 7JQ
Tel 020 7490 1555
Fax 020 7490 0881
info@foe.co.uk
www.foe.co.uk

Eco Design
Environmental issues for the design
professions and related industries.
Ecological Design Association, The
British School, Slad Road, Stroud,
Glos GL5 1QW
Tel 014 5376 5575
Fax 014 5375 9211
ecological@designassociation.freeserve.co.uk

EG
Planning, sustainable development,
Local Agenda 21, urban regener-
ation, transport and policy.
The Environment Resource and
Information Centre, University of
Westminster, 35 Marylebone Road,
London NW1 5LS
Tel 020 7911 5000 ext. 3135
Fax 020 7911 5171
rossa@wmin.ac.uk

**EIRIS (The Ethical Investment
Research Service)**
Research to help people invest
according to their ethical principles.
71 Bondway, London, SW8 1SS
Tel 020 7840 5700
Fax 020 7735 5323
ethics@eiris.org
www.eiris.org

Green Events
Green and holistic concerns. Lists
upcoming events and classes.
93 Fortess Road, London, NW5 1AG
Tel 020 7267 2552
Fax 020 7813 4889
pmccaig@onet.co.uk
www.cerbernet.co.uk/greenevents

*Green Futures
Information, opinion and debate on
progress towards sustainable
development. Focus on solutions
and best practice.
Subscriptions, Circa, 13-17 Sturton
Street, Cambridge CB1 2SN
Tel 012 2356 8017
Fax 012 2335 4643
greenfutures@circa-uk.demon.co.uk

Green Pepper
European-wide activist magazine.
EYFA PO Box 94115, 1090 GC,
Amsterdam
Tel 31 20 665 7743
Fax 31 20 692 8757
eyfa@eyfa.org
www.eyfa.org

Habitat
Summarizing notes on
environmental issues.
The Environment Council, 212 High
Holborn, London WC1V 7VW
Tel 020 7836 2626
Fax 020 7242 1180
info@envcouncil.org.uk
www.the-environment-council.org.uk

Letslink UK News
Newsletter on Local Exchange
Trading Systems.
UK LETS Development Agency,
Basement Flat 54 Campbell Road,
Southsea, Hants PO5 1RW
Tel 017 0573 0639
Fax 017 0573 0629
LETS@letslinkuk.demon.co.uk
www.LETSLINKUK.org

Living Earth
Sustainable food, farming and
forestry.
Soil Association, 86 Colston Street,
Bristol BS1 5BB
Tel 011 7929 0661
Fax 011 7925 2504
info@soilassociation.org
www.soilassociation.org

***Living Lightly and Positive
News**
Highlights achievements
and innovation.
No 5 Bicton Enterprise Centre, Clun,
Shropshire SY7 8NF
Tel 015 8864 0022
Fax 015 8864 0033
positive.news@btinternet.com
www.positivenews.org.uk

Local Environment
Environmental and
sustainability policy, politics
and action.
Carfax Publishing,
Taylor and Francis Ltd,
Customer Services Dept,
Rankine Road, Basingstoke,
Hants RG24 8PR
Tel 012 5681 3000
Fax 012 5633 0254
enquiry@tandf.co.uk
www.tandf.co.uk

London Environment Alert
Bulletin of London
Friends of the Earth.
Friends of the Earth, 26-28
Underwood Street, London N1 7JQ
Tel 020 7490 1555
Fax 020 7490 0881
Info@foe.co.uk
www.foe.co.uk

Netnews
Newsletter of
the European Housing
Ecology Network.
Housing ecology-projects
/ ideas from all countries
in Europe.
Anna Rodregez Gabriel
80T/Research Institute for
Buildenvironment
PO Box 6500 02015 HUT Finland
Tel 00 3 58 9451 4468

News from the new economy
Newsletter of
the New Economics Foundation.
New Economics Foundation,
Cinnamon House,
6-8 Cole Street
London SE1 4YH
Tel 020 7407 7447
Fax 020 7407 6473
info@neweconomics.org
www.neweconomics.org

New Internationalist
Poverty and inequality.
Tower House, Lathkill St,
Market Harborough LE16 9EF
Tel 018 5843 9616
Fax 018 5843 4958

Newsletter of the London Forum of Amenity and Civic Societies
70 Cowcross Street, London,
EC1M 6EJ
Tel 020 7250 0606

People and the Planet
Each issue focuses on a particular topic's relevance to humans and nature. For example, water, forests, waste, the family, education.
Planet 21, Suite 112 Spitfire Studios 63-71 Collier Street London N1 9BE
Tel 020 7383 4388
Fax 020 7383 2398
planet21@netcomuk.co.uk
www.peopleandplanet.net

Planning in London
The Journal of the London Planning and Development Forum.
149a Grosvenor Road, London
SW1V 3JY
Tel 020 7834 9471
Fax 020 7834 9470

Red Pepper
Left and green monthly on politics, economics, ecology, consumer issues, culture and society.
16 Waterlow Road, London N19 5NJ
Tel 020 7281 7024
redpepper@redpepper.org.uk
www.redpepper.org.uk

Social Economy
Cooperative movement and new economics in banking, finance, energy, environment, regeneration, trading and investment.
Malcolm Lynch Solicitors, 19 High Court Lane, The Calls, Leeds LS2 7EU
Tel 011 3242 9600
Fax 011 3234 2080

Sustainable Energy Developments
Sustainable energy and environment policy.
GSR Publications, 72C Old Dover Road, Blackheath, London
SE3 8SY
Tel 020 8305 1831

Sustainable Energy News
Imminent problems faced and caused by the energy sector internationally. Sustainable alternatives, practice, contacts.
International Network for Sustainable Energy
Gl. Kirkevej 56,DK-8530, Hjortshotj, Denmark
Tel 45 86 227 000
Fax 45 86 227 096
ove@inforse.org
www.inforce.org

The Ecologist
Ecology and related matters.
c/o Cissbury House,Furze View, Five Oaks Road, Slinfold,
W. Sussex RH13 7RH
Tel 014 0378 6726
Fax 014 0378 2644
sgc@mag-subs.demon.co.uk

Town and Country Planning
Planning, community involvement and sustainable development.
TCPA, 17 Carlton House Terrace, London SW1Y 5AS
Tel 020 7930 8903
Fax 020 7930 3280
editor@tcpa.org.uk

UK Climate Impacts Programme Newsletter
Coordinates assessment of the impacts of climate change in the UK.
Union House, St Michael's Street, Oxford OX1 2OU
Tel 018 6543 2076
Fax 018 6543 2077
enquiries@ukcip.org.uk
www.ukcip.org.uk

Urban Environment Today
Fortnightly magazine on the management, planning, design and economy of urban centres.
Landor Publishing, Quandrant House, 250 Kennington Lane London SE11 5RD
Tel 020 7735 4502
Fax 020 7735 1299
subs@landor.co.uk
www.landor.co.uk

Urban Nature and Environment
Ecology, biodiversity, and sustainability within the urban environment
23 Crosbie Road, Harborne, Birmingham, B17 9BG
Tel 019 0232 2177
P.Jarvis@wlv.ac.uk

Vision for London
Diary of upcoming events and activities
1 Queen Anne's Gate, London SW1H 9BT
Tel 020 7222 6400
Fax 020 7222 4440
visionforlondon@compuserve.com

Waste Paper News
Newsletter for the European Recovered Fibre Industry. Recycling.
Brunton Business Publications Ltd, Thruxton Down, Andover Hants SP11 8PR
Tel 01264 889 533
Fax 01264 889 622

publications@brunton.co.uk
www.brunton.co.uk

Warmer Bulletin
Sustainable management of, and the recovery of resources from, post–consumer wastes.
The World Resources Foundation, Bridge House, High Street Tonbridge, TN9 1DP
Tel 017 3236 8333
Fax 017 3236 8337
wrf@gn.apc.org
www.wrfound.org.uk

Quarterly WEN News
Newsletter of the Women's Environmental Network. Educates, informs and empowers women who care about the environment.
PO Box 30626, London, E1 1TZ
Tel 020 7481 9004
Fax 020 7481 9144
wenuk@gn.apc.org
www.gn.apc.org/wen

These are all useful, but beware information overload! I have asterisked the two I would select.

Bibliography

Recommended for reading or reference:
I have grouped these under five heads but there is obviously some overlap.

London

Mike Considine, Kate Brady, Marijke Acket eds. *Survivors London* Alternative Press, London 1989

Jerry White, Michael Young *Governing London* The Institute of Community Studies 1996

Michael Hebbert, Tony Travers eds. *The London Government Handbook* Cassell, London 1988

Stephen Inwood *A History of London* MacMillan, London 1998

Ian Jack ed. *London: the lives of the city* Granta *65* special issue Spring, London 1999

Nick Rennison ed. *Waterstone's Guide to London Writing* Waterstone's Booksellers Ltd 1999

Andy Thornley ed. *The Crisis of London* Routledge, London 1992

Tower Hamlets Arts Directory 1999 published by London Borough of Tower Hamlets Arts and Events

Sustainable Cities

The EU Commission's Expert Group on the Urban Environment *European Sustainable Cities* Report March 1996 part I October 1994

Herbert Girardet *The Gaia Atlas of Cities: new directions for sustainable urban living* Gaia Books, London 1992

Herbert Girardet *Creating Sustainable*, Schumacher Briefings No 2, Green Books Totnes, Devon 1999

Graham Haughton, Colin Hunter *Sustainable Cities* Jessica Kingsley for the Regional Studies Association, Regional Policy and Development series 7, London 1994

Mayer Hillman, Tim Elkin, Duncan McLaren *Reviving the City: towards sustainable urban development* Friends of the Earth with Policy Studies Institute 1991

Charles Landry, Franco Bianchini *The Creative City* Demos, London 1995

Harley Sherlock *Cities are good for us: the case for close-knit communities, local shops and public transport* Palladin, London 1991

Ken Worpole, Liz Greenhalgh *The Richness of Cities* Comedia 1999

Sustainability generally

C J Campbell *The Coming Oil Crisis* Multi-Science Publishing 1997

Peter Draper ed. *Health through Public Policy: the greening of public health* Green Print, London 1991

Jennifer Elliott *An Introduction to sustainable development* Routledge, London 1999

Allen Hammond *Which World? Global destinies, regional choices* Earthscan, London 1998

Tim O'Riordan, Heather Voisey eds. *Sustainable Development in Western Europe: coming to terms with Agenda 21* Frank Cass, London 1997

Ben Rogaly, Thomas Fisher, Ed Mayo *Poverty, Social Exclusion and Microfinance in Britain* Oxfam 1999

Poverty and Development: an inter-faith perspective World Faiths Development Dialogue booklet

The Independent Commission on Population and the Quality of Life *Caring for the Future* Oxford University Press, Oxford 1996.

The World Commission on Environment and Development *Our Common Future* Oxford University Press, Oxford 1987

New Economics

Robert U Ayres *Turning Point: the end of the growth paradigm* Earthscan, London 1998

Herman E Daly *Beyond Growth* Beacon Press, 1996

Richard Douthwaite *The Growth Illusion: how economic growth has enriched the few impoverished the many and endangered the planet* Lilliput Press, Dublin 1992 revised 2000

Richard Douthwaite *The Ecology of Money*, Schumacher Briefings No 4, Green Books, Totnes Devon 1999

Richard Douthwaite *Short Circuit: strengthening local economies for security in an unstable world* Green Books, Devon in association with the Lilliput Press, Dublin 1996

Paul Ekins, Mayer Hillman, Robert Hutchison *The Gaia Atlas of Green Economics* Gaia Books, London 1992

Paul Ekins *Economic Growth and Environmental Sustainability: the prospects for green growth* Routledge 2000

Viviane Forrester *The Economic Horror* Polity Press, Cambridge 1999

Friends of the Earth *Capital Punishment: UK insurance companies and the global environment* report prepared by FM Research for Friends of the Earth January 2000.

Susan George *A Fate Worse than Debt: a radical new analysis of the third world debt crisis* Penguin Books, London 1989

Paul Hawken, Amory B Lovins, L Hunter Lovins *Natural Capitalism: the next industrial revolution* Earthscan, London 1999

Hazel Henderson *Beyond Globalisation* New Economics Foundation 1999

Peter Kellner *New Mutualism: the third way* The Co-operative Party, London 1998

David C Korten *The Post-Corporate World* Kumarian Press, San Francisco and Berrett-Koeehler Publishers, West Hartford, Conneticut, 1999)

Peter Lang *Ethical Investment: a saver's guide* Jon Carpenter Publishing, Charlbury, Oxfordshire 1996

Jerry Mander, Edward Goldsmith *The Case against the Global Economy* Sierra Club Books, San Francisco 1996:

Diane Harker, Ed Mayo, Perry Walker, Catherine Unsworth eds. *Community Works!: a guide to community economic action* The New Economics Foundation, London 1999

Robin Murray *Creating Wealth from Waste* Demos, London 1999

Robin Ramsay *The Prawn Cocktail Party: the hidden power of New Labour* Vision Paperbacks, London 1999

James Robertson *Transforming Economic Life, a millennial challenge*, Schumacher Briefings No 1, Green Books in association with the New Economics Foundation, Totnes, Devon 1998

James Robertson *Beyond the Dependency Culture: people, power and responsibility* Adamantine Press, Twickenham, 1998

Ernst von Weizaecker, Amory B Lovins, L Hunter Lovins *Factor Four: doubling wealth, halving resource use* Report to the Club of Rome, Earthscan, London 1997

CDRom The New Economics Foundation's *Brave New Economy, how to grow a better world*

New Democracy

Dick Atkinson *The Common Sense of Community* Demos, London 1994

Murray Bookchin *From Urbanisation to cities: toward a new politics of citizenship* Cassell, London 1995

Elaine Brass, Sophie Poklewski Koziell *Gathering Force: DIY Culture, radical action for those tired of waiting* The Big Issue, London 1997

Barbara Benedict Bunker, Billie T Alban *Large Group Interventions: engaging the whole system for rapid change* Jossey-Bass Inc, San Francisco 1997

Michael Jacobs *The Politics of the Real World* Earthscan Publications London 1996 (written and edited for the Real World Coalition)

Simon Jenkins *Accountable to None: the Tory nationalisation of Britain* Hamish Hamilton, London 1995

Adam Lent ed. *New Political Thought: an introduction* Lawrence and Wishart, London 1998

Alex MacGillivray, Candy Weston, Catherine Unsworth *Communities Count!: a step by step guide to community sustainability indicators* New Economics Foundation 199

The Environment Trust Associates and the Local Government Management Board *Creating Involvement: a handbook of tools and techniques for effective community involvement* pamphlet 1994

Paul Hirst, Sunil Khilnani eds. *Reinventing Democracy*, The Political Quarterly series Blackwell, Oxford 1996

New Economics Foundation staff *Participation Works!: 21 techniques of community participation for the 21st century* New Economics Foundation 1999

Michael Mason *Environmental Democracy* Earthscan, London 1999

Harrison Owen *Expanding our Now: the story of open space technology* Berrett-Koehler, San Fransisco 1997

David Prior, John Stewart, Kieron Walsh *Citizenship: rights, community and participation* Pitman London 1995

James P Troxel ed. *Government Works: profiles of people making a difference*, Miles River Press, Alexandria, Virginia 1995

Desmond Tutu *No Future without Forgiveness* Rider, London 1999

Nick Wates ed. *Action Planning: how to use planning weekends and urban design action teams to improve your environment* The Prince of Wales Institute of Architecture, London 1996

David Wilcox *The Guide to Effective Participation* Partnership Books, Brighton 1993

David Wilkinson, Elaine Applebee *Implementing Holistic Government: joined-up action on the ground* The Policy Press 1999

Index

Pathways to the future